SPECIAL EDUCATIONAL PROVISION

Meeting the Challenges in Schools

Janice Wearmouth

Hodder & Stoughton

A MEMBER OF THE HODDER HEADLINE GROUP

Orders: please contact Bookpoint Ltd, 78 Milton Park, Abingdon, Oxon OX14 4TD. Telephone:
(44) 01235 827720, Fax: (44) 01235 400454. Lines are open from 9.00–6.00, Monday to Saturday,
with a 24 hour message answering service.
Email address: orders@bookpoint.co.uk
British Library Cataloguing in Publication Data
A catalogue record for this title is available from The British Library

ISBN 0340 780568

First published   2000
Impression number   10 9 8 7 6 5 4 3 2 1
Year   2005 2004 2003 2002 2001 2000

Cover photo from Photodisc
Typeset by Multiplex Techniques Ltd, Brook Industrial Park, Mill Brook Road, St. Mary Cray,
Kent BR5 3SR
Printed in Great Britain for Hodder & Stoughton Educational, a division of Hodder Headline Plc,
338 Euston Road, London NW1 3BH by Redwood Books, Trowbridge, Wilts.

Contents

This book is for my family, past, present and future.

Acknowledgements

This book is based on the Open University course *E831. Professional Development for Special Educational Needs Co-ordinators.*

I would like to acknowledge all the support and assistance I have received from friends and colleagues at the Open University, members of the E831 Course Team and the SENCO Support Group, and those who contributed directly to the course materials whose work I have referenced in the text. In particular I would like to thank Liz for her endless encouragement, and John and Janet for their time and patience in proof-reading the draft manuscript and in offering invaluable critical comment on it.

Introduction

The co-ordination of special educational provision in schools is multi-faceted and challenging. There is endless variation in the ways that teachers and whole schools choose to work with children who have been identified as requiring additional or alternative provision from what is normally available in mainstream schools. The *Code of Practice for the Identification and Assessment of Special Education Needs* (DfEE, 1994) acknowledges that the work-patterns and professional experiences of different special educational needs co-ordinators (SENCOs) are likely to differ '... the detail of what they decide to do may vary according to the size, organisation, location and pupil population of the school' (p.ii). There are official protocols laid down in the *Code of Practice* (DfEE, 1994) and in the set of *National Standards for Special Educational Needs Co-ordinators* (TTA, 1998a). However, it is doubtful whether the function of any two SENCOs are the same (Garner, 2000).

The context within which those responsible for co-ordinating provision are required to operate has been characterised as one 'of zero tolerance' (Davies, Garner & Lee, 1998). An 'increasingly inspection-, evaluation- and performance-led approach to education has led to far greater accountability than ever before in the history of education' (Garner, 2000). OFSTED has produced review reports evaluating the implementation of the Code of Practice (OFSTED, 1996; 1997). This implies that the Code has become an overt component of central policy in the area of special educational needs, even though, by law, it has the status of guidance only (Garner, 2000).

A new statement on inclusion in the revised National Curriculum for 2000 (QCA, 2000) is to be statutory. This statement sets out three principles for inclusion which relate to 'setting suitable learning challenges', responding to 'diverse learning needs' and 'overcoming potential barriers to learning'. Schools are urged to 'take action at all levels of curriculum planning' to meet the learning needs of individuals and to offer 'relevant opportunities' to all pupils.

SENCOs often find they have insufficient time to attend to set of duties. OFSTED (1996) reported that 'Many SENCOs have an over-demanding workload' exacerbated by the requirement in some schools, particularly at primary level, for SENCOs to undertake other responsibilities. In a recent interview (Wearmouth, in press) three highly experienced special needs co-ordinators, 'Cindy', in a mainstream primary school, 'Carol' and 'Paula', in secondary, summarised their feelings about their function and role within their own schools. All three saw their roles largely in terms of management:

- co-ordination of resources

- staff development and training

- liaising with other professionals and ensuring that special programmes are carried out within school

- management of conflict between staff and pupils through student advocacy.

The sheer complexity of the role can be illustrated by the work of 'Carol'. The responsibilities involved in co-ordinating provision for pupils across two sites had been divided up according to Key Stages. In order to maintain the integrity of the team it was essential to have in place a clear schedule of meetings. Even so, 'Carol' described herself as 'galloping between sites' in order to maintain cohesion for the team for which she was responsible. 'Cindy', employed in a junior school with additional provision for pupils who experience complex difficulties in learning, described a 'cobweb system' for organising the work of the special needs team in the school. This system she saw as performing a twofold function: supporting pupils in class, both individually and through advice offered to classroom teachers, and also bringing back information to the whole support team for further discussion and evaluation. The three SENCOs mentioned above acknowledge their own practice of working very long hours. At the same time they were actively looking for ways to use their time efficiently by:

- setting up clearly and tightly organised structures for sharing and dissemination of information

- expecting other staff to take on responsibilities for particular pupils

- finding 'quality time to think', given the amount and complexity of the information with which they have to deal.

Central government is promoting school 'improvement' through competition and market-oriented practices. However, the fact remains that in many centres of population a pyramid of schools is seen as serving the community at large. Given the current focus on inclusion within a context of 'Standards' (TTA, 1998a) for the co-ordination of special educational provision, all schools need to be aware of the challenges facing them in facilitating the learning of pupils who experience difficulties. This book discusses the debates and dilemmas associated with a number of these challenges and offers practical suggestions for dealing with them. The aim is that those responsible for co-ordinating special educational provision in schools should be in a better position to make decisions about issues that are sometimes contentious and difficult to resolve.

Since the introduction of the Code of Practice a number of concerns have become apparent in identifying, assessing, and making appropriate and sensitive provision for, the special learning needs of pupils. These concerns are a focus of interest in the revisions to the new Code proposed for the year 2001 (DfEE, 1999). Many of the challenges facing schools in addressing these concerns are discussed in this book: the development of 'more inclusive' approaches to meeting pupils' learning needs; 'good practice' in collaborative working arrangements between Education, Health and Social Services; the role of school governors in the area of special educational needs; the issue of pupil disaffection; the relationship between special educational needs, the National Curriculum and the National Literacy Strategy; appropriate use of information and communications technology; approaches to identification and assessment of pupils difficulties in learning; the design of Individual Education Plans; the issue of target-setting; the relationship between home and school; pupil self-advocacy, irelated to the law and the formal appeals procedure.

Chapter 1 sets the scene with a discussion of the concepts of 'need', 'sameness' and 'difference', an outline of the historical development of the special sector in education and critiques of it, and reflection on the current situation in schools. Chapter 2 outlines the law relating to special educational needs in England and Wales, sets out and critiques the requirements of Code of Practice for the identification and assessment of special educational needs (DfEE, 1994) and briefly refers to the law and the Code (DENI, 1998) in operation in Northern Ireland. There is an outline of the statutory duties of those with responsibilities for the co-ordination of special provision in schools in Chapter 3, and discussion of the challenges facing those in the role of SENCO. In Chapters 4 and 5 issues of national, local and school policy are discussed, with a particular focus on the dilemmas posed for schools when different policy initiatives from central government appear, in practice, to be at variance with one another. For example, the move towards an inclusive approach expressed in the Green Paper (DfEE, 1997) is not comfortably compatible with the encouragement of competition between schools. Chapter 6 outlines in-school issues with which those planning special provision for individual pupils will need to be familiar. Practical and theoretical questions related to engaging with the views of pupils, parents and carers are raised in Chapter 7. Issues of assessment and planning and practical suggestions for implementing statutory requirements are included in Chapters 8 and 9. Chapters 10 to 12 incorporate considerations of the allocation of additional or special resources, both human and physical, to pupils identified as experiencing difficulties in learning.

At the end of each chapter there are suggested activities for further reflection on theoretical and practical issues related to the co-ordination of special educational provision. Additionally, included in the Appendix is a set of needs analyses of various aspects of school special needs provision for those interested in undertaking an evaluation of the provision in their own institution.

1 Setting the scene

This book is designed to address issues of the co-ordination of in-school provision for pupils' 'special educational needs'. Schools have 'special educational needs co-ordinators'. The expressions 'children with special educational needs', 'SEN children', or even, 'SENs' are often used in educational contexts. The continued outpouring of government publications, regulations, official circulars, consultation, advice and guidance documents, academic texts and articles, on the topic of 'special educational needs' reinforces an impression that there is common understanding of what the term implies. However, this apparent consensus serves to conceal the complexity of meaning underlying this term. This book therefore begins by considering, first, what is meant by 'special educational needs'. Only when we have a clear definition can we begin to answer questions about how those 'needs' can be addressed and 'special' educational provision co-ordinated.

Defining 'need'

In common parlance there is a variety of ways to define 'needs'. On the one hand a 'need' can be seen as a lack of something in an individual which gives rise to difficulty. For example, lack of sustenance might constitute a need for someone who is starving or lack of sight for a blind person. On the other hand 'need' can mean the thing the individual requires to satisfy that lack. Food and drink would satisfy an immediate need for sustenance for the starving. In the educational context, for the pupil without sight, the need might be for text in braille, 'talking books' or support from a classroom assistant to enable access to the school curriculum.

Ostensibly, the notion of fulfilment of 'need' conveys a sense of benevolence. In practice, however, in the context of difficulties experienced by pupils the concept is 'deeply problematic' (Salmon, 1995). There is often an assumption of agreement between all the interested parties about what is 'needed' which ignores 'crucial issues' of the degree of power allowed to pupils and parents in the decision-making process. What is termed 'need' has often not been negotiated with learners and/or their parents or carers. The assumption also ignores the implied value placed on pupils by the kind of special, or additional, provision which a pupil is deemed to 'need' - or deserve. The dominant values of an educational institution can all too easily be translated into pupil 'need' as if this is unproblematic.

Schools are required to operate within the law pertaining to education. In England and Wales, the aspect of law currently relating to special educational needs is Part IV of the 1996 Education Act (Part II of the Education Order 1996 in Northern Ireland). Under the terms of this Act a child 'has *special educational needs* if he or she has a *learning difficulty* which calls for *special educational provision* to be made for him or her'. That is, a child only has 'special educational needs' when special provision is required to meet them: learning difficulties do not in themselves constitute such a need. Learning difficulty and 'special educational need' are, in law at least, not synonymous. In law, the learning difficulty creates the need. The need is 'special' if the provision required to satisfy that need is 'special'. 'Learning difficulty' is commonly construed in schools as a general, overall, global 'difficulty in learning', a slowness to grasp new concepts and ideas. Or the problems experienced by a pupil in the development of literacy might be seen as a 'learning difficulty'. However, there are other, less obvious, interpretations of this term in law. A pupil might have a 'learning difficulty', for example, if he or she has a physical disability which makes it hard to move around the school to engage in the same learning activities as other pupils.

How we see what lies at the root of a 'learning difficulty' in school is of crucial importance because it has a very strong influence on what we will see as an appropriate way to respond to it. Over the years, different social or psychological perspectives on the root of the difficulty have given rise to different approaches. Particular approaches to provision for pupils seen as 'having difficulties' may often be interpreted as reflecting the norms and values of society as much as what might be in the long term interest of future life chances.

Constructions of difference between people

Fulcher (1989) has identified four discourses, or ways of speaking, which people use to describe disability. These discourses reflect a range of ways in which differences between individuals have been conceptualised. The distinctions she makes can also be applied to the varying ways that 'special educational needs' have been viewed. There are recognisable parallels in the ways in which 'special educational provision' for pupils regarded as 'different' has developed:

- **the medical discourse** which sees difficulties as diseases or deficits to be treated. The language of this discourse depends on the notion of deficiency and negativity, which, in turn, has connotations of being in some way inferior or distant from the norm (like dis-, un-, -challenged, difficulty, impairment). The language of this medical discourse may in itself prevent a positive approach to diversity and difference. This why the 'medical model' of pupils' difficulties is identified with a 'deficit model' (see above)

- **the charity discourse** which assumes those in difficulty need the help of others. This 'special provision' may be seen to embody paternalistic values of nurturing and care (Corbett, 1996)

- **the lay discourse** which is associated with the fearful, prejudiced or resentful response of the ordinary person towards the disabled gives rise to the view that children who are different must be separated off from the majority

- **the rights discourse** which assumes equality while interpreting discrimination as oppression. Garner and Sandow (1995) point out that the development of human rights legislation in Britain has been piecemeal. Consequently, lobby groups representing the interests of 'minority' groups have presented issues related to provision and participation in terms of human rights, but policy makers and service providers have seen those same issues as problems only for the organisation concerned. These authors cite Beresford and Campbell's (1994) opinion that:

… the providers of services and the recipients thereof have a different 'world view'; the first being preoccupied with services and people's relation to them as consumers, the latter are concerned with rights, empowerment and appropriate support to meet people's needs and maintain their independence.

(Garner and Sandow, 1995, p. 13)

The discourses identified by Fulcher provide a useful way of distinguishing between different interpretations of the way in which current special educational provision has evolved. For example, some might argue that special schools remove children with disabilities from the mainstream of society thus not only reinforcing superstitious beliefs and fears on the part of those in the mainstream but also preventing children with disabilities from accessing the curriculum to which they are entitled. However, others argue that one very humanitarian aim of special schools is to develop specialist methods used to help children overcome the effects of a disability. Vygotsky, for example, at the Institute of Defectology in Russia saw special schools as places where special methods could be used to achieve the common goals of schooling. Humanitarian as this aim might have seemed in the past, contemporary critics might challenge the whole idea of 'normalisation' as a desirable goal, not to mention the name of the Institute itself. It is possible, therefore, to view the existence of special schools from entirely opposite perspectives, as anyone reading parental responses to the 1997 Green Paper would confirm. There is fuller discussion of this Paper in Chapter 2.

From my own experience of teaching in eight different schools, it appears to me that pupils who experience difficulties or who may seem threatening to the system are often seen from one of these four perspectives. When I thought about some of the pupils I have known personally, it seemed to me that the perspective from which they had been viewed seemed to be highly influential on the kind of provision made for them and sometimes clouded our professional judgment.

- 'Jason' was the first dyslexic pupil whose learning needs I really tried to engage with and understand. In a previous school he had been pitied because he could not achieve as highly as his two brothers and was given construction toys to play with instead of being expected to do any written work. The 'treatment' applied to his 'condition' in his secondary school was individual one-to-one tuition in reading and spelling together with in-class support for him personally. Jason was 12 years old at the time, was embarrassed at the sudden individual attention in class and was very rude to his support teacher. If he had been regarded as a person with rights we would have tried to understand his point of view and negotiated the kind of provision made for him from the beginning.

- A second pupil, 'Melvin', was small, thin, frequently hungry and often dirty. Several times he was caught stealing from peers, staff, the local shops and people queuing at the bus stop near the school. Some of his teachers felt that what he really needed was food, clean clothes and then he would be 'sorted out' – a charitable perspective. Others wanted him to be excluded permanently because they saw him as a threat to his peers as well as to the smooth functioning of the school. The educational psychologist offered him counselling, a 'medical' approach which set out to 'treat' and 'cure' him.

What these two examples illustrate is the way in which the perspective from which we view any situation carries with it its own constraints and limitations as well as clear advantages. Currently, questions about 'underachievement' and 'social exclusion' are being raised at a national level. It is pertinent, therefore, to examine what might lie at the root of difficulties in learning faced by individuals and groups of pupils in a broader context. One might ask, for example, what part economic deprivation and poverty play in creating these difficulties, and think about the extent to which 'learning difficulties' might be seen as 'obstacles to learning' arising from the society in which they live.

At the level of the individual school, often the dominant perspective on the difficulty in learning faced by a pupil, is this so-called 'medical', 'deficit' or 'within child' view of difficulty. The law also adopts this view of individual need. Any 'special educational need' identified on a pupil's Statement of Special Educational Need must be matched to provision in a quantifiable, prescription-like way. However, the medical model of difficulty is only one out of a number of perspectives discussed in the following chapters.

Discourses around sameness and difference

The principle of universal access to education and, within that, the inclusion of all pupils in mainstream schools wherever possible, is now enshrined in public policy. To put this principle into operation, policy makers are faced with the fundamental dilemma of how to make educational provision for all pupils, which takes full account of 'sameness' and, at the same time, pays due regard to 'difference' and 'diversity' amongst individuals (Norwich, 1996). Focusing on difference can be discriminatory: for example there is evidence that in a few local education authorities pupils with Downs Syndrome are automatically placed in special schools at secondary level, whatever the pupil's level of academic achievement. At the same time, failing to acknowledge difference can be counterproductive to individual learning needs and be seen as disrespectful to life experiences. How any individual will view particular kinds of educational provision for particular groups of learners will be influenced by his or her own set of values as a human being and as a professional educator.

There are many different ways in which a national education system might be designed to address the learning needs of all children. In the current system, most pupils are expected to be able to cope with the curriculum offered in mainstream schools. Why some pupils fail can be explained in a range of ways. The problem might be interpreted as rooted in social factors, for example, family poverty and unemployment or in cultural differences in understanding and expectations between family and school. Alternatively, the child's difficulties might be seen as arising out of the immediate learning environment, for example inappropriate teaching methods or texts, or inadequate school resources. Another view might be to see the problem as located at the level of the learner him or herself and an individualised approach taken to identifying and assessing his or her 'special' learning needs. There are examples of central government acknowledging all of these interpretations by promoting interventions at societal level and at the level of the whole-school, as well as supporting the notion of 'special' provision for individual pupils. The focus of this book is the co-ordination of special provision in schools to facilitate pupil learning, meet current statutory criteria, support other staff and promote positive working relationships between school and home. Against this will be set reflections on what sometimes appears to be a fragmented central approach to raising the achievement of all pupils with government policies, sometimes at odds with one another, operating at different levels simultaneously.

Development of the 'special' education sector for the few: a historical perspective

The way in which educational provision is currently organised is a product both of its own history and of the values, beliefs and political ideology of our society. The Warnock Report (1978) contains a very useful summary of the history of the special sector in England and Wales. Warnock outlined the stages at which special schools were introduced for the various groups of pupils seen as 'different' and the kind of education deemed to be appropriate for these groups over various periods. Warnock commented on the relatively recent origin of special education for those pupils deemed to have difficulties of various sorts. She noted the time lag between provision for various groups: the first 'special' group for whom schools were founded were the blind and the deaf, then came schools for pupils with a physical disability, then schools for 'mentally handicapped' pupils and, finally, special provision for the 'maladjusted' and for those having speech impairments. These first special schools were solely vocational as befitted the societal context where child labour was the norm.

The Elementary Education Act of 1870 marked the beginning of compulsory state education. Subsequent education laws improved and expanded the system of state education, increasing access for the next hundred years. This continually evolving and expanded notion of who was entitled to schooling put pressure on schools to evolve as institutions capable of including all pupils. Historically local education authorities responded to this challenge by creating and maintaining a dual system of mainstream and special schooling built upon the pre-existing structure which had developed out of voluntary enterprise.

After the 1870 Act made attendance at school compulsory, the question of what to do with children who made little or no progress and whose presence in the classroom was felt to be holding others back, now became important. The 1896 Committee on Defective and Epileptic Children experienced considerable difficulty in defining its own terminology in relation to pupils seen as having some kind of cognitive difficulty. There were three groups who came under this general heading, 'feeble-minded', 'imbeciles' and 'idiots'. It was not thought possible to educate idiots. Admission to asylums was considered suitable for 'imbeciles', whilst the 'feeble-minded' should be educated in special schools or classes.

Categorisation of pupils was a major element of developing legislation: the labels used to describe particular groups of pupils reflect the way in which they were generally viewed. To trace the use of particular labels can give an interesting insight into social perspectives on pupils with particular difficulties. In his report Warnock shows the difference in status and respect given to the various groups of pupils seen as 'different' from the rest. 'Idiots', 'feeble-minded' and 'imbeciles' should be separated off from the rest for the good of the majority. The deaf and blind, however, were to be educated in separate institutions to receive the specialised form of education which teachers should be specially qualified to deliver. The changing social and historical context of provision has meant that many labels once attached to pupils ('imbeciles' and 'feeble minded') have become unacceptable.

In further sections of this report Warnock notes that once the old school boards were abolished and the two-tier system of local education authorities for elementary and secondary education was established in 1902, the statutory foundation of special provision continued broadly until the 1944 Act. Responsibility for special education was transferred to the authorities for elementary education although the authorities dealing with secondary education also had the power to provide for blind, deaf, defective (the physically disabled) and epileptic children.

The tensions within the national education system are very clearly reflected in the changes that have taken place in the 'special' education sector since 1944 in Britain. Clark, Dyson, Millward and Skidmore (1997) trace the 'optimistic, committed and values-driven perspective that has ... been a constant theme within the field of special needs education in recent decades' (p. 2) back to the education system created by the 1944 Education Act.

In seeking to develop a common national framework for the education of (nearly) all children, the creators of the 1944 Act were faced with the dilemma of how to construct an educational framework that would support the learning of a diverse pupil population. The legislators addressed it by formalising a system of selection and segregation based on the results of assessment techniques that, they believed, could differentiate different 'types' of learners. Different curricula could then be designed for different learning 'types' to be educated in separate sectors of the system.

In the area of special education, the 1944 Education Act, Sections 33 and 34, set out the legal basis for subsequent provision. It adopted the 'medical model'. The difficulties in learning experienced by pupils were conceptualised as disabilities of body and mind and intrinsic to the pupils themselves. The Handicapped Pupils and School Health Service Regulations 1945, developed a new framework of eleven categories of pupils, including that of 'maladjusted' for the first time. Local education authorities were required to ascertain the needs of children in their areas for special educational treatment. Blind, deaf, epileptic, physically handicapped and aphasic children were deemed educable only in special schools; those children thought to have a severe mental handicap were perceived as ineducable and dealt with by health authorities. During the years which followed the two groups which continually expanded in numbers were those pupils considered 'educationally sub-normal' and those identified as 'maladjusted' (Warnock, 1978).

Segregation operated between mainstream and special schools, and selection between types of secondary school in mainstream: grammar, technical and secondary modern. Within individual mainstream schools pupils were selected into ability 'streams'. Pupils might be directed into academic or work-related programmes according to measured 'ability'. The educational hierarchy that developed was seen by many as both equitable, because pupils appeared to be able to rise to a level which reflected their ability, and stable because it was based on psychometric testing considered at that time to be largely reliable and valid.

However, as Clark et al (op cit) note, the credibility of the system was undermined by a number of factors:

- differing proportions of pupils were selected for each type of school in different local education authority areas

- considerable doubt was increasingly thrown on the reliability and validity of the psychometric tests being used

- there was obvious overlap between the learning needs of pupils in mainstream and special schools

- movement between school types was very difficult indeed, regardless of the amount of progress made by individual pupils.

In addition to the factors militating against the stability of the selective system there was a growing concern for equality of opportunity and social cohesion in society at large. The result was that many commentators in education came to view this system as divisive and functioning to sustain the position of some already advantaged groups over others, rather than as a rational and equitable response to scientifically-measured differences between pupils (Douglas, 1964, Hargreaves, 1967).

Education for All

The net outcome of all this was the establishment of comprehensive schools in mainstream, the importation of special school methods and curricula into mainstream through the introduction of special classes and 'remedial' provision, and the integration of some children from special to mainstream schools.

Within the realm of the special sector, the 1970 Handicapped Children Education Act transferred responsibility for children with severe handicaps from health to education authorities and finally established the concept of education for all in law. For the first time, children perceived to have severe cognitive disabilities were entitled to a school-based education.

The 1978 Warnock Report reviewed educational provision in Great Britain for children and young people who, up to that time, were considered 'handicapped by disabilities of body or mind'. It introduced the concept of 'special educational needs', recommending that it should replace categorisation of handicap. Previously around 2 per cent of children had been legally classified as 'handicapped', but now this report suggested that up to 20 per cent of pupils might have a 'special educational need' at some time in their school career.

The 1981 Education Act attempted to translate the Warnock Report into legislation. The old categories of handicap were replaced with the idea that difficulties occur on a continuum, and that a 'special educational need' existed if a child had 'significantly greater difficulty in learning' than peers, or a disability that hindered him or her from using educational facilities normally available in the local school. Local authorities were given responsibilities to identify needs which called for special provision that is, provision in addition to that normally available in the school. Parents' rights were addressed in that they were to be consulted and could appeal against a local authority's decision about appropriate provision. This Act also reaffirmed the principle of integration. All children should be educated in mainstream schools but with certain provisos: that their needs could be met there, and that it was compatible with the education of other children and with the 'efficient use of resources'.

Two Education Acts were passed in 1986. In the second of these governors were to 'use their best endeavours' to ensure that children with special educational needs were identified and suitable provision made.

The main features of the 1988 Education Reform Act which affected special education were the introduction of the National Curriculum, local management of schools, Grant Maintained Status and open enrolment in schools. In a sense the introduction of a National Curriculum for all was the first time that functional, rather than simply 'locational', integration was realised for pupils (Bines, 1998). In that this Act intervened in the area of the curriculum it had far-reaching consequences for pupils who experience difficulties. The new curricular framework was compulsory and subject-based and a national system of assessment based on norms and focused on results which could be used to evaluate the 'effectiveness' of schools was introduced. The new 'market' approach encouraged by this Act encouraged competition, consumer choice and pressure on resources. Notions of 'norms' have led to a greater emphasis on making additional provision for those pupils who experience difficulties.

The Elton Committee was established in 1989 to recommend action to secure the orderly atmosphere necessary in schools for teaching and learning. It offered no simple diagnosis of the cause of pupils' indiscipline but instead made wide-ranging recommendations on effective classroom management and on the creation of a sense of community and shared values. The management style of head teachers should encourage a sense of collective responsibility amongst their staff and commitment to school among pupils and parents. Parents should provide firm guidance and positive models of behaviour, and pupils should be given more responsibility.

The 1993 Education Act replaced the 1981 Education Act in all but a few minor details, although it covered much the same ground. It introduced a Code of Practice for the identification and assessment of special educational needs (DfEE, 1994), new procedures for assessing 'needs' and specifying resources in 'statements of special educational needs' and a new tribunal system to hear appeals against these formal assessment procedures. Parents were given legal remedies against decisions about their children in assessment and statementing. The old local educational authority appeals panels which heard complaints from parents were replaced by 'independent' tribunals chaired by lawyers, following the model of industrial tribunals. These tribunals are more powerful than the appeals panels because they can amend the statement and their decisions are binding on LEAs. The introduction of the Code of Practice gave the tribunals a shared text to guide their practice in hearing appeals about formal assessments.

This Act gave the responsibility for co-ordinating special education provision solely to local authorities irrespective of the type of school attended by the pupils concerned. It introduced the requirement that all schools should produce a distinct 'special needs policy' as part of their general school policy and altered the terms under which pupils could be excluded from schools. The category of indefinite exclusion was abolished. Local authorities must provide education for excluded pupils in Pupil Referral Units which must offer a broad balanced curriculum, but not necessarily the full National Curriculum.

The 1994 *Code of Practice on the Identification and Assessment of Special Educational Needs* and its associated Circulars, will be discussed in more detail in Chapter 2. Suffice to say at this point that the model of pupils' difficulties in learning in these documents is seen in terms of identifying, assessing and resourcing the perceived needs of individual pupils rather than the adoption of a whole-school approach.

Issues of labelling pupils by category to access additional provision

One issue which often generates strong views is that of the kind of categorising and labelling of pupils that is often used to justify a request for additional provision. The early 1990s witnessed heated academic debate about disability-related labelling, for example (Soder, 1991; Booth, 1991; Reindal, 1995). Essentially, this debate focused on the significance of labels and language in recognising, challenging and changing the everyday experiences of disabled people.

The use of labels is extremely sensitive. It is not simply the label itself but the associations (prejudices) that accompany it. The names we use to describe people and things are not neutral. Further, the relationship between educational expectations and student achievement, self-esteem and development has been well documented (Rosenthal and Jacobson, 1968).

In a reflection on how the 'special educational needs' label is used in common parlance, Salmon comments on her perception of the discrepancy between the rhetoric that sees 'special needs' language as empowering and the reality that such language actually removes power from individuals (Salmon, 1995, pp.73–74). She feels that the term is now 'equated with failure to come up to the mark'. So far from signifying belonging and entitlement, these terms *special* and *need* have turned out 'weasel words' with 'connotations of helplessness and inadequacy justifying segregation'. They are used to 'justify exclusion and relegate the problem to a specialist', whilst at the same time leaving teachers 'feeling helpless and deskilled'.

Many have argued that language, particularly the words or labels we use to describe people are themselves a factor in the oppression of others. Corbett (1996) explores the relationship between language and the concept of disability. Through a 'deconstruction' of the language of special needs she shows how pupils can become marginalised rather than valued by schools:

> **What does *'special'* mean? If we detach this word from its anchor in *'educational'* we can see that 'special' does not mean especially good and valued unless we use a phrase like, 'you are a special person'. It is linked to 'needs' which implies dependency, inadequacy and unworthiness**

> *(Corbett, 1996, p.3)*

Here, as Corbett shows, the language of special needs both sentimentalizes and prejudices our view of disability.

The case of 'maladjustment'

The brief history below, of the rise and demise of the term 'maladjusted' within special education, illustrates how far labels relating categorical notions of problems as belonging to the child become pervasive and fixed to suit the existing national context. In reality they are perceptions of deviance as seen against some assumed norm.

The problem of disruptive, challenging behaviour by students in schools is long-standing. Furlong (1985) notes that in the seventeenth century pupils were often armed and occasionally took part in violent mutiny. There appear to be recorded instances of pupils destroying all of the most famous public schools at least once (Ogilvie, 1953, in Furlong, 1985). Challenging behaviour has a history 'as long as mass education itself' (ibid). There is a record from the nineteenth century of a schoolteacher in a primary school on the Isle of Wight requesting money from the school managers for shin pads for himself because his pupils hated school so much that every time they came into the classroom they kicked him. They would rather have been earning money working on the land.

However, pupil 'maladjustment' is an invention of the twentieth century. Once education became compulsory for all children, the issue of how to control potentially difficult pupils assumed increased importance and politicians looked to medicine and the growing profession of psychology for solutions to behaviour in schools that was construed as deviant (Ford, Morgan and Whean 1982). 'Maladjusted' is an example of a professional explanation of pupil behaviour which carried with it the expectation of certain forms of treatment. Until 1945 there was no formal category of 'maladjustment' enshrined in Ministry of Education regulations. Galloway et al., remark that the category had its origins both in early labels of mental deficiency:

> The 1913 Mental Deficiency Act created a category of moral imbeciles or defectives, and children who displayed emotionally disturbed or disruptive behaviour came to be associated with both mental defect and moral defect.
>
> *(Galloway et al., 1994, p.110)*

in the unstable, nervous child identified in Board of Education Reports in the 1920s, and also in the:

> ... 'difficult and maladjusted' child recommended in the 1929 Board of Education report as in need of child guidance.
>
> *(Ibid, p.112)*

After 1945 all LEAs had a responsibility to establish special educational treatment in special or ordinary schools for pupils defined in this way. The concept was still relatively new when the Underwood Committee was set up in 1950 to enquire into 'maladjusted' students' medical, educational and social problems. The Committee referred to modes of behaviour outside the realm of the 'normal'. The Underwood Report (Chapter IV, para 96) lists six symptoms of 'maladjustment' requiring professional help from psychologists, child guidance clinics or doctors. These include four 'disorders', one category labelled 'difficulties' and one 'psychotic':

- nervous disorders, e.g. fears, depression, apathy and excitability

- habit disorders, e.g. speech defects, sleep-walking, twitching and incontinence

- behaviour disorders, e.g. defiance, aggression, jealousy and stealing

- organic disorders, e.g. cerebral tumours

- psychotic behaviour, e.g. delusions and bizarre behaviour

- educational and vocational difficulties, e.g. inability to concentrate or keep jobs.

The nearest this report could come to an overall definition read as follows:

> In our view, a child may be regarded as maladjusted who is developing in ways that have a bad effect on himself or his fellows and cannot, without help, be remedied by his parents, teachers and other adults in ordinary contact with him.

(Ibid, p. 22)

There has never been a consensus on what defines 'problem behaviour', of the sort categorised by the term 'maladjusted':

> ... the common point to emerge from attempts to clarify behavioural disorders and types of maladjustment is that it is a ragbag term describing any kind of behaviour that teachers and parents find disturbing.

(Galloway and Goodwin, 1987, p. 32)

Rutter, for example, points out that the term 'maladjustment' has been used pragmatically to justify special educational provision (Rutter, Tizard and Whitmore, 1970):

> ... its chief purpose (in the country) has been to provide a label under which special education may be provided according to the Handicapped Pupils and School Health Service Regulations.

(Ibid)

Invent the category, create the pupil. Ravenette identified three situations where the word 'maladjustment' was commonly used:

1. There is a breakdown in the relationship between a child and others which is chronic rather than transitory.

2. The adults in the situation are worried by the behaviour which points to a breakdown and by their inability to do anything about it.

3. It is then a signal to others that the situation is intolerable, that the institution is entitled to some special help or relief and that perhaps the child should be placed in a more appropriate institution, or be rendered 'normal' by treatment.

(Ravenette, 1984, p. 4)

Between 1945 and 1960, the numbers of pupils classified as maladjusted rose from 0 to 1742. Estimates at the time of Rutter's et al (1970) epidemiological study, which attempted to assess the prevalence of specific categories of difficulties in the school student population, varied from 5 to 25 per cent of the child population:

> **Psychiatrists have sometimes been prone to see pathology in all kinds of variations of personality and styles of life … Most investigations have shown that between 5 per cent and 12 per cent of children are "maladjusted" or show some kind of psychiatric disorder (Ministry of Education, 1955), but rates of up to 25 per cent have occasionally been reported (Brandon, 1961).**

> *(Rutter et al., p. 178)*

> **By 1975, there were 13,000 pupils labelled as maladjusted (Furlong, 1985).**

The term 'maladjusted' is no longer used. It has been replaced by terms such as 'emotional and behavioural difficulties', which was first formally applied to groups of school pupils whose behaviour was perceived as difficult to manage by Warnock (1978), which suffer from the same difficulties of lack of definition but which enable pupils to be removed from the mainstream.

With regard to the effect the label may have had on pupils, the 'maladjusted' label is one with 'which has a powerful history of stigma, being associated with undesirable personal and social characteristics' (Galloway, Armstrong and Tomlinson, 1994). It is very likely, therefore, that pupils might be damaged by their awareness of the attribution to themselves of a descriptor with such negative connotations.

Change and development in mainstream schools

By the time of the Warnock Report (1978) the boundaries between special and mainstream education had become permeable; many schools had adopted pragmatic solutions to coping with the diversity of the pupil population. There was a growing awareness that the barriers to learning pupils might face were not simply the result of personal deficit, and some of those associated with the area of special educational needs began to discuss an alternative 'interactive' model of difficulties (Wedell, 2000). In this model, difficulties are seen to arise as a result of the interaction between what the child brings to her or his learning and what is offered to her or him through the method of teaching, the content of the particular activity, the supporting resources, and so on. A much greater emphasis could then be placed on the learning environment as potentially creating barriers to learning. Where the learning environment is viewed as a part of the problem, more focus can be placed on the responsibility of schools and local authorities to identify the pupil's learning needs and support her or him in accessing the curriculum (Wedell, ibid). In mainstream schools, some large secondary schools developed a proliferation of alternative forms of curricula, for example academic courses leading to externally-accredited qualifications, non-examination vocational and/or life skills courses and 'remedial' tuition in withdrawal groups.

The move away from 'remedial' education to a 'whole school approach' has been well documented (Bines, 1986). Clark et al., argue that the 'whole-school approach' constituted the first attempt at a coherent structural merger of special and mainstream education (Clark, 1997). It appeared to engender sufficient optimism amongst those who supported mainstreaming to look forward to a time when the merger would be complete. However the criticism began to be voiced that this provision still amounted to a 'bolt-on' extension of what was planned for the majority, rather than part of an integrated whole designed to address the entire diverse body of pupils. Many commentators felt that for the most part mainstream schools remained inhospitable places for some pupils. The major obstacle to inclusive education (Wedell, 2000) is that the current system is not yet geared to meeting the diversity of children's learning needs. For example, traditionally, one teacher stands in front of a class of thirty or more children of similar age. Recognising pupils' individuality in these circumstances is extremely problematic. Wedell's major hope for the future is that the education system will at some stage be planned to recognise the diversity of children's learning needs, rather than the minority of children being made to fit a structure intended for the majority. He advocates moving to a school system where teachers can respond to children in a variety of ways and with greater flexibility, where:

- the teacher might assume a management function and co-ordinate collaboration between peers, helpers from the external community and information and communications technology

- pupil groupings would be by learning needs or subject/content areas and each individual would be encouraged to become an autonomous learner

- schools rely on the local community to support children's learning

- staff teach cross-age groups of pupils.

The current position

As has already been discussed, within our current system, from a legal perspective, learning needs are 'special' only if they require 'special' provision to be made:

A child has special educational needs if he or she has a learning difficulty which calls for special educational provision to be made for him or her.

(DfEE, 1994a, 2:1)

The individualised view of 'learning difficulties' is only one perspective on how to structure provision for the diversity of the pupil population. It carries with it certain underlying assumptions that must be clarified in order to understand the implications of this particular approach. In principle the law is based on individually-defined need. If the pupil has the need then this must be addressed. However, in practice, resource limitations have meant that only a proportion of individuals have been covered by the legislation. A study by Rutter, Tizard and Whitmore (1970) enquired into the incidence of difficulties in learning in the school population. The report from this study showed teachers' perceptions that, on average, 20 per cent of their pupils were experiencing difficulty of some kind. Since that time, the figure of 20 per cent has been used to estimate the number of children nationally who might experience difficulties.

Nationally, about 20 per cent of children may have some form of special educational needs at some time. For the vast majority of children such needs will be met by their school with outside help if necessary – and school governing bodies have statutory responsibilities to ensure that those needs are met. Only in a small minority of cases – nationally, around two per cent of children – will a child have special educational needs of a severity or complexity which requires the LEA to determine and arrange the special educational provision for the child by means of a statutory statement of special educational needs. These figures are broad national estimates: the proportion of children with special educational needs varies significantly from area to area.

(DfEE, 1994a, 2:2)

Of the total number of pupils, approximately 2 per cent are seen by policy makers as likely to have difficulties which require additional or extra resources to be provided for them. This figure of 2 per cent is clearly useful to resource-providers, for example local education authorities, to estimate what proportion of their budget they are likely to have to set aside to support individual pupils' educational needs. However, it is an arbitrary one, drawn from a count of pupils in special schools in 1944. The law, focusing as it does on individual need, gives no such figures for the incidence of children likely to need statutory assessment. However, LEAs, whose duty it is to implement legislation, have used such DfEE guidance to establish general criteria for assessment.

Criticisms of a 'special' perspective

Sociological critiques

A crucial issue in the debate around inclusion in mainstream schools is the question of whether there is ever any place for a 'special' sector within the education system. A sociological approach to the study of differences between people focuses on the factors at the level of society which marginalize and oppress disabled people. Since the 1980s, a number of critiques of the special sector in education have been elaborated from this perspective. Some of the issues raised have been that:

- the development of special education may be seen as the outcome of the conflict of interests between professionals with a vested interest in the expansion of pupil numbers in the special sector (Tomlinson, 1985)

- difficulties in learning have been attributed to the characteristics of the individual student rather than to the school and societal context in which the difficulties have arisen. One of the criticisms made of the Warnock Report (1978) is that it neglected the importance of social factors in the creation of learning difficulties.

- many students categorised as 'having emotional and behavioural difficulties' and removed from mainstream education into special segregated provision, come from working-class families whose parents find it much harder to negotiate with professionals than middle-class parents (Tomlinson, 1982, p. 5)

- society maintains a state of equilibrium between its interrelated parts. From this viewpoint, special education is seen as a safety valve for the rest of the education system. Order within the education system is maintained:

... by removing potentially troublesome children which upset the smooth running (of the education system) ...

(Tomlinson, 1981, p. 209)

and special education is used as a form of social control:

Is the establishment of special educational facilities, particularly those concerned with problems of behaviour, a pernicious system of social control?

(Ford, Mongon and Whelan, 1982, p. 27)

- educational institutions maintain social stratification by reinforcing class identities among young people. In this way they contribute to the production and reproduction of social and cultural inequality (Wexler, 1992). Tomlinson concludes that in this respect traditional and existing practices benefit the current social order.

A sociological view has both strengths and weaknesses in its ability to explain the development of special educational provision. Particular strengths are its analysis of:

- the implications of the existence of a special system side by side with a mainstream (Booth, 1981)

- provision made for pupils whose behaviour is seen as disruptive and therefore challenging to the social order

- the societal and organisational factors which prevent some students from learning and produces barriers for others.

It also has a number of weaknesses. Clark, Dyson and Millward (1998, p. 162), for example, point out that this orientation tends to be preoccupied with critique: 'substantially unchanged recycling of their critiques continues to appear on a regular basis'. A fundamental claim that students' special learning needs are a social product rather than a description of what students' experiences are really like means that 'there are, therefore, no really-existing "special needs" which necessarily cause problems for educators and call for some carefully worked-out response' (Ibid, p. 162). Once the special-ordinary distinction is shown through critical analysis to be irrational, mainstream practices, it is argued, should be shown capable of supporting the learning of all students. Such a position runs counter to the classroom experience of many teachers.

Sociological perspectives do not necessarily allow for the views of individual users of the system on the place of the special sector. Two groups of pupils about whom teachers often express very serious concerns are those whose experience profound and complex difficulties in learning who may also have acute physical disabilities, and those whose behaviour is perceived as very threatening and disruptive. With regard to the first group, it may be that some students are so vulnerable that the overriding consideration for them is a protective environment where their individual care needs can be considered together with their education. Whether the actual location is a mainstream or special site may be of less relevance than the quality of the specialist facilities to support their physical requirements, the level of understanding established between students and staff and the effectiveness of the system of communication between home and school. In relation to the second, the proviso that pupils 'with special educational needs' should be educated in maintream schools provided that this is compatible with the education of peers is often seen as the justification for placement in an alternative location.

Parental views

There were over 3000 responses to the 1997 government Green Paper 'Excellence for All Children', a document which took a strongly inclusive perspective. The ratio of parental responses favouring special as opposed to mainstream provision for students who have Statements of Special Educational Needs was 20:1. The sample of parents responding cannot be considered a cross section of those who children have a Statement. Mostly these Statements referred to educational needs arising from sensory impairments or multiple and complex difficulties in learning. Nevertheless, these parents' views must still be taken very seriously. Some of the reasons given for supporting special provision were:

- bullying in mainstream. Physically disabled children are often perceived to suffer at the hands of non-disabled peers. 'Children can be treated like, and feel like, a freak if they are integrated as individual disabled children' (letter from parent). One parent wrote: 'The worry caused when your child is being bullied or feeling depressed affects the whole family. Taking an Asperger child out of that environment greatly increases the quality of the child's life as well as the family.'

- a perception that, although the same opportunities are often not available to pupils in special schools as those in mainstream, this does not mean these opportunities automatically become available if the child is moved into mainstream schooling. These opportunities must be made available within the special schools rather than transferring the children to mainstream.

- a perception of intolerance by children and staff

- a perception that special schools constitute a 'reservoir of shared knowledge and expertise in teaching' of pupils with specialist needs

- gross dissatisfaction with perception of levels of resourcing, staff training, awareness and understanding in mainstream.

The minority of parents wanting a mainstream education for their children had equally strong views on their children's rights to be respected as full members of society. In preparation for this they felt it most appropriate that they should be included in local mainstream schools with additional provision to meet their individual needs. In a recent interview (Wearmouth, 1996, 2000) the mother of a blind child was very upset when it was suggested that her daughter should be transferred from mainstream to a special boarding school. She expressed her very firm opinion that her daughter who had been supported through local lower and middle schools by a very competent classroom assistant should continue to be educated in her local neighbourhood upper school. She had developed close friendships with peers living close by and attending the same school. Her mother saw the development of these relationships as an essential part of her child's education and was concerned that these friendships would weaken and her daughter would no longer be seen as an accepted member of the local community if she was forced into a special school.

Summary

Over the years, the ways in which differences between people have been conceptualised, notions of entitlements and human rights have developed, and the focus of, and on, education itself has altered, have all contributed to the complexity and changing nature of the field of special educational needs.

The term used in legislation since 1983, 'special educational needs', is part of the discourse which, according to Salmon and Corbett, for example, suggests a deficit model. At the same time we must recognise, along with the Disability Movement, that failing to acknowledge difference can be counterproductive to the learning needs of a student and be interpreted as disrespectful to that person's life experiences. Whatever an individual's view, parents, teachers and other professionals in education have to conform to aspects of the official definitions when engaged on formal processes under the Act such as assessment and statementing.

Sometimes, ensuring that a pupil is identified as 'having a special educational need', perhaps even that his or her needs are specified on a Statement and thus risking labelling, could be the best way to protect a mainstream placement for a child experiencing difficulties. Paradoxically, 'including' a child in a mainstream school might need to be accompanied by more labelling and categorising of individual pupils, using basically the same medical and psychological perspectives mentioned, above than would be the case if the same learner attended a special school.

Suggested Activities: Reflection and discussion

1. Constructions of 'special educational needs'

How far do you agree with Salmon (above) that there is a discrepancy between the rhetoric of 'special needs' language as empowering and its reality as disempowering? How significant do you consider the terminology that we use?

2. Constructions of difference between people

Think about examples from your own experience of pupils in school who have been seen by other staff, and perhaps also yourself, from one of the four perspectives outlined by Fulcher. Reflect on how the particular perspective influenced the way in which teachers responded to them. Consider whether alternative responses to learning needs might have been made if a different perspective were adopted for each.

2 Understanding the legal context

The law currently in operation is based on individually defined need. All students of school age have the statutory right to have their 'special educational needs' assessed and met.

In the British education system all students of school age have a legal entitlement to access to the National Curriculum. Local Education Authorities are required to make special provision at school level available for those students identified as needing it. There is an irony here, however. As we have already seen, labelling the student as different creates the possibility that she or he may feel stigmatised. Lack of identification, however, means that she or he may be denied access to additional support. A similar dilemma accompanies the choice of appropriate curricula. Young people sharing identical learning aims and curricula may be deprived of the opportunity to develop competencies appropriate to their needs. Yet they may be made to feel inferior if their curriculum is different.

The law relating to special educational needs in England and Wales

The 1996 Education Act repealed and replaced the 1993 Act; however, Part IV of the new Act incorporated all the provisions of Part III of the 1993 Act. Despite the political changes that have taken place since the enactment of the 1996 Act, the legal situation remains unchanged.

There are a number of documents associated with current special education law, only some of which are binding. Regulations provide a legally binding interpretation of clauses in the Act. After an Act has been passed Circulars, which do not carry the force of law, may be issued to offer further advice about it. The *Code of Practice on the Identification and Assessment of Special Educational Needs* itself (DfEE, 1994a) also has advisory status only. The Act requires educational institutions to 'have regard' to this Code. Having said this, however, OFSTED also uses it as a shared text to evaluate policy and practice in the area of special educational needs during school inspections, so school staff would be well advised to pay heed to it. The Code quotes extensively from the law, for which it uses the convention of blue print. In addition, some other sections of the Code are also legally binding because they reflect established case law. For example, the specification that the special provision described on a student's Statement of Special Educational Needs should 'normally be specific, detailed and quantified' (DfEE, 1994a, para. 4:28) became a legal requirement after the case referred to in law as *R v Secretary of State for Education and Science Ex parte E.*

The 1996 Act does not apply in Scotland or Northern Ireland. A circular has been produced in Scotland on 'children and young persons with special educational needs' which brings about changes to the 'recording' process and revises the advice and guidance connected to the Education (Scotland) Act 1981 (SOED, 1993). In Northern Ireland a new Code of Practice came into effect in September 1998.

Part IV of the 1996 Act

In this Part of the Act, 'child' is taken to mean any registered school pupil under 19 years of age. The male pronouns 'he' and 'him' refer to both sexes.

The child's 'special educational needs'

Part IV of the Act defines 'special educational needs' and 'special educational provision'. As set out in Section 312 of the 1996 Education Act, a child has 'special educational needs' if he has a 'learning difficulty' which calls for 'special educational provision' to be made for him (sic). A child has a 'learning difficulty' under the Act if:

a. he has a significantly greater difficulty in learning than the majority of children of his age,

b. he has a disability which either prevents or hinders him from making use of educational facilities of a kind generally provided for children of his age in schools within the area of the local education authority, or

c. he is under the age of five and is, or would be if special educational provision were not made for him, likely to fall within paragraph (a) or (b) when of or over that age.

Children must not be identified as having a 'learning difficulty' solely because the language spoken at home is different from the language in which they are taught.

Under the Act, 'special educational provision' means (S.312 (4))

a) in relation to a child who has attained the age of two, educational provision which is additional to, or otherwise different from, the educational provision made generally for children of his age in schools maintained by the local education authority (other than special schools) or grant-maintained schools in their area, and

b) in relation to a child under that age, educational provision of any kind.

Unless it is 'incompatible' with the wishes of his parent, education for a child identified as having special educational needs must not take place in special schools, with certain provisos. Section 316 of the Act lists these provisos:

The conditions are …

a) **his receiving the special educational provision which his learning difficulty calls for,**

b) **the provision of efficient education for the children with whom he will be educated, and**

c) **the efficient use of resources.**

The Act also provides for a code of practice giving 'practical guidance' on this Part of the Act to which local education authorities, school governors and, in the case of an appeal, the Tribunal, should 'have regard'.

Duties of local authorities

Local education authorities must:

- review special education provision

- in co-ordinating provision, consult funding bodies and school governors, where appropriate

- formally assess all those children who have special educational needs under the terms of this Act and who require special provision other than that already provided by their schools. This requirement applies whether a child is registered at a maintained or non-maintained school, or is not registered in school, provided those needs have been drawn to the local authority's attention

- provide statements of special educational need for those children who require such provision, in the view of the LEA. The statement must specify the special provision to be made, the type of school and the name of a suitable school. The procedures must be completed within six months

- ensure the provision set out in the statement is made and can require the named school to take a particular student

- arrange appropriate specialist provision outside England and Wales.

LEA officers must be granted access to any school which educates a child with a statement of special educational need, for example a grant-maintained or private school, to fulfil their responsibilities to oversee such education.

Duties of governing bodies

Governors must:

- 'use their best endeavours' to *secure that* special education provision is made for those whose learning difficulties call for it

- ensure that that teachers are aware of the special learning needs of identified pupils

- ensure that teachers are aware of the importance of identifying and providing for special needs

- ensure that children identified as having special needs engage in activities with others not so identified, subject to the three provisos above

- in the annual report on the school for parents, include a report on the school's policy for pupils with 'special educational needs' as to admission and access arrangements for disabled pupils.

Appeals procedures

When a statement is first issued, when an amendment to it is proposed, or after an assessmnent, parents can go to the Tribunal to challenge the LEA's decision not to assess or to reassess, the decision not to make a statement, the contents of a statement, and any amendments to the statement made by the local authority. The decisions of the Tribunal are binding.

Parents can express a preference for a particular maintained mainstream or special school. LEAs can overrule in either case in accordance with the provisos above. Parents can also make representation for a non-maintained (independent) school. The LEA has no duty in law to respond to this request.

Regulations

Regulations associated with Part IV of the Act specify procedures for formal assessment, statements and annual reviews. They also require that a transition plan be produced and reviewed after the fourteenth birthday of a child who is the subject of a statement. This plan is discussed below.

In addition, Regulations set out the precise list of issues that must be addressed in writing a school's special education policy. This list is to be found in Section 2:10 of the 1994 Code of Practice and in Circular 6/94, and is discussed further in Chapter 5.

There is a requirement that statements should 'substantially correspond' to the example set out in the Regulations.

The Circulars

Circulars 10/99 and 11/99 on 'social inclusion', outline the role of schools and LEAs in supporting children 'at particular risk', for example children 'with special educational needs', those who are looked after, travellers, those from families under stress and teenage mothers. Circular 10/99 explains the law and good practice on pupil behaviour and discipline, reducing disaffection, school attendance, detention and exclusion, and introduces pastoral support programmes for disaffected pupils. Circular 11/99 includes the legal responsibilities of LEAs for managing attendence, providing education outside schools, reintegrating excluded pupils and 'pupil referral units'.

The Parents' Guides

In addition to the documents about the details of the law and the advice to professionals, the Department for Education produced two documents for parents: *Special Educational Needs; a guide for parents* and *Special Educational Needs Tribunal: how to appeal*. These documents can be seen as part of the recent trend towards increasing accountability to the consumer.

The Code of Practice

The Code of Practice came into effect in September 1994 and provides advice on most aspects of Part IV of the 1996 Education Act. The 'fundamental principles' of the Code are listed on page 2 of the Code itself (para. 1:2). These principles include children's rights to having their special learning needs addressed, the notion of a 'continuum of need' and a corresponding 'continuum of provision', children's entitlement to a broad curriculum, inclusion in mainstream schools where possible and appropriate, early intervention, parental choice and partnership with parents.

The injunction to 'have regard' to the Code applies only where it provides advice on matters *in addition* to those required by law. A good definition of its status was provided by Lady Blatch when the House of Lords considered the Code:

> **In justifying their actions, those to whom the Code applies will have to show that the alternative action they took produced results which were at least as beneficial as those which would have resulted from their following the code.**
>
> *(Lady Blatch, Lords Hansard, 29 April 1993, column 487)*

Not withstanding its 'advisory' status, tribunals rely heavily on the Code in reaching their judgments. OFSTED uses it as a template when assessing good practice in schools (OFSTED, 1996).

The five stages of assessment

The principal innovatory element in the Code, compared to the law and the Regulations, was the introduction of a five-stage model of assessment which will be discussed in detail in Chapter 9. In paragraph 2:119 of the Code, schools are enjoined to establish clear procedures to identify children whose 'academic, physical, social or emotional development is giving cause for concern', in consultation with parents and the child, develop and review individual education plans designed to address individual needs, assess children's performance and make use of outside specialist advice particularly from Stage 3. This staged model reflects that set out in the Warnock Report (DES, 1978, pp. 60–63), versions of which some local education authorities subsequently adopted (Booth, 1996).

The Individual Education Plan

The term 'Individual Education Plan' (IEP) follows the American model outlined in the 1975 special education law in the USA (Public Law 94–142) where a plan for a child perceived as having difficulties had to be drawn up in order to attract additional federal funds.

In the Code of Practice, the Individual Education Plan (IEP) is introduced at stage 2. It summarises action to be taken at home and at school to address difficulties in learning (p. 28, para. 2:93). It focuses on the nature of the child's learning difficulties rather than other elements of the school context which impact on learning. There is further discussion of this plan in Chapter 9 below.

Statutory assessment (stages 4 and 5)

In the years following the 1981 Education Act a number of deficiencies in the procedures for assessing pupils thought to 'have special educational needs' became apparent. The Audit Commission and Her Majesty's Inspectorate identified three key problems:

- **lack of clarity about what constitutes special educational need and about the respective responsibilities of schools and LEAs**

- **lack of systems to ensure that schools and LEAs are accountable for their work in the area of special needs**

- **lack of incentives for LEAs to implement the 1981 Act.**

    (Audit Commission/HMI, 1992, para. 126)

The Code attempts to make the statementing process clearer, more useful to parents and teachers, and faster. It suggests that when the learning difficulties 'are significant and/or complex; have not responded to relevant and purposeful measures taken by the school and external specialists, and *may* call for special educational provision' outside resources normally available to mainstream schools, 'the LEA should consider very carefully the case for statutory assessment' (paras 3:59 to 3:94).

A request for an assessment can come from a head teacher or a parent. In the case of a request from a head teacher, 'except in a small minority of cases' (DfEE, 1994a, para. 3:6) a student will be considered for a statutory assessment only if they have passed through the three school-based stages. Schools are expected to submit full records of the views of parents, evidence of health checks and of involvement with social services and other outside agencies, if appropriate, together with records of Individual Education Plans. If the request is from a parent it will be considered only if the student has not been assessed in the previous six months.

The timetable for the process

Booth (1996) has paraphrased the steps in the process of assessment as outlined in the Code:

> The Regulations set time limits for statutory assessment. Unless, for example, a period of school holidays coincides with the time for educational advice or a child is out of the country, the assessment must take, in total, no more than 26 weeks. It has the following steps:

1. Considering whether a statutory assessment is to be carried out

> When an LEA decides to consider whether to carry out a statutory assessment, an officer must write to the student's parents setting out what an assessment would entail, who would be consulted, and the time limits for both the assessment and the stages in drawing up a possible consequent statement. Parents must be given at least 29 days to respond to this suggestion by, for example, agreeing with or contesting the need for an assessment. They must be given the name of an LEA officer whom they can contact for clarification and advice, and it is recommended that they are also provided with the name of an independent Named Person from a voluntary agency. Where a parent has requested an assessment and the authority decides not to go ahead with one, the parents must be informed of their right to appeal to the Special Educational Needs Tribunal. Unless there are exceptional circumstances, the LEA must decide whether to go ahead with the assessment within *six weeks*.

2. Making an assessment

> The LEA must seek parental, educational, medical, psychological and social services advice as well as advice from relevant others. The LEA's experts must advise on the provision appropriate to the child. The Code also recommends that 'the views of young people themselves should be sought wherever possible'. The time scale for collecting the advice must normally be no longer than six weeks. 'Normally' this is included within a maximum of *ten weeks* from notifying parents that an assessment is pro-

posed to notifying them of the LEA's decision on whether to draft a statement. If the authority decides not to issue a statement a parent may appeal against the decision to the Tribunal.

3. Drafting the proposed statement or note in lieu

A statement has to be set out 'substantially' according to the format in the Regulations reprinted at the end of the Code. The Code states 'LEAs should draft clear, unambiguous statements' (DfEE, 1994a, para. 4:26). Part 1 contains personal details of the student. Part 2 sets out 'each and every one of the child's special educational needs as identified by the LEA during the statutory assessment' (para 4:24). Part 3, the section which outlines the special educational provision considered necessary to meet the child's needs, is divided into three sub-sections. The first describes the objectives which the provision should aim to meet; the second, the educational provision necessary, including any modifications to or disapplication from the national curriculum; and the third, arrangements for monitoring the success of the provision. The Code adds that it may be useful to specify exactly which elements of the provision are to be made by the school and which by the LEA. It also states that the description of the provision 'should normally be specific, detailed and quantified (in terms, for example, of hours of ancillary help or specialist teaching support), although there will be some cases where some flexibility should be retained in order to meet the changing special educational needs of the child concerned' (para. 4:28). Part 4 sets out the type and name of the school where provision is to be made. It has to be left blank when the draft statement is sent to parents so as not to pre-empt their wishes concerning placement. Part 5 identifies non-educational needs and Part 6 non-educational provision, effectively defined in terms of provision that is made by an agency other than the educational authority. The time allowed for drafting the proposed statement is no more than *two weeks*.

If the LEA, having completed the statutory assessment process, decides that a statement is not appropriate, the Code recommends that a note in lieu of a statement is issued to the child's parents, school and any other professional involved. In law, the issuing of a note in lieu is the equivalent of a refusal to assess, and parents are able to appeal against this outcome. This should allow the information collected during statutory assessment to be used by the school in augmenting their own provision for the child.

4. Finalizing the statement.

The draft statement must be accompanied by a letter which is set out 'substantially' in accordance with the example given in the Regulations, and included as the first page of Appendix B. Included with the letter must be a list of all mainstream and special schools in the area, as well as relevant independent schools. Parents can express a preference for a school in the maintained sector from these lists, or make 'representations' for a place in an independent school. Though the LEA is under no obligation to fund a place at an independent school if they can recommend a suitable mainstream or special school, in the case of a state school, the LEA must comply with parental wishes, unless, in the words of the law:

the school is unsuitable to the child's age, ability or aptitude or to his special educational needs, or

the attendance of the child at the school would be incompatible with the provision of efficient education for the children with whom he would be educated or the efficient use of resources.

(Education Act 1996, Schedule 27, Section 3(3))

It is argued in the Code that if a parent expresses a wish for a particular mainstream school but the above conditions apply in that school then the LEA must fulfil its duty to integrate by suggesting another mainstream school, if possible, where they do not apply. In January 1994, in England about 95,000 or 1.30 per cent of students aged 5–16 were in special schools. This percentage varied between LEAs from 0.42 per cent in Cornwall, 0.62 per cent in the London Borough of Newham, 2.35 per cent in Manchester and 3.14 per cent in the London Borough of Lambeth (Education, 2 June 1995, p. 22).

When the proposed statement has been received a parent has 15 days in which to comment and state a preferred school (for example, the school the student is already attending), or to request a meeting with an LEA officer, and then a further 15 days after the last LEA meeting to send further comments which the LEA has to consider. These time limits are included in an overall maximum period from the issue of the draft statement to the issue of the final statement of *eight weeks*.

If parents disagree with the final version of the statement they can appeal to the Tribunal under Section 326(1) of the 1996 Act against:

Part 2, the description of their child's 'special educational needs';

Part 3, the special educational provision;

Part 4, the school named, or if no school has been named, that fact.

The Tribunal can reject the appeal or rewrite the statement. Its decision is binding on the LEA.

(Booth, Simmons and Wearmouth, 1996)

Annual reviews

The LEA must initiate a review of the statement within 12 months of its issue and then annually thereafter. Thie requirement is discussed more fully in Chapter 9.

The Transition Plan

Regulations require that a Transition Plan is drawn up at the review following a young person's fourteenth birthday, in consultation with the student, the parents, teachers, the careers service, and other professionals, as appropriate. The Transition Plan is intended to ensure a coherent pattern of provision to smooth the student's transition from school to subsequent activities including college and employment.

Social services and the health authority

The Code also recommends improved liaison and communication with social services and the health authority to aid the assessment process (para. 3:16). However, the Code does little to resolve disputes over speech therapy. There remains a difficult issue of whether the responsibility for the provision of speech therapy lies with LEAs or the NHS. The Code says only:

> **Prime responsibility ... rests with the NHS ... Where the NHS does not provide speech and language therapy for a child whose statement specifies such therapy as educational provision, ultimate responsibility for ensuring that the provision is made rests with the LEA, unless the child's parents have made appropriate alternative arrangements.**
>
> *(DfEE, 1994a, paras 4:34 to 4:35)*

This issue was re-opened by the Green Paper but remains unresolved.

The individual and the law

Simmons (2000) offers some interesting reflections on the relationship between the individual child and the law:

> The courts continue to uphold the notion of individual need, even though many LEAs, encouraged by the Audit Commission/HMI report *Getting in on the Act*, have attempted to shift the focus of their special education provision away from individually based resourcing to funding based on formulae or on allocation of cash sums to schools (Audit Commission/HMI, 1992). What the Audit Commission did not point out, however, was that such formulae-based allocations should be made within the context of the existing law. The courts have subsequently made

this point clear, in *R v. Cumbria County Council Ex parte P* (1994). In this case, P's statement referred to speech therapy in Part 3 but did not specify how much help P was to receive. However, the statement was specific about the amount of money that would be spent on P's provision: 'P's needs entitle him to extra funding at Band level 3. This is now £6,000 per year.' The judge said that although it was interesting for parents to know how much was being spent on their child, citing a figure in itself did not discharge the LEA's duty to specify what the child would be getting:

If in the present case nothing other than a sentence on the lines of '£6,000 is allocated to pay for all P's needs' had appeared in Part 3 of the statement, I would have regarded this as not complying with the requirements of specificity contained in the statute and regulations.

The judge's comments have been significant for those LEAs who have introduced resource ladders, matrices or other resourcing devices based on formulae. While there is nothing intrinsically unlawful about such devices, if statements do not also contain details of specific provision, then they are likely to be challengeable. So for example, when a tribunal was asked to consider Part 3 of a statement which read 'Sam should have additional support equivalent to Level C on the Resource Ladder', the Tribunal judgement stated:

'It is the view of the Tribunal that specifying Sam's special educational provision in terms of a level on the (Resource) Ladder does not fulfil the LEA's statutory obligation to specify the special educational provision to be made. In reaching this conclusion we have had regard to S168 of the Education Act of 1993, the Education (Special Educational Needs) Regulations 1994, paragraphs 4:24–4:29 of the Code of Practice and the decision in R v. Secretary of State for Education and Science, ex p. E (1992).'

So while some LEAs may argue that formula funding is a 'fairer' way of resourcing special education, it is not a serious option for those LEAs wishing to avoid challenge at tribunals or in the courts.

(Booth, Simmons and Wearmouth, 2000)

In principle, provision made for children identified as 'having' special educational needs is not subject to the vagaries of local 'discretion' or cuts in funding, though parents may have to struggle to secure their child's individual entitlement. The law is based on individual need, which means that individual parents or carers must act on their child's behalf. There is a view that the law as it stands is 'unfair' to those children whose parents or carers are less able, for one reason or another, to promote their child's interests. The voluntary sector has argued the importance of supporting such parents in securing their child's entitlement. The Action Plan which followed the 1997 Green Paper, stated that the Government intended to expand local parent partnership services and to give guidance on a new service to parents through Independent Parental Supporters schemes. If parents or carers fail to respond to letters within the time limits set out, they lose their right of appeal to the SEN Tribunal. It may be that the school could refer a parent to the new parents' support services, once these become established throughout LEAs. These services have the advantage of being local and easy to access. However, it is unclear as yet just how independent they will be and they are likely to vary. Schools will need to develop their own knowledge of independent services, in order to give parents help in finding outside agencies who can advise them.

Simmons (op cit.) reflects that what these legal definitions mean in practice is that the law sees children as falling into one of several different categories.

First, there are children who do not have any kind of "learning difficulty" as defined under the Act. Second, there are those who, although they have learning difficulties as defined under the Act, do not need special educational provision and therefore do not legally have special educational needs. Think, for example of an able hearing-impaired child who can adjust his own hearing aid and who can access the whole curriculum without additional help. Thirdly, there are children who have learning difficulties and who need special educational provision to meet their learning difficulties but whose school can itself arrange the special educational provision they need. An example here would be a child who has a speech and language problem but whose SENCO trained as a speech therapist and is able to work individually with her. A child in a situation like this would not need the LEA to arrange their provision, though the situation might change if the child changed schools or if the teacher left. Fourthly, there are children who have learning difficulties which can only be met by special educational provision and whose schools cannot arrange that provision themselves. An example here would be a child with serious language and literacy difficulties, who needs individual help in most lessons in his mainstream school, although the school can only afford to provide him with that help in the mornings. Arranging this child's provision would be likely to become the direct responsibility of the LEA, following formal assessment and the issuing of a statement of special educational need.

(Ibid)

Simmons uses the following two examples to exemplify why, given current statutory requirements, in terms of the legal definition of 'special educational need', a child in one school might have a Statement while in another a child with similar needs might not:

1. Jane is 8 and has Down's Syndrome. Her classroom teacher has attended several courses on the education of children with Down's Syndrome and has organised a circle of friends who play with Jane at lunch and break times. Jane has an individual learning support assistant in the mornings and shares another child's helper in the afternoon. She is making good progress though there are increasing concerns about her ability to communicate. She has speech therapy weekly at the local health centre.

2. Arwah is 13: she is very clumsy and has difficulty holding a pencil and organising her work. She finds it difficult to understand what is going on in class and her reading is poor. However, she has an excellent knowledge of Urdu, which she reads and speaks fluently.

There is no national 'benchmark' for the issuing of a statement, although the DfEE has commissioned a study aimed at national guidance criteria for statements. The Code of Practice has attempted to introduce some consistency into judgments of whether a child needs a statement or not. However, decisions should be based on individual need not on externally imposed criteria. Whether a child needs a statement or not could vary considerably from school to school, depending on the level of resources in each school and how those resources are deployed. In School A, a child with a high level of additional need could have those needs met as part of the general provision within the school. In School B, less well geared to individual need or less well resourced, the same child would need to have their provision arranged by the LEA through the statementing process.

(Ibid)

Simmons explains that:

Children with an 'obvious' difficulty such as Jane would only need a statement if their needs could not be met within the resources generally available to their school. There are LEAs, with a clear commitment to inclusion, who have put enough resources into schools so that children with Down's Syndrome, for example, do not necessarily need a statement. During the consultation period on the 1997 Green Paper, some respondents argued that such arrangements are to be preferred, since they avoid the 'stigma' of a statement.

The option of the statement, of course, remains, if the level of school-based resourcing falls. Many parents seek a statement simply because it is the only guarantee they have that a level of support will be maintained.

In Jane's case, the real cause for concern is her speech therapy. Currently it is being provided through the Health Authority: her parents could argue that since language is such a crucial part of her education, then it should be part of her educational programme in school. Unless such provision already exists in Jane's school, then the only way it could be guaranteed as part of her educational programme would be by means of a statement. In such a statement, the need for speech therapy would be included in Part 3 and the provision detailed in Part 4. Should Jane require a statement, then all her needs would be set out in it, including needs that are currently being met by her school. The school would continue to meet those needs but if in the future it found it could not continue to do so, then the responsibility for arranging provision would fall to the LEA. Whatever happened, Jane's provision would be secure. Jane's parents might need to seek independent advice on whether they wished to request an assessment with a view to a statement.

With Arwah, the difficulties arising out of her use of English as a second language would not entitle her to a statement. However, she appears to have other problems that are holding her back. She would need to be on one of the school-based stages; regular review should show whether she is making progress with the resources available to her school. If she is not, then she would be entitled to assessment.

(Ibid)

SEN Tribunal as the focus of differences

The Special Educational Needs Tribunal, with its focus on the child's needs on the day of the hearing, relies heavily on the evidence available from LEA personnel – teachers, SENCOs, educational psychologists. It is one arena where the differences in opinion between parents on the one hand and the local authority and/or the school or the other are likely to become apparent. The Select Committee Report (House of Commons, 1996) cites evidence that in some LEAs such people are subjected to considerable pressure to support the LEA case. Some teachers and head teachers have been told that they 'cannot attend' a hearing to give evidence in support of parents' cases, some have had pension rights docked and there is evidence that some teachers on short term contracts have not been re-employed.

The President of the Tribunal himself recognized this problem in his Annual Report:

> In the spirit of parent partnership engendered by the Code of Practice I had thought that those most closely concerned with the child in question

would have no hesitation on coming forward to offer their help. It turns out that in some cases local education authorities are reluctant that any of their employees, and this will particularly apply to teachers, should give evidence for the parents and 'against' the authority. This takes a confrontational view of the appeal to the Tribunal which seems unfortunate.'

(SEN Tribunal, 'Annual Report', 1995, p. 14)

Reactions to the Code of Practice

Parents' views of the assessment process

A study of the responses of parents with children with special needs to the assessment and statementing process by the Independent Panel for Special Educational Advice (IPSEA) in 1995, showed high levels of parental dissatisfaction with the process of assessment (Simmons, 2000). Parental concerns related to:

- worries about vaguely worded Statements

- increasing difficulty experienced in convincing local authorities that children should be assessed

- unpopularity in mainstream schools of children identified as 'having special needs'

- disagreement with the LEA over school placement

- a perceived shortage of resources, hardly surprising, since the new legislation had brought no new funding with it.

A year into the new framework, the House of Commons Education Committee investigated the working of the Code and the Tribunal. It sought the views of a wide range of people involved in implementing the new framework and published a document containing the report itself, the minutes of the Committee recording their questioning of witnesses, and appendices which were written evidence supplied by local authorities, voluntary organizations, teachers' unions and academics, among others.

Different groups expressed conflicting models of learning in their evidence. The medical model of a child *with* a difficulty that should be treated in an individual specialist manner was endorsed, for example, by the British Dyslexia Association in a reference to the statementing process:

It is established in Case Law that Part 2 should be a 'diagnosis'. The medical analogy is a helpful one and should enable understanding and an effective 'prescription' or provision.

(House of Commons Education Committee, 1996, Appendix 10, p. 29)

The BDA rooted its position very firmly in the law in advocating that provision for individual pupils should be quantified:

> The provision should normally be specific, detailed and quantified (in terms, for example, of hours of ancillary or specialist teaching support) ...

(DfEE, 1994a, para. 4:28)

The medical model of learning difficulties is further reinforced when psychologists use standardized psychometric tests to diagnose pupils' difficulties as an expected part of the assessment procedure. Evidence from the British Psychological Society (Division of Educational and Child Psychology) questioned the assumption that problems can always be diagnosed in this way:

> The question as to whether psychometric tests should be a necessary prerequisite for the allocation of resources continues to be raised. The DECP feels that this is a nonsense and that psychologists must be able to assess a child as is most appropriate in the given situation.

(House of Commons Education Committee, 1996, Appendix 11)

Other evidence makes the assumption that a student will experience difficulties where there is a mismatch between that individual and teaching methods, approaches and resources. A social and interactive model of learning which takes context very firmly into account was supported for example by evidence from Canterbury Christ Church College which was based on research funded by the DfEE to investigate individual education plans :

> There is a consensus of opinion that the Code will fail if 'bolted on' to a school setting which does not have the philosophy, staffing and structures to support an inclusive approach to SEN pupils.

(House of Commons Education Committee, 1996, Appendix 12, p. 34)

and by Professor Alan Dyson:

> ... the Code runs counter to developments in some schools which were attempting to meet the children's needs by enhancing the quality of provision for all pupils within ordinary classrooms. The Code, therefore, unwittingly reinforces the establishment of separate special needs systems characterized by somewhat narrow 'remedial' aims.
>
> I suggest that the positive aspect of the Code could be maximized by emphasizing: the principles of the Code rather than its detailed procedures; the scope for legitimate interpretation of those principles; and the key contribution to be made by the quality of mainstream classroom provision at stage 1 and 'stage 0' (which is currently missing from the Code).

(House of Commons Education Committee, 1996, Appendix 17, p. 44)

This social perspective is also compatible with the view expressed by Harrow Education Services Committee (House of Commons Education Committee, 1996, Appendix 23, p. 53) that learning support staff have an important role in developing materials and approaches that are appropriate for all pupils. The Code should therefore be established as integral to the national curriculum, rather than as a separate entity.

Schools' reactions

The introduction of the Code provoked a mixed reaction in schools. On the positive side the emphasis on individual need was welcomed by some as providing a clear framework for the identification and assessment of particular children 'with special needs' (Cocker, 1995; Bradley and Roaf, 1995). This led to reports of 'greater quality of assessment and the planning of appropriate provision' (House of Commons Education Committee, 1996, para. 6, p. vi). Evidence from primary and secondary schools in one local authority in southern England also suggested that many teachers regarded the Code as fulfilling the function both of evening out the allocation of extra resources for children and of highlighting the need to take the difficulties in learning experienced by some pupils more seriously (Loxley and Bines, 1995).

However, schools also reported disadvantages in the individual approach to identification and assessment. Practitioners cited continued problems of negative labelling, unquestioning acceptance of the dominant deficit model of the child and stigma associated with some of the practices recommended in the Code (Dyer, 1995; Wheal, 1995). In some schools there have been problems, for example categorization, heightened perception of difference and lack of confidentiality, associated with the practice of maintaining a school special needs register (Wearmouth, 1996). Teachers also blamed the Code for a huge increase in administration. A survey among special needs co-ordinators in the south east of England revealed that less than half expected to remain in the same or similar position in five years' time. The majority cited burdensome administrative requirements and lack of time for curriculum development as reasons why they were unlikely to stay (Male, 1996). Schools also drew attention to lack of funding within the school to support pupils who experience difficulties in learning but who are not statemented (Loxley and Bines, 1995). Not all LEAs kept separate the additional 'special needs' element in the school's capitation allowance. The LEA might be satisfied that it had allocated sufficient funds to a school, but the school might say it did not have the necessary resources for additional support for a child (House of Commons Education Committee, 1996, p. vii, para. 8).

The Code's acknowledgement that schools can create difficulties for children as well as meet their needs (para. 3:65) did little to clarify the confusion which has existed in the roles of many special needs co-ordinators since the advent of the 'whole-school' approach. On the one hand, they might be perceived as support teachers for individual pupils and staff. On the other, they might be expected to promote curriculum change and development to bring about an integrated inclusive approach to facilitate the learning of all pupils. 'As the *special* teachers in *ordinary* schools they have to be, at one and the same time, the advocates of the new movement towards inclusion and part of the separate apparatus of separate education' (Dyson and Gains, 1995).

Evidence, for example from some OFSTED inspectors, has indicated that the work of many learning support staff is having only a minor impact on curriculum development anyway: 'There is now less incentive for SEN staff to act as partners to other teachers in developing a proactive, differentiated curriculum for all' (Greenhalgh, 1996).

Local authorities' reactions

The Association of County Councils and the Association of Metropolitan Authorities submitted comments to the House of Commons Education Committee from over forty local authorities which presented both positive and negative reactions to the introduction of the Code (House of Commons Education Committee, 1996, Appendix 3, pp. 18–19). On the positive side, LEAs generally welcomed the Code. They viewed schools as more willing to acknowledge responsibility for the progress of pupils who experience difficulties in learning, as having improved school-based identification and assessment and as having raised the status of special needs co-ordinators. In addition, the perception of Bedfordshire LEA was that local authorities were now making more detailed and better informed statements of special educational needs, parents were better informed and had become more involved with the education of their children, annual reviews are now carried out with more diligence than before, and LEAs were working more closely than previously with other statutory agencies (House of Commons Education Committee, 1996, Appendix 6, p. 24).

Other comments expressed negative views, however, with LEAs saying that they were experiencing some difficulties in fulfilling their statutory obligations towards individual students. These difficulties were blamed on resourcing. LEAs said that meeting the requirements of the legislation was costing more, despite the government's assertion that the effect of the Act would be 'cost-neutral'. They cited additional bureaucracy, for example because the LEA instead of the school had to arrange the 14+ review, so that money was spent on office staff rather than direct support for children. One of the biggest problems to LEAs was whether LEAs or health authorities were responsible for providing services which might be interpreted as related both to education and health, for example speech therapy, in spite of the case law stemming from the Lancashire judgement.

The effect on LEA support services of shifting primary responsibility for provision for students during the school-based stages on to schools themselves has been considerable. Previously LEAs made the decision about which model they would use to deliver support services to schools. Now the relationship has been reversed. The school-based stages of assessment and identification of the learning needs of pupils have placed responsibility for provision for pupils firmly in the hands of school governors and staff. It is their duty to call upon assistance from outside agents, purchased from the provision which is 'generally available' through the schools' budget. Schools must then decide how external support will be most appropriately used. LEAs have been given the duty to 'consult all schools regularly about their need for support services and provide clear information to schools about their availability' (DfEE 1994b, paragraph 63). The model of provision is clearly market-oriented. As providers of these services LEAs must be 'able to conclude service level agreements with schools and ... able to maintain services which are staffed and equipped at a level which will efficiently meet demand' (DfEE 1994b, paragraph 87(1)). The 1996 OFSTED report on how the Code was being implemented in schools indicates inadequacies in service use. In most LEAs schools were uncertain how to access centrally held support services, and the amount and kind of support offered to schools from LEA services is between and within LEAs.

> The criteria and procedures for schools to obtain access to the centrally held support services should also be made more explicit in most LEAs. In some LEAs, the range of support services enables provision to be made at Stages 1 and 2, whilst other LEAs have very limited provision even at Stage 3 owing to financial restraints or funds having been previously delegated to schools.

(OFSTED, 1996)

The brief of the House of Commons Education Committee was to report on how the Code and the Tribunal were working in practice, rather than to undertake a fundamental re-appraisal of the conceptual framework of Part III of the 1993 Education Act. Specific recommendations made by the Committee were related to the situation as it exists and the fact that the law is based on the rights of the individual. Its members did not consider how far this view might inhibit the encouragement of the potential of all students.

The Committee recommended that there should be a review of:

- responsibility and funding for the training of special education teachers

- the role of special needs co-ordinators

- criteria used by LEAs for initiating statements

- provision for specific learning difficulties

- the implications of Tribunal decisions for LEA policies and resources.

- what the President of the Tribunal should say to Tribunal chairs on how they should advise parents' befrienders (following this recommendation, the President of the Tribunal wrote to the chairs advising them on how to make the best use of parent befrienders)

- the most appropriate LEA employee to give evidence to Tribunal hearings.

The Code of Practice in Northern Ireland

The responsibility of the Department of Education, Northern Ireland (DENI), for educational provision is devolved to the five Education and Library Boards. Membership of these Boards is at the discretion of DENI. There is a clear division between school along religious lines. 'Controlled' schools tend to be Protestant, maintained schools are Catholic and integrated schools are inter-denominational. The selective system makes the grammar schools the preferred choice at secondary level for most parents. The system of special schools is seen as separate and distinct. The number and type of special schools varies across Boards. The policy of each Board determines the special system in each area.

The Northern Ireland Code is a more succinct version of that in England and Wales. One important difference is that of time limits within which local authorities have to assess a student whose needs may require a Statement. In England and Wales the law relating to time limits for the various stages in the process is made clear. However, there is only one time limit underpinned by law in Northern Ireland which is that there should be no more than eighteen weeks between the Education Board's decision to assess a child's educational needs with the intention of going through the Statement process, and issuing the draft Statement. The rest are given as guidance in the Northern Ireland Code which does not carry the force of law. The implication of this is that if the process is delayed parents have no recourse to the Tribunal because they have not received full notice of the proposed provision. The 'named person' in the Code in England and Wales is the 'named Board officer' in Northern Ireland. The significance of 'Education Plans' in Northern Ireland, rather than the term 'Individual Education Plans' as in England and Wales is that teachers in the Province have the chance to consider group education plans rather than solely plans for individuals.

In many schools in the province provision is in the process of development, although most schools now have a special needs policy. Overriding all, however, is the fact that the system is driven by the selection procedure at 11+, as already mentioned. Many primary schools are streamed as are many secondary.

Quite frequently there is a 'special needs' stream, or pupils are withdrawn from classes, thus rendering problematic the notion of 'inclusion'. There is, however, a sense in some schools that responsibility for meeting children's learning needs rests with all teachers. The Code has also proved the impetus for new initiatives, and in some schools there is targeted support to meet specific needs.

Proposed Changes to the 1994 Code of Practice: the revised Code

A revised Code of Practice is proposed for the year 2001 to take account of some of the concerns expressed during the operation of the 1994 Code. In a document entitled *The SEN Code of Practice and Associated Legislation – proposed changes and areas for revision* (DfEE, 1999) the DfEE has indicated its intention to 'expand' the guidance given on a number of topics and 'revise' the Code in certain respects to take account of particular issues. The discussion below relates to the proposals as outlined in this document.

Expanded guidance

Among the topics on which it is proposed to offer expanded guidance are: the development of 'more inclusive' approaches to meeting pupils' learning needs; 'good practice' in collaborative working arrangements between Education, Health and Social Services; support for the learning of 'looked-after' children; the role of school governors in the area of special educational needs; support for the under-fives; school exclusions; the relationship between special educational needs, the National Curriculum and the National Literacy Strategy; disabled children's entitlements to personal support; arrangements for conciliation between home and the education service; the use of information and communications technology in maintaining records; the 'implications for SEN of the National Childcare Strategy and changes to the NHS', and the 'new school framework' (ibid).

Areas for revision

It is proposed in the DfEE (1999) document that the revised Code will offer guidance on a number of areas, among which are

'Flexibility': the new Foreward will emphasise that schools may interpret the guidance given in the Code to suit their own context.

'Secondary schools': a number of teachers teach secondary pupils. There will be a focus on target-setting and monitoring of progress.

'Special educational needs co-ordinators': the time required to co-ordinate special provision, including that of administrative staff, in typical primary and secondary situations will be discussed.

'Individual Education Plans': Model IEP formats will be set out together with advice that 'IEPs are most helpful when they are crisply written and focus on three or four short-term targets for the child'.

'Stages of the Code': the revised Code will 'recommend a framework which includes only two school-based' stages – 'School Support', where the school is expected to make provision from its own resources, and 'Support Plus', where additional resources will be provided. It will also develop the guidance given on statutory assessment and statementing procedures.

'Children whose first language is not English': more guidance will be given on identifying and assessing the special learning needs of these pupils.

'Parent Partnership Service': the Government expects 'Independent Parental Supporters' to provide 'a similar service to parents as that offered at present by Named Persons'. Advice will be offered on the role and functions of local parent partnership services.

'Criteria for making statutory assessments': many of the criteria for making a statutory assessment of a variety of needs given in the 1994 Code, paragraphs 3:55 to 3:94 are common to all needs. This material will be rationalised.

'Child's views': LEAs and schools will be further encouraged to engage with the child's views throughout the process of identification and assessment.

'Appeals to the SEN Tribunal': the Act will be amended to allow appeals from schools, as well as parents, against LEA decisions not to assess a child's special educational needs, and to treat a request from a school in the same way as a parental request 'when parliamentary time permits'.

'Local conciliation arrangements': guidance will be given on ways to resolve disgreements between parents or carers and the school and/or LEA before an appeal stage is reached.

'Speech and language therapy': this area is clearly still contentious and there are serious issues yet to be resolved (ibid).

Summary

Implicit in these discussions of the Code of Practice and the Tribunal are issues of equality of opportunity in education, fairness in allocation of resources and the question of whether individual learning programmes for students or a whole-school approach to learning support is more likely to encourage all learners to reach their potential. Neither the Code, nor the 1993 Act or the subsequent 1996 Act, re-examined the definition of 'special educational need' or 'learning difficulty' enshrined in the 1981 Act.

Following the period of consultation after the publication of the 1997 Green Paper *Excellence for All Children*, the government's Action Plan *Meeting Special Educational Needs* proposed a number of significant changes to the Code.

Suggested Activities: Reflection and Discussion

1. Reactions to the Code of Practice

Re-read the section *'Reactions to the Code of Practice'*. Reflect on:

- how far your own experiences of working within the recommendations of the Code mirror the evidence outlined here

- what additional or alternative recommendations you would make to improving or amending the Code.

2. Meeting legal requirements

Reflect on:

- why, in terms of the legal definition of 'special educational need' a child in one school might have a Statement while in another a child with similar needs might not

- what problems, if any, this relativist notion of 'special need' might create in schools. What practical solutions can you see, from your own experience or those of colleagues?

- what is meant by 'legal entitlement'. What is it that children with special educational needs are entitled to?

3. The responsibilities of the governing board

Reflect on the extent to which members of the governing board at a school with which you are familiar are aware of their statutory responsibilities towards pupils identified as experiencing special educational needs, or who might experience such needs.

If this issue is problematic, discuss with colleagues what might be done to raise greater awareness in the short-, medium- and long-term.

---

3 Complexities, tensions and demands of the co-ordination role

The task of co-ordinating school provision labelled as 'special' is highly complex. To meet the demands successfully, necessitates an awareness and understanding of issues of policy development, management of personnel and physical resources, curriculum, pedagogy, assessment and planning for pupil learning. It may be that the governing body 'might be led to think that a school's special needs co-ordinator could look after all aspects of the school's special needs practice' (Cowne, 1998). However, 'special needs is too broad and too pervasive of the curriculum and ethos of a school to be any one person's sole responsibility' (ibid). In addition, the law is very clear in its delineation of statutory duties for securing pupils' entitlement to special provision in school to address identified learning needs. The governing body retains this duty, however a particular school chooses to make the arrangements. The Code advises that, in practice:

... the division of responsibility is a matter for individual schools ... but schools should bear in mind the following:

– the governing body should ... with the head teacher, determine the school's general policy and approach ... establish the appropriate staffing and funding arrangements and maintain a general oversight

– the governing body may appoint a committee to ... closely monitor the school's work

– the head teacher has responsibility for the day-to-day management of all aspects of the school's work ... the head teacher will work closely with the school's SEN co-ordinator or team

– the SEN co-ordinator or team ... has responsibility for the day-to-day operation of the school's SEN policy and for co-ordinating provision for pupils with special educational needs, particularly at stages 2 and 3

– all teaching and non-teaching staff should be involved in the development of the school's SEN policy and be fully aware of the school's procedures for identifying, assessing and making provision ...

(DfEE, 1994, 2:7)

The duties involved in the co-ordination role

The multi-faceted demands of the co-ordination role are demonstrated by reference to the list of duties of the Special Needs Co-ordinator outlined in *The Code of Practice* (DfEE, 1994a):

- **the day-to-day operation of the school's SEN policy**

- **liaising with and advising fellow teachers**

- **co-ordinating provision for children with special educational needs**

- **maintaining the school's SEN register and overseeing the records on all pupils with special educational needs**

- **liaising with parents of children with special educational needs**

- **contributing to the in-service training of staff**

- **liaising with external agencies including the educational psychology service and other support agencies, medical and social services and voluntary bodies.**

(DfEE, 1994a, 2:14)

One way of looking at this role is that it represents an attempt to mediate the tensions and dilemmas inherent in an approach to special provision in school which adopts a whole-school view of curriculum support at the same time as meeting individual needs. On the one hand the co-ordinator is expected to take a proactive part in identifying, assessing and organising provision appropriate to meeting individual needs. On the other hand, she or he is also expected to support curriculum differentiation in order to meet a diversity of need in every classroom. In terms of these issues, the duties outlined above might be represented as follows:

Meeting individual need	Curriculum support
Fulfilling the law: upholding individual pupils' entitlement to having their 'special educational needs' identified, assessed and met.	Supporting learning for all: upholding common entitlement to accessing the broad, balanced curriculum.
Maintaining a managerial role which pays due regard to the Code of Practice.	Maintaining a role as manager/co-ordinator of curriculum support which may be defined as anything that facilitates pupils' learning.
Sustaining a system for identifying, assessing and meeting the 'special needs' of individual children.	Actively working with other staff to identify areas of the curriculum which could be made more inclusive of pupils' learning.

Liaising with staff, parents and outside agencies with regard to individual pupils' difficulties.	Promoting differentiated approaches to teaching and assessment for all pupils within the classroom.
Negotiating, reviewing and evaluating Individual Education Plans	Team and support teaching in-class to reduce barriers to learning.
Advocacy for individual children.	Advocacy of curricular improvements for all.

The manner in which the duties of the co-ordinator are described may be seen to represent a dual approach to meeting pupils' learning needs, highlighting again the tension between supporting the notion of learning for all, and making special provision to meet the needs of an identified special few.

In 1998, the Teacher Training Agency issued a set of 'Standards' for the effective co-ordination of special educational provision in schools. Implicit in these Standards is a recognition of the broad-ranging nature of this role. They essentially define a set of core duties for the special needs co-ordinator within the areas of:

- strategic direction and development of SEN provision in the school

  SENCOs co-ordinate, with the support of the headteacher and within the context of the school's aims and policies, the development and implementation of the SEN policy in order to raise achievement and improve the quality of education provided (TTA, 1998a).

- teaching and learning

  SENCOs seek to develop, with the support of the headteacher and colleagues, effective ways of overcoming barriers to learning and sustaining effective teaching through the analysis and assessment of pupils' needs, by monitoring the quality of teaching and standards of pupils' achievements, and by setting targets for improvement (ibid).

- leading and managing staff

  SENCOs support staff involved in working with pupils with SEN by ensuring all those involved have the information necessary to secure improvements in teaching and learning and sustain staff motivation (ibid).

- the efficient and effective deployment of staff and resources

  SENCOs identify, with the support of the headteacher and governing body, appropriate resources to support the teaching of pupils with SEN and monitor their use in terms of efficiency, effectiveness, and safety (ibid).

Indicators of successful co-ordination of special educational needs provision in schools are defined as:

a. pupils on the SEN register who

make progress towards targets set in their individual education plans; show improvement in their literacy, numeracy and information technology skills; are helped to access the wider curriculum; are motivated to learn and develop self-esteem and confidence in their ability as learners;

b. teachers who

are familiar with and implement the school's SEN policy and approaches to meeting the needs of pupils with SEN; identify pupils who may require special provision e.g. those with EBD, and help to prepare individual education plans as appropriate; communicate effectively with the parents, the SENCO and all other staff with responsibilities for SEN, including those from external agencies; have high expectations of pupil's progress, set realistic but challenging targets which they monitor and review, and provide appropriate support;

c. learning support assistants who

whether employed by the school or LEA, understand their role in the school in relation to pupils with SEN; work collaboratively with the SENCO, teaching staff and staff from external agencies; through opportunities to develop their skills, become increasingly knowledgeable in the ways of supporting pupils and help them to maximise their levels of achievement and independence;

d. parents who

understand the targets set for their children and their contribution to helping their children achieve them; fell fully involved as partners in the education process;

e. headteachers and other senior managers who

recognise that the curriculum must be relevant to all pupils by taking SEN into account in the formulation and implementation of policies throughout the school; understand how best to support those with responsibility for SEN co-ordination;

f. governors who

understand their role in relation to pupils with SEN (and their parents) through the discharge of their statutory responsibilities; develop mechanisms for liason with the headteacher and the SENCO to ensure that they receive regular updates on the implementation of the school's SEN policy and the outcomes from the regular reviews; monitoring and evaluation of the provision made for pupils with SEN;

g. LEAs and other responsible bodies who

receive timely information about the progress made by pupils with SEN, including those with statements; ensure that time spent in the school by external staff is effectively used in support of pupils with SEN.

(Ibid)

The implication here is that successful outcomes of a school's special educational provision are the result of the work of the co-ordinator alone. However, the kind of provision in schools which secures the quality of teaching and learning that raises the standard of pupils' achievement is a shared endeavour. Success or failure in the task is not directly attributable to the co-ordinator alone. The work of any individual member of staff within a school is influenced as much by factors which impede or expedite his or her plans and intentions as by his or her personal attributes. Three specific problems arise. First, there is insufficient clarity or emphasis in this document of the extent to which the work of the special needs co-ordinator depends on the degree to which staff in a school, and the school system as a whole, is open to reflection and change. Second, there is little acknowledgement of how far external constraints influence the extent to which school managers feel the curriculum can be adapted, or differentiated, to enable the whole pupil body to engage more fully in formal learning activities. Where there is great resistance to new initiatives the SENCO may find his or her role very uncomfortable. Third, insufficient recognition is paid to the degree to which the head teacher and governors must actively and openly support the co-ordinator's work if she or he is to be seen to have the personal status required to influence the curricular changes and developments needed to reduce the barriers to pupils' learning. Support for the co-ordinator *cannot* be assumed, as is implied here.

The SENCO as change-agent

The successful discharge of the co-ordinator's role is highly dependent on his or her ability to perform the function of change-agent. She or he is reliant on co-operation from other staff, positive support from the governors, head teacher and senior management and on direct involvement in whole school planning. An increasing number of pupils identified as experiencing particular difficulties in learning are now included in mainstream schools as a result of the government focus on inclusion. The demands made of SENCOs as the agents of change in schools may also intensify. The extent to which SENCOs are in a position to effect change will depend on a number of factors including:

- the terms of the job description

- the co-ordinator's status and position in the school

- the expectations of the head teacher and senior management team

- the co-ordinator's relationship with the rest of the staff.

For any school there is a challenge in thinking through the way in which change might be developed and implemented, whilst simultaneously harnessing sufficient support throughout the school for it to be sustained.

Fullan and Hargreaves (1996) believe that staff development designed to bring about change in pedagogy must take account of the teacher's purpose in his or her work. 'Teachers' purposes motivate what teachers do' (p. 19). Every day in the constantly shifting environment of the school, teachers make innumerable decisions about, for example, discipline in the classroom, fairness, pupil autonomy and the organisation of support for pupils' learning. All these decisions encompass personal, philosophical and moral judgments. Change which either cuts across what teachers feel is in the best interests of those they teach, or which appears impractical, is likely to be resisted and/or resented. This is not to say that teachers are always right or always have a well-developed sense of purpose in their work. The issue here for those involved with professional development is how to develop procedures which respect teachers' knowledge, ideas and existing capacity to make informed discretionary judgments and at the same time to encourage them to reflect on their own work and be open to adopting new practices. This must include the opportunity for teachers to investigate the beliefs underlying their own practices and also a consideration of a reward structure which will sustain teachers' sense of worth in their work. The issue for teachers themselves is to become critical in their adoption of external initiatives so that these initiatives are integrated with their own purposes and practices. Learning therefore should be two-way.

School factors significant in the process of change

In the past, educational change in schools has been dependent as, Fullan (1992) states, on 'what teachers think – it is a simple and complex as that'.

Collaboration or 'experimentation' with colleagues 'is linked with opportunities for continuous improvement and career long learning'. Good teaching is a process of professional development involving collaborative learning close to the job. The capacity of schools to improve the quality of education for all the pupils who attend, that is become more inclusive, as Hopkins and Harris (1997) argue, is dependent on a school's capacity for continuous change and development. It would seem that good teachers, and hence good schools, do see professional development and hence school improvement as an attitude and a way of working (Hewton and Jolly 1991). If it were, inspection or rather evaluation would then be something done in partnership with schools rather than to them (Boothroyd et al 1996). It is unfortunate that what teachers think or say appears to receive little recognition in the OFSTED guidance.

Too often policy change in education has failed to effect change in practice because it has failed to take into account the teaching force which has to put the change into operation (Fullan, 1992). The current attempt to bring about reform in education has created tension by imposing demands on teachers and schools which are not entirely compatible with one another. This approach simultaneously expects teachers to take greater ownership of policies and practices at school level by engaging more with decision-making processes involved in school-based management. At the same time it has imposed a National Curriculum and external assessment schemes to appraise both pupils and teachers which may not fit comfortably with the thinking of the practitioners themselves. Fullan and Hargreaves (1996) identify six problems in what they see as the struggle between reform stemming from teachers themselves and that which is centrally imposed.

Firstly, teachers are 'dangerously overloaded' as a result of curriculum innovation, the changing profile of class groups with its implications for more complex planning and preparation, greater accountability and the explosion of knowledge with which to keep pace. The authors pinpoint two particular factors as causing 'particular concern': 'the effects of special education legislation and the mainstreaming of special education students into regular classes' (p. 3) and also 'fragmented solutions' to problems, 'faddism and other bandwagon shifts, massive multi-faceted, unwieldy reform' (p. 4).

Secondly, teacher collaboration itself contains implicit paradoxes which are insufficiently recognised. On the one hand it can contribute to sustained improvement in schools, particularly where individuals within the group are prepared to take the lead in sharing ideas, knowledge and experience without attempting to dominate others. On the other hand, members may feel constrained to go along with the majority and suppress their own ideas. The pressure of the group can reduce creative solutions to problems either through desire to maintain the status quo or through susceptibility the most recent fashion.

Thirdly, there is currently an 'unseen pool of existing talent' among teachers which is yet untapped. The anxiety created by formal evaluation that encompasses the whole staff in order to detect the incompetence of the very few can constrain the achievement and excellence of the many.

In addition, traditionally, the only way for a teacher to gain promotion has been to move out of the classroom into administration. Where responsibility is not shared between classroom teachers and senior management, imposed solutions may not address the problem properly.

Furthermore, most attempts at reform in education are unsuccessful because:

- the complexity of the problems is often poorly understood
- policy makers may be interested only in immediate results
- solutions which rely on modifications to the curriculum and assessment ignore their implications for teacher development
- the technology required to support policy initiatives is not provided
- the frequent imposition of a multitude of reforms alienates those expected to put them into effect.

Finally, there is a problem of professional isolation which is maintained by school architecture, timetabling and overload, all of which militate against creating opportunities for teachers to learn from each other. This isolation constrains access to new ideas, exacerbates the stress felt by individuals and fails to recognise both outstanding competence and incompetence

Many teachers are reluctant to be observed in their classrooms and to share their ideas and experiences. It is interesting to speculate on reasons why this might be so, whether there are any negative consequences of this private-ness among teachers and what might be done to reduce this isolationism.

Some teachers may not wish to share their ideas because they do not want to appear overly arrogant or boastful. Some are reluctant because they are unclear about the purpose of the observation and uncertain about whether it will lead to improvement of some kind. Others, especially in a climate of competition, do not wish others to take the credit for their ideas. Some may feel that observation of their practice is intrusion. Others again may not want to admit that they are having difficulty in a situation in case they are construed as incompetent. Support may often be confused with assessment and control. The negative effects are to support the resistance to change and to increase stress.

Planning change

Gosling, Murray and Stephen (1996) note two important questions relating to factors supportive of, or resistant to, change that need to be addressed in the initial stages of planning any new initiative in schools:

What change?

- **What do those who desire the change think is unsatisfactory at present?**

- **Who desires the change (i.e. who thinks the present situation is unsatisfactory)?**

- **Who might not desire the change?**

- **What would those who desire the change like to see happen as a result?**

What constrains and what facilitates the change?

- **What will happen if those desiring the change are either in the minority or in personal or professional positions which do not allow them to lead or manage change?**

- **How will those who desire the change convince or motivate those who might not desire it?**

- **What is the minimum requirement for the change to be successful in terms of the different people involved (i.e. what could there be consensus around)?**

(Gosling, Murray and Stephen, 1996, p. 27)

Institutional change tends to happen in stages (Torrington, Weightman and Johns, 1989) which those responsible for any in-school developments might do well to bear in mind:

i. The collection of information about whether a change is necessary by talking to peers on courses or in other schools, gathering data from government documents and local authority sources, and reading reports of research in journals.

ii. Consulting with other interested parties through face to face or group meetings and circulating draft documents for discussion.

iii. Putting the plan into operation, patiently explaining and repeating what will happen to the various interest groups, and offering training where appropriate.

iv. Monitoring the progress of the initiative and asking for feedback both formally and informally.

Their suggestions reflect the action research approach to bringing about and embedding change in schools. First there is an assessment of need then, on the basis of this assessment, an initiative is planned to address the identified need. The initiative is put into effect and evaluated. The cycle is then repeated, taking this evaluation and any needs subsequently identified into account.

Tensions implicit in the special needs co-ordinator's role

Garner and Sandaw (1995) note the 'role tensions' implicit in the work particularly of teachers involved in the area of special educational needs. For the special educational needs co-ordinator, commitment to the work may derive from an aggregation of personal value-systems and past experiences. The greatest sense of achievement may occur when an individual pupil begins to make quantifiable progress in some respect. However, to survive, the co-ordinator will have to recognise the forces outside and inside the school which may, from time to time, operate to undermine and devalue what she or he regards as important. The current education system may be perceived as inequitable. Many of the pupils to whom the co-ordinator may devote a great deal of care and attention are not popular in the system. The co-ordinator may have a host of different, and contrasting, loyalties: to colleagues, to pupils and to the school. Some colleagues may regard SENCOs as less-than-teachers, those with the 'easy ride', who do a bit of support work in class from time to time. Others may regard their work very highly and make constant demands on their time. Some co-ordinators may be given precious little time in which to carry out their functions and experience feelings of guilt and anxiety as a result. Outside inspection of school practices, with 'success' judged against externally-imposed criteria, may subject special educational needs co-ordinators to a high degree of uncertainty in their role, stress and a sense of de-skilling (Garner and Sandow 1995).

The tensions inherent in meeting the guidance requirements of the Code of Practice have been highlighted in a number of studies (Evans, Docking, Bentley & Evans, 1995; Lewis, Neill and Campbell, 1996; OFSTED, 1996: Derrington, Evans & Lee, 1996; Davies, Garner & Lee, 1998). In the 1994 Code of Practice, considerable emphasis was placed on collaborative work in schools. Of the seven functions envisaged for the SENCO, four of them are directly connected with that process, whilst the remainder are reliant on effective collaboration to succeed:

- **liaising with and advising fellow teachers**

- **co-ordinating provision for children with special educational needs**

- liaising with parents of children with special educational needs

- liaising with external agencies, including the educational psychology service and other support agencies, medical and social services and voluntary bodies (para 2.14, pp. 9–10).

Garner (2000)

The National Standards for Special Educational Needs Co-ordinators (TTA, op. cit.) include as a 'core purpose' for the SENCO that of 'supporting, guiding and motivating colleagues' (p. 5). However, the set of 'Standards for Subject Leaders' does not include as a 'core purpose' that of their role collaborative practice with regard to pupils who experience difficulties in learning. By inference, therefore, developing collaborative practice is to be initiated and sustained by the SENCO. This is no easy task, given that:

… there may well be those who are diffident or even hostile to greater involvement with children with learning difficulties, whatever the statutory guidelines specify. Mittler (1993) is categorical about this, observing that whilst '… the slogan that everyone is a teacher of children with special educational needs is true … it is very far from being accepted in practice'.

Garner (2000)

Survey data from research by Lewis (1995) has suggested that primary school co-ordinators found it easier to maintain an effective working partnership with their classroom-teacher colleagues than co-ordinators in secondary schools. The latter reported some difficulty in obtaining the co-operation of subject-teachers. Garner (2000) reports work by Bearn & Smith (1998) and Digby, Lewis, Taylor & Yates (1999) indicating that some secondary subject teachers see some pupils to be 'outside of their teaching range'. Teachers in certain areas, for example, science and technology, might even hold a jaundiced view of the work of the special needs co-ordinator (Digby, Lewis, Taylor & Yates, op. cit.).

One of the implications drawn from the above might be that the SENCO has little hope of influencing colleagues unless she or he has considerable status in the school. The three co-ordinators mentioned above felt that status can result from both the head teacher's and governors' attitudes and also the individual co-ordinator's self confidence in carrying out the role. They also pointed out that the credibility of a co-ordinator often depends on proven ability as a classroom teacher. Clearly this raises again the huge issue both of time management and also of knowledge: one person is expected to have the skill to manage her or his time in order to carry out all the co-ordination functions as well as spend some time teaching in the classroom, and at the same time acquire sufficient knowledge to fulfil the role successfully.

Conflict resolution and problem solving

In their role, SENCOs may well find themselves either in conflict with somebody else over the way they view situations, or, alternatively, having to behave as the mediator between other parties who are in disagreement with each other.

Elsewhere (Wearmouth, 1997) I have reported on an initiative in an upper school where unexpected achievement by so-called 'less able' pupils was received by many staff in a similarly negative manner to that reported by Rosenthal and Jacobson (1968). In this article, a special needs co-ordinator introduced laptop computers to assist pupils who experienced difficulty in expressing themselves in writing. The upper school concerned had maintained its very strong academic traditions from its days as a grammar school and an expectation of a stratified model of pupils' ability. When the pupils using the word-processing programme on the new laptops began to produce written work of a higher standard than some other pupils, this disruption to the anticipated hierarchy of achievement appeared to cause considerable feelings of discomfort. Some staff expressed concern at the lack of equity in the new arrangements for supporting pupils' learning: word-processing facilities should be available to everybody, not just the few who experienced the most difficulties. At the time this approach was impractical because there were insufficient resources in the school. The following year there was considerable resistance to the special needs co-ordinator working in the same way. I concluded that there is very strong pressure to maintain equilibrium in the school system. This conflicts with any role that the SENCO may have in promoting curriculum change which challenges the belief system of individual teachers or the institutional view of the school as a whole:

> **For how is it possible to change a whole belief system without threatening or undermining the whole organisation? The SENCO who fails to recognise this is bound to make matters much worse for pupils who experience difficulties in learning. Insecure systems will clamp down to protect themselves. Insecure teachers may well tighten their grip around teaching techniques and styles which are tried and tested. Children who do not achieve in the conventional sense in school are always a challenge to a teacher's sense of self worth anyway.**

> *(Ibid)*

One way of resolving a problem is to frame it as a conflict between different agenda. Some of the literature on conflict resolution offers strategies which might have offered a way forward in this particular conflict situation. Heitler (1990) suggests that the process of co-operative talking which addresses the concerns of all participants has three phases:

- the expression of an initial position stating what one wants

- the exploration of underlying personal concerns about the position

- the selection of mutually satisfying solutions for addressing these concerns.

An opportunity to stand back from the situation she was in and to reflect on how she might address each of these phases might have been helpful to this co-ordinator.

An example of the kind of conflict with which many involved in special provision in schools might be familiar is that of one-to-one tuition for a pupil as expected by parents and carers versus whole-class support from a classroom assistant (Florian, in press). If the SENCO were to attempt a phased approach to conflict resolution she or he might try to determine the concerns underlying the initial position. It is possible that the incompatibility of the initial positions is derived from similar concerns: how to ensure the inclusion in a mainstream school of a pupil experiencing particular difficulties in learning. The class teacher's position might be that one-to-one tuition inhibits rather than facilitates inclusion, and that, in any case, she or he will be overseeing the work of the individual pupil whilst the classroom assistant is assisting other class members. In this case, the underlying concerns of parents and/or carers, local authority providers and the class teacher and/or SENCO are not incompatible. As a result, solution-building will depend on generating options which involve the skilful deployment of the classroom assistant in support of the pupil with the statement when viewed as a member of the class group.

If the underlying concerns are different, for example if the teacher is opposed to having an additional adult in the classroom, or if the specification of the classroom assistant is based on a belief that one-to-one tuition is the only way the pupil can progress through the curriculum, then a different solution will have to be sought. This will depend on more sophisticated problem-solving strategies. Heitler (1990) reminds us that opposition needs to give way to co-operation; although this may not be easy in what might be an emotionally-charged atmosphere of parental and/or carer concern for the child's welfare and future life chances, and teachers' own senses both of equity and preferred way of working. The latter is often derived from years of experience and careful thought and evaluation. Re-stating the problem at a level of abstraction with which all parties can agree might well help the process. In the above example this might be 'How can we provide a good all-round education for this child?' The tone of co-operation established by this re-statement will permit further exploration and lead to the generation of solutions satisfying to all parties.

Friend and Cook (1996) adopt a slightly different approach to interpersonal problem-solving. Their review of research suggests that the first step, problem-identification, is the key to successful resolution. They recommend several strands to this initial stages:

- phrase the problem as a question in order to communicate that a solution is possible

- think of problem identification as having both divergent and convergent elements as a means of creating the opportunity for reformulating the problem

- describe the problem precisely, ensuring commonality of understanding of key concepts, for example what 'inclusion' means

- confirm the existence of a problem by looking to its sources of information;

- allow adequate time for problem-identification

- ensure that participants remain committed to solving the problem.

It is interesting to note the differences between the approaches of Heitler and of Friend and Cook. Experienced practitioners may well be able, from personal experience, to think of conflict situations where either or both of these approaches would have enabled an effective resolution of the issue.

Teacher support groups

One way in which teachers in some schools have sought to further the development of pupils' learning, in particular of those who experience difficulties, is through the introduction of collaborative, problem-solving, self help groups among staff members. Ysseldyke and Christenson's (1987) review of the literature on learning environments identified a number of factors thought to be related to positive student outcomes. 'Within School Conditions' included the degree of collaboration between the staff, that is, how far teachers worked together, shared tasks and discussed issues and problems. Norwich and Daniels (1997) have reported on a project aimed at increasing teacher 'tolerance of', and 'active engagement' with, pupils with special learning needs in primary schools through the use of such self-help groups, termed Teacher Support Teams for Special Educational Needs. There are, of course, a variety of ways of interpreting a word such as 'tolerance'. To some it might imply that certain pupils are perceived as a burden or a strain which must be borne by teachers, and use of this term is therefore stigmatising and disrespectful to the pupils concerned. To others it might imply a clear sense of realism. The behaviour of certain pupils is often experienced as stressful. Sharing the burden with others allows the individual teacher to become more tolerant. Alternatively, it might imply that responding to increasing diversity among the pupil population necessitates open-minded flexibility on the part of individual teachers. This flexibility, tolerance, can be strengthened in discussion with others who may be able to offer a range of possible courses of action in facilitating pupil learning and help to restore a sense of balance in difficult situations.

Ownership by the staff themselves was seen to be important in the success of this approach. Any special needs co-ordinator interested in setting something up on similar lines would have to take the issue of ownership very clearly into account.

Summary

The law is very clear in its delineation of statutory duties for securing individual pupils' entitlements to special provision in schools to address identified learning needs. However arrangements in individual schools are organised, the governing body retains this duty. In practice, governors may expect the SENCO to undertake responsibility for all aspects of provision. However, schools are complex institutions. In addition to their own knowledge, understanding and skills, to carry out their role SENCOs rely on support from head teachers and the senior management team and co-operation from colleagues, and this is not always forthcoming. Change in schools must first be clearly justified, then planned carefully and possible resistances acknowledged. Some schools have made considerable progress towards developing self-help groups among staff to support each other in generating solutions to potentially problematic situations.

Suggested Activities: Reflection and Discussion

1. Planning a change in school

Think about a particular change that you have tried to make in school in the past. Note down:

- how successful you consider the change to have been

- how well you addressed the kind of questions posed by Gosling, Murray and Stevens above when you initiated this change

- how different the outcome might have been if you had addressed these questions first

- how far the way in which you considered the stages of development of your initiative compares with the four stages outlined by Torrington, Weightman and Johns.

(Cont...)

2. In-school needs analysis

Evaluating awareness of roles and responsibilities in the area of special educational needs.

Those interested in evaluating the extent to which colleagues in their own schools are aware of roles and responsibilities for special educational provision, might like to carry out *Whole-school needs assessment 1: Responsibilities and roles in special educational provision in schools* which is included in the Appendix.

4 National and local policy constraints

What is policy?

The government has the power to determine the structure of the national system of education and the content of a national curriculum. Education, therefore, is bound to be highly politicised. Research gives a strong indication of the importance of educational achievement on future life chances. A study sponsored by the Basic Skills Agency on the impact of poor basic skills on the lives of 37 year olds examined their literacy and numeracy skills. It concluded that there is a strong relationship between poor basic skills and qualifications, unemployment, type of job, amount of workplace training, promotion and wage levels. Following the 1997 General Election, the government has made it clear that its over-riding priority in education is what it would see as the improvement of pupils' achievement overall.

Whose interests does policy serve?

'Policy', as exemplified by schools 'Special Educational Needs' policies (DfEE, 1994a, 1994b), comprises the philosophical beliefs underpinning the statement of principles which are intended to guide the actions of people within an institution, the plans drawn up to put these principles into operation, and, very often, the process through which the policy itself can be monitored and evaluated. At any level within the education system, national, local education authority, school, department, individual policy should be compatible with the policies operating at any other level in the same domain as well as with general overarching policies in education. Policy at national level which impinges on provision made for, and the learning of, pupils who experience difficulties in learning is by no means straight forward, however. At times, government policy as it affects pupils who experience difficulties gives the impression of being fragmented. Attempting to recognise and respond to perceptions of individual 'need' as well as the 'needs' of groups, whole school populations and the community, local and national, means engaging with complex issues of sameness and difference, equity and discrimination which, ultimately, are very difficult to reconcile. Initiatives at one level sometimes are at variance with others at the same, and across, levels. For example, moves to 'include' in mainstream schools more pupils identified as having special learning needs do not fit easily with policies advocating competition between schools and the publication of academic league tables.

The influence of current national priorities in education

Major questions that always hang over any decision-making process in education include:

- In whose interest(s) is any particular outcome?

- What are the advantages to politicians at national and local level, local government officers, pupils, teachers and parents of adopting one solution to a problem rather than another?

It is clear that pupils in some schools and/or in some socio-economic groups achieve much less highly in terms of academic qualifications than in others. Whether the difficulties in learning faced by such pupils should be seen as arising from the broader social and economic context, the school environment or as belonging to them as individuals, is debatable. In the 1970s, schools were often viewed as subject to social and economic processes in society. There was a conceptualisation of innate difficulties in learning faced by pupils, as well as those difficulties that related to an alien school environment, as rooted in an inequitable class structure (Dyson, 1997). The new government in 1979 heralded a series of changes which has resulted in the socio-economic perspective being overtaken by an individual focus and various forms of consumer accountability (ibid). Pupil outcomes have often been narrowly conceived in terms of examination results and used as evidence of school 'improvement'. Research into specific factors thought to have a bearing on pupils' attainments have replaced concerns with the wider societal context within which schools operate. Examples of the kind of research which tends to the assumption that factors operate in isolation from each other are the literature on school 'effectiveness' which focuses solely on internal issues, such as leadership qualities, and interpretations of boys' underachievement solely as questions of academic achievement in schools. This is not to say, of course, that the results of work focusing on in-school factors relating to effectiveness or factors relating to poorer achievement by boys in academic terms in school are not important. It is just that this kind of research appears to assume that schools operate in a vacuum, in isolation from the context of the wider society.

The effect of poverty

The introduction of competition and league table performance in the UK after 1988, and nationally-organised inspection procedures, assume that the extent of all pupils' achievement can and should be judged on common criteria. This approach has been exemplified in a press release from the Department for Education and Employment dated May 1998, Stephen Byers, the then Minister of State for Education, was quoted as saying:

We want no excuses for failure. Many LEAs are in deprived areas, but poverty is no excuse for under-achievement ... There is clear evidence that some schools in depressed areas are already reaching above the national average - if they can improve, all schools can improve.

(Press Release, DfEE, May 1998)

In legislation relating to special educational needs, pupils' difficulties in school are understood in terms of individual children's characteristics and equated with individual disability. It is the reverse of the view that barriers to learning can be generated by the way in which the education system is organised, and that difficulties facing individuals and schools are located within broader socio–economic patterns of disadvantage. Dyson (1997) links feelings of disaffection, under-achievement and disruptive behaviour with societal patterns of inequality rather than to notions of individual special educational needs. He suggests it is inappropriate to liken the effect of stresses on families, such as the effects of unemployment, poor health and poverty, that stem from society and impinge on children's learning to individualised disability. The move towards integrating pupils into mainstream schools was part of a wider process of liberalisation and commitment to equity rather than one stage in the process of transformation of education generally into provision suited to the whole pupil body. As a result, an 'army' of special educators has 'colonised' rather than transformed mainstream schools (Dyson, op cit.).

Mittler (1999) also notes that policy makers have conceptualised special educational needs in terms of disability rather than disadvantage. He feels that the effects of social and economic disadvantage have been ignored in the discourse relating to 'special educational needs', partly because those people directly affected have no status or power. Mittler refers to tackling poor educational achievement within a 'wider strategy which addresses gross social inequalities and aims to reduce poverty'. He proposes that special educational needs should be 'reconceptualised' so that poverty, marginalisation and social exclusion are seen as 'the major obstacles to children's learning'. They should not be simply accepted as a taken-for-granted relationship between low achievement and social and economic deprivation.

Government attempts to ameliorate the effects of poverty and social exclusion

Mittler (op cit.) notes that the government's response to the issue of poverty is to dismiss it as an insufficient 'excuse' for under-achievement but to hold out the promise of 'targeted support' at a social level. This approach offers resources to some groups of pupils which are not made available to others in similar circumstances. One example of the 'targeted support' offered currently is that of funds for supporting 'Education Action Zones' in areas of urban or rural 'educational under-performance'. These are local clusters of primary, secondary and special schools working in partnership with the local authority, parents, businesses and local training providers, with a grant from the DfEE to help with running costs and to fund particular local initiatives. Whether Education Action Zones prove to be successful will be heavily dependent on the extent to which members of the local community see potential and purpose in taking up an initiative proposed by an outside agency, central government, and feel a sense of ownership for them.

Where 'effective' is also inclusive

Mortimore et al. (1988) assert that schools which are effective for one group will also be effective for everyone else:

> ... we have shown that, in general, schools which were effective in promoting progress for one group of pupils (whether those of a particular social class, sex or ethnic group) were usually also effective for children of other groups. Similarly, those schools which were ineffective for one group tended to be ineffective for other groups ... school effectiveness does not seem to depend on pupils' backgrounds... By attending a more effective school all pupils will benefit, even those who are at an initial educational disadvantage because of their particular background characteristics.

> *(p. 217)*

School effectiveness research has concluded, repeatedly, that when the intake characteristics of pupils and other environmental factors are controlled, individual school processes have a statistically significant association with the outcome measures:

> ... children were more likely to show good behaviour and good scholastic attainments if they attended some schools than if they attended others. The implication is that experiences during the secondary school years may influence children's progress.

> *(Rutter et al. 1979, p. 178)*

This view has been supported consistently in other major studies (Reynolds, 1976; Mortimore et al., 1988, and Smith and Tomlinson, 1989). Sammons, Hillman and Mortimore (1995, p. 8) identified eleven factors that appear from the literature to be conducive to effective schools:

1. 'Professional leadership' which is 'firm and purposeful', employs a 'participative approach', and is clearly in possession of knowledge about pedagogical and curricular issues (Rutter et al., 1979).

2. 'Shared vision and goals' where staff have 'unity of purpose, consistency of practice, collegiality and collaboration'.

3. A 'learning environment' in which there is an 'orderly atmosphere' and an 'attractive working environment'.

4. 'Concentration on teaching and learning', where 'learning time' is maximised and there is an 'academic emphasis' and 'focus on achievement'.

5. 'Purposeful teaching' characterised by 'efficient organisation, clarity of purpose, structured lessons (and) adaptive practice.

6. 'High expectations all round ... providing intellectual challenge'.

7. 'Positive reinforcement' of 'clear and fair discipline' with 'feedback' to pupils.

8. Monitoring and evaluation of pupil progress and evaluation of school performance.

9. Clear communication of pupils' rights and responsibilities with an emphasis on 'raising pupil self-esteem'.

10. 'Home-school partnership' and 'parental involvement in their children's learning'.

11. Involvement by all personnel in the school as 'a learning organisation'.

They feel that Factors 4, 5 and 6, which are concerned with the quality of teaching and expectations, are the most significant influences on pupils' learning, progress, educational outcome and future life chances.

Practitioners, especially those working in the special needs area who have an interest in how a particular school might become more inclusive and effective, would do well to consider the extent to which:

- the factors identified by the Sammons research are reflected in the work of the school

- significant changes that would need to occur for the school to become more effective in responding to the learning needs of all its pupils

- these changes could be addressed immediately, in the medium term and in the long term.

Some of these changes might be extremely sensitive. One of the major aspects of any whole-school initiative is that the change-agent has to think about what she or he has the authority to influence directly within the school system, and what she or he can bring to the attention of others but over which she or he may have no control.

Approaching boys' under-achievement

On many measures of academic performance in schools, formal or informal, the achievement of girls is superior to that of boys. In January 1998 the Government announced that each education authority would be required to have plans to tackle boys' under-achievement.

Weiner, Arnot and David (1996) suggest conceptualising this issue simply as that of raising boys' achievement in school is simplistic. Examination performance by boys in schools is poorer than that of girls. The extent to which this may be termed male 'under-achievement' is questionable. These authors note, for example, that different explanations are offered where girls achieve poorly in comparison with boys than where boys achieve relatively poorly. Much more important in terms of life chances is the statistical over-achievement of men in terms of career opportunities. Equally, different explanations are given for the comparatively poorer achievement of working-class males than for poorer achievement by middle-class males. Highlighting the relatively poorer performance of boys therefore ignores the 'continuing subordination of many women', the issue of working class under-achievement and, within that, the demise of manual occupations in many areas, and the enhanced career opportunities of males. If there is a much greater disparity between the educational achievement of the working classes and that of the middle classes than between boys and girls, arguably there is a case for putting any additional resourcing into raising the achievement of this group. Whether this should be at the expense of resources for raising the achievement of boys, or whether it is a totally separate issue is problematic.

One important issue that has not been raised in the discussion above is that of the existing large imbalance of resources used to meet the special educational needs of boys in proportion to that used to support girls. In research undertaken in primary schools Daniels, Hey, Leonard and Smith (1995), for example, note a large disparity in the identification of need and provision of resources when comparing boys with girls. They found that formal testing and informal teacher-referral indicated that there were twice as many boys as girls who experienced some kind of difficulty in learning. Despite this apparently clear evidence, between three and five times as many boys as girls were being given extra help in the later years of the two primary schools. Whether or not any over-allocation of resources to boys is interpreted as discrimination in favour of, or against, girls will depend on the kind of provision made through this additional resourcing. If additional resources are used to support the identification and 'treatment' of boys as 'unacceptable deviants', as Daniels et al. point out as one possibility, this may well be construed as positive discrimination in favour of girls.

Raising achievement through competition: target setting and league tables

As noted above, recent UK governments have taken a market-driven approach to the raising of standards for all. Setting targets to improve the general level of children's achievements and the establishment of league tables of test results comparing one school with another have been key features of government policy since the 1988 Education Act.

Benchmarking

One national policy which is likely to have a strong impact at all levels of the education system is that related to 'benchmarking'. From September 1998, schools have been required to set and publish annual targets for their students' performance in National Curriculum assessments and public examinations, using 'benchmark information' of results achieved by 'similar' schools.

Benchmark information is provided in the form of tables of pupils' results which group schools on particular sets of factors. In order to identify 'similar' schools, the government uses given indicators.

At Key Stages 1 and 2 the key indicators are:

- the proportion of children in the school known to be eligible for free school meals

- the proportion of children for whom English is an additional language.

At Key Stages 3 and 4, they are:

- the proportion of children in the school known to be eligible for free school meals

- whether the school is selective or not.

For pupils who experience barriers to their learning there are advantages and disadvantages implicit in the practice of setting targets based on common benchmarks for individual schools' overall achievements in external assessments. Teachers might find it very helpful to have a clearly-defined goal against which to judge the progress of pupils and towards which they might direct their efforts in raising their overall achievement. Regular evaluation of practice judged against the extent to which pupils can be shown to have made progress is a very important aspect of the job of all professionals associated with schools. There are, however, problems associated with the kind of target-setting outlined here.

First, these targets rest on an assumption that the results of assessments, and therefore the assessments themselves, which underpin the targets are valid in respect of every pupil, that is that they test what they are intended to test. Some teachers may feel that this is not always a justifiable assumption. Secondly, a school's attempts to raise pupil performance in particular areas for which there are benchmarks may lead to a narrowing of the curriculum. Furthermore, some schools have small year groups whose attainment may fluctuate from one year to the next. Year on year comparison can therefore be inappropriate. In addition, the publishing of results may lead to competition between schools which results in lower-attaining pupils becoming unpopular to schools. Finally, focusing on the mean average of all pupils ignores the special learning needs of individual pupils.

Target-setting against benchmarks may be in the interests of pupils if it results in a sharpened focus on ways to improve teaching practices to raise overall standards. It is also a relatively straightforward way of making comparisons between schools. Parents and carers may see a value in being able to compare the results of their children's school in comparison with what is 'expected'. However, individual schools may feel that comparisons of this sort work against their interest because they cannot take into account the complexity of their own situation, and this includes the special learning needs of their pupils.

The aim of such an approach is to raise standards for all through encouraging competition between institutions as the following extract indicates:

News & opinion Benchmark tables 'will puncture complacency' **by Nicholas Pyke**

The long-awaited national data system showing schools how well they are performing was published this week. A set of "benchmarks" has been sent to every primary and secondary school.

The benchmarks, a series of statistical tables, allow heads and governors to compare their results in national curriculum tests and GCSE exams against the national averages for schools in similar social and economic circumstances.

From next September, they will be obliged to set their own school targets for academic improvement, using this week's publication as a guide.

The Government's curriculum quango, the Qualifications and Curriculum Authority, said the new statistical tables would "puncture complacency" across the system.

"For too long schools have been in the dark about how others like them are performing nationally," said David Hawker, head of the QCA's curriculum and assessment division.

"This has often meant that underachievement is not properly recognised and tackled. Now for the first time this information is available in easy-to-read tables. They will throw into sharp relief the disparity between schools in similar circumstances," he said.

The tables are grouped according to factors such as the number of pupils taking free school meals, and the proportion speaking English as an additional language.

At Key Stage 2, for example, a head would be able to examine the national averages for the category of schools where more than 50 per cent of pupils speak English as a first language, but where between 36 and 50 per cent are eligible for free school meals.

The benchmark tables show the cut-off points for the bottom 25 per cent of pupils ranked by achievement, the top 25 per cent, the top 5 per cent and the median.

(TES, January 30 1998)

Initiatives which have increased competition between schools may well affect pupils who experience difficulties in learning of some kind:

- Special needs co-ordinators may sense pressure from parents or colleagues to put pupils forward for formal assessment, in order to access the additional resources that may be made available through a Statement.

- There may be an added impetus to exploring ways of differentiating materials and teaching approaches for those pupils who experience difficulties.

- There may be some feeling that certain pupils' attainments should not be included in the school's overall results.

- Schools may be becoming reluctant to admit children whose impact on the overall mean achievement rating may be negative.

- In some schools there is a strong emphasis on helping groups whose achievements lie just below one threshold to reach the next level, rather than putting the main effort into helping all children to achieve more. This has a stultifying effect on meeting the diversity of pupils' needs.

(Wearmouth, quoting Wedell, in press.)

In response to the Green Paper, (DfEE, 1997) one parent wrote:

> We live in an area containing many high quality mainstream schools which are oversubscribed. These schools are very competitive and strive to achieve high measures in success rates primarily measured by the number of GCSE and A level passes gained by each pupil. Such measurements are meaningless as far as our son is concerned, except to say that the more competitive and academic the classroom, the less likely it would be able to educate our son effectively because he would not be able to cope with or comprehend the situation and would hold the rest of the class back. This is not a criticism of such a school but a recognition that they have chosen to specialise in the education of 'mainstream' children to the detriment of children who, for one reason or another, do not fit that mould ... We have found that most mainstream schools are not really interested in adequately catering for children with SEN. They pay lip service to concepts, aims, policy and ideals but the underlying attitude is that SEN children are a problem (– or the school). In contrast the special schools we visited had a completely different attitude to educating children with SEN. They recognised that focusing on exam-based achievement is a waste of time for certain children and would serve only to brand them as failures when, in fact, it would be the system that has failed, not the child. The key to successfully educating the children is to identify what each child can do and then build on that ability. Measuring success for these children using exam results is as pointless as using a ruler to measure the length of an hour ... A competitive secondary school classroom is one of the hardest environments for a child with SEN to contend with.

At the same time as this heightened focus on the raising of standards through competition, the government has also issued proposals to move towards an inclusive approach to providing for all pupils' learning needs. How far the effect of imposing additional pressure on schools to improve their overall academic standards will result in raising the level of everything that educationalists might consider 'achievement' among all pupils, or in squeezing out of the system pupils perceived as 'lower-achieving' remains to be seen. What is clear from these apparently conflicting signals is that considerable thought will have to be given to the changes which individual schools will have to make at the level of whole-school policy if they are to raise mean achievement levels and include all pupils.

Developments towards an inclusive approach

Schools operate within a number of different contexts each of which may constrain how far a school's policies can be inclusive:

- They are products of their own history, both as individual institutions, and as institutions within the history of the British education system. Some in-school conventions will have developed within the local history of the school, and some within national history.

- They form part of a locality where there may be particular expectations of schools and particular constraints on possibilities for institutional development, for example, as noted above, local socio-economic conditions.

- They belong to the national education system and, as such, are highly politicised, being subject the control mechanisms of central government. How an individual working within this system responds to such control may well depend on how far she or he is in sympathy with any current government's general perspective and direction.

Although, as some writers have pointed out (Salmon, 1998), there are many factors militating against the inclusivity of schools, there are also many examples of schools operating practices which clearly are intended to engage with the needs of all pupils.

Corbett (1999) has investigated the responses of two multi-cultural inner-city schools, A and B, to overcoming low achievement resulting from poverty and social exclusion. Like Mittler, she notes that some schools in very poor areas have been able to raise the achievement of their pupils seemingly against the odds.

Corbett notes certain differences in the way the two schools, A and B, attempt to promote high expectations amongst pupils. School A takes a pastoral approach to the issue of raising pupils' expectations through role models among the staff and mentoring from successful employees in the city. School B adopts a dual approach related both to pastoral support and more directly to the academic curriculum. It uses black mentors who have improved their own educational and social status and also supports learning through an Open Learning Centre and through introducing the academic study of subjects related to the pupils' own culture.

Local community groups come into School A, most notably at the weekend. School B is also used by its community during weekends. In addition it is proactive in confronting racial tensions by requesting that the police protect pupils on their way to and from school and also by training teaching staff in conflict resolution between different racial groups.

In order to address appropriately learning needs of all pupils, Corbett advocates 'connective pedagogy'. By this she means taking a holistic view of the individual pupil. The teacher must understand both the current level of attainment of the pupil and also the nature of the community to which the school and the learner within it belong.

The initiatives instigated in these two schools sprang from the inside from the beginning. The links advocated by the DfEE between school and the community and between pupils and employers, and the development of information and communications technology have already been established by the two schools. The crucial factor in the schools' success was the deep commitment of the two head teachers to their local communities and the educational advancement of their own pupils and their business-like ability to seize opportunities to promote the interests of their schools.

The influence of the local education authority

Sometimes local education authorities promote particular initiatives in their own areas which have a strong impact on schools, teachers and individual students. Birmingham City Council, for example, still retains a number of selective secondary schools and special schools designated as catering for a range of particular learning needs. However, in the past few years this local education authority has initiated a series of strategies on inclusion intended to achieve the aim of offering as many pupils as possible the opportunity for education in a mainstream school alongside peers from their local community. 'Inclusion' was, and is, seen by Birmingham Local Education Authority as vital to the well-being of the city and its inhabitants.

> the economic prosperity of the City and its social and moral climate depend on the reality of social inclusion in a multi-ethnic, multi-faith community. Educational inclusion is clearly a central pillar of our commitment to equality of opportunity.

(Birmingham Local Education Authority, 1996)

These strategies were designed to provide additional resources for inclusion and to support greater engagement of students in their own learning in mainstream schools wherever possible. Birmingham's 'strategy' documents are intended to be practical as well as philosophical and contain details of how initiatives are intended to be put into operation. Particular strategies that have been developed have included, for example, the 'Supported Places Initiative' and 'New Outlooks, Framework for Intervention', a behaviour support strategy. The first of these, the 'Supported Places Initiative', was trialled by the local authority in fourteen schools. When pupils had been identified as experiencing serious barriers to their learning, the additional support required to support these pupils, calculated on set criteria for specific types of perceived needs, was converted into a cash amount and transferred to the school. The school could then appoint its assistants or other support according to the level of assistance required within it. In all the other schools, additional support hours were allocated centrally by the local authority. 'New Outlooks, Framework for

Intervention' adopted the view that problem behaviour in schools is usually a product of the interaction between the individual pupil, the school, the family, the local community and wider society. It advocated school behaviour policies which indicate rewards and consequences which are seen to be fair and effective and involve pupils, their carers and the community in sharing responsibility for pupils' behaviour. Within this framework, the first step in any intervention was always an audit of the learning environment to identify any mismatch between pedagogy and pupils' learning.

In 1997, Birmingham LEA supported a number of its teachers on the Open University MA (Ed) module *Developing Inclusive Curricula*. During this course the teachers' work on projects related to policy-making pointed to the need for development in a number of areas but particularly in communication between all those involved in the implementation of a policy and in awareness-raising in respect of any policy. The teachers felt that development with regard to the first of these should include:

- Better liaison in gathering information from all the 'stakeholders'. It appeared that LEA support agencies usually came together as a reaction to a situation rather than for evaluating success.

- A reconsideration of the nature of partnership with parents. It appeared that, although information existed, parents had limited influence. Even those few parents of children who experienced difficulties in learning who were aware of the 'system' and confident about what they wanted for their children had little influence on policy.

- Greater availability of parental leaflets which should, as a matter of policy, be given to all parents who are concerned about the difficulties experienced by their children.

- Schools' policy should be clarified to include a summary of the LEA policy on school placement and explain school procedures for finding out if the school can meet pupils' needs.

- Both the LEA and school policy should explain how it is decided whether a child's admission into mainstream is interpreted as an efficient use of resources and not as a source of interference with the education of other children in the school.

- Both the LEA policy and the school policy should state how pupils who experience difficulties in learning receive the same treatment as other pupils and the facilities provided which enable access to the mainstream curriculum.

The experience of the teachers strongly indicated that the second should include:

- Raising awareness of the requirements of the inclusive policy with all involved, particularly head teachers.

- Greater awareness of the challenges faced by support assistants, the major resource for inclusive strategies.

- Interpreting the role of support assistants in innovative ways and supporting them.

- The involvement of all teaching and non-teaching staff in a school in a special needs policy review to promote shared values and understanding between themselves and with parents.

Summary

It is important for all those in maintained schools with responsibilities in the area of special educational needs to be aware of the way in which national and local authority policies influence school practices in relation to pupils who experience difficulties. Competition and inspection procedures which presuppose that like is being compared with like do little to further the interests of pupils who experience difficulties. On the other hand many would argue that schools must be accountable to the general public for the quality of education they provide for the nation's children. One way to evaluate quality is compare results across institutions and evaluate in-school practices on common criteria. Where policies, national and local, attempt to promote both the individual and the majority, the conflict of interest that sometimes arises is very difficult to resolve.

Suggested Activities: Reflection and Discussion

1. The effects of schools in competition on the individual student

Note down ways in which you feel that increased emphasis on competition between schools is affecting pupils who experience difficulties in learning of some kind. Discuss your ideas with colleagues.

2. Gender issues in special provision

Reflect on the disparity in the identification of need and provision of resources when comparing boys with girls in the two primary schools described by Daniels, Hey and Leonard. Then:

- investigate how far this disparity in the allocation of resources exists in your own school

(Cont...)

- discuss with colleagues how far you agree with the explanations focused on gender inequalities that are offered in this chapter.

3. The effectiveness of the individual school

Discuss with your colleagues what you feel about how the factors identified by the Sammons research are reflected in the work of your own school.

What are the most significant changes that would need to occur for your school to become more effective in responding to the learning needs of all its pupils?

Which of these factors could be addressed immediately? - in the medium term? in the long term?

Draw up a list of priorities.

4. The effects of target-setting against benchmarks

Consider your responses to the following questions:

- What, in your experience, are the advantages and disadvantages of setting targets based on common benchmarks for individual schools' overall achievements in external assessments?

- In whose interest is target setting against a set of common benchmarks?

5. Putting LEA policy into practice

Those interested in the link between local education policy and school policy might like to:

- collect together and read the local authority policy documents on behaviour and any other aspects of special educational needs

- consider what impact LEA policies have on what happens in a school with which they are familiar

- look at the list of points that the teachers in Birmingham felt needed development in the area of policy and tick those that are particularly important in their location and for themselves.

5 Policy and inspection at school level

In the past few years schools have been operating in a context of far greater accountability than was apparent previously. As we have seen, the statutory detail to be set out in schools' special educational needs policies is outlined in the Code and used by OFSTED as a shared text to evaluate policy and practice during inspections. Since the 1988 Education Reform Act there has been a requirement for schools to develop an overall School Development Plan which will also be open to scrutiny during an official inspection. The special educational needs policy, amongst others, should form an integral part of this Plan. It is vital, therefore, that those responsible for special provision in schools should be aware of the statutory requirements of school policies, should be actively involved in the process of planning at whole-school level, and should be conversant with OFSTED inspection procedures.

Developing and evaluating school policy

The Code of Practice for the Identification and assessment of Special Educational Needs (DfEE, 1994) sets out the information required of mainstream schools in Section 2:10.

School SEN Policy

1. Basic information about the school's special educational provision:

- the objectives of the school's SEN policy

- the name of the school's SEN coordinator or teacher responsible for the day-to-day operation of the SEN policy

- the arrangements for coordinating educational provision for pupils with SEN

- admission arrangements

- any SEN specialism and any special units

- any special facilities which increase or assist access to the school by pupils with SEN.

2. Information about the school's policies for identification, assessment and provision for all pupils with SEN: ►

- the allocation of resources to and amongst pupils with SEN

- identification and assessment arrangements, and review procedures

- arrangements for providing access for pupils with SEN to a balanced and broadly-based curriculum, including the National Curriculum

- how children with special educational needs are integrated within the school as a whole

- criteria for evaluating the success of the school's SEN policy

- arrangements for considering complaints about special educational provision within the school

3. Information about the school's staffing policies and partnership with bodies beyond the schools:

– the school's arrangements for SEN in-service training

– use made of teachers and facilities from outside the school, including support services

– arrangements for partnership with parents

– links with other mainstream schools and special schools, including arrangements when pupils change school or leave school

– links with health and social services, educational welfare services and any voluntary organisations.

These guidelines were further elaborated for schools in England by The Education (Special Educational Needs) (Information) (England) Regulations 1999, Regulation 3(1), 3(2) and 3(3).

Davies, Garner and Lee (1998) investigated the quality of school policies on special educational needs and concluded that many schools have experienced difficulty in both writing and revising their policies. The following guidelines have been suggested by Tarr and Thomas (1998):

• Write clearly with an audience for the policy in mind.

• Ensure everything that should be in the policy is included; follow Circular 6/94 rather than the aide-memoir in the Code.

• Ensure that the policy is specific about spending and provides clear budget statements.

- Ensure the policy gives clear guidelines on how parents are involved, and provides information on how parents can process complaints.

(Tarr and Thomas in Davies, Garner and Lee, p. 163)

Cowne (1998) notes that if a school policy is to 'remain active and dynamic' it must be viewed 'as a *process* of development'. The SEN policy should be seen as part of the School Development Plan and show clear links with other school policies also, for example policies on behaviour, assessment and equal opportunities. Planning for school development is intended to enable a school to answer four questions:

- **where is the school now?**

- **what changes do we need to make**

- **how shall we manage these changes over time?**

- **how shall we know whether our management of change has been successful?**

(DES, 1988)

The underlying rationale of a School Development Plan is that:

> **... it brings together, in an overall plan, national and LEA policies and initiatives, the school's aim and values, its existing achievements and its need for development. By co-ordinating aspects of planning which are otherwise separate, the school acquires a shared sense of direction and is able to control and manage the tasks of development and change. Priorities for development are planned in detail for one year and are supported by action plans or working documents for staff. The priorities for later years are sketched in outline to provide the longer term programme.**

(DES, 1988)

There are four sequential stages in the year-on-year planning cycle:

- audit: a school reviews its strengths and weaknesses

- plan construction: priorities for development are selected and then turned into specific targets

- implementation: of the planned priorities and targets

- evaluation: the success of implementation is checked.

These stages are common to any policy development within a school, whether it is the overall School Development Plan, or the policy for special educational needs. Tarr and Thomas (op cit.) offer the following advice to anyone intending to review and improve a school policy for special education needs:

- **Establish a policy review and development team which includes at least one governor.**

- **Attempt to involve senior management and class teachers in areas of provision which will promote and foster inclusive practices in the school.**

- **Clarify the process of collaboration with external agencies and other schools, grouping together with SENCOs from other schools, in order to share ideas.**

(op cit., p. 163)

Taking account of OFSTED requirements

Any framework for inspection of special educational provision in schools will necessarily have to be based on a view of what constitutes effective provision for both the sum total of pupils as well as the diversity of individual pupils' needs. There is clearly a dilemma here of whether a national inspection framework should be the same for all schools and the quality of teaching and learning within them, or should be different, depending on the context of the individual school and the diversity of its pupil population.

OFSTED's perspective of one common inspection framework has the potential for inspectors not to report on the attainment of pupils defined as 'having special needs'. Whilst a common framework with this flexibility appears to be equitable it also stands the criticism of being less able to respond flexibly and appropriately to individual differences and as marginalising and undermining the value of pupils whose attainment is not seen as worthy of inclusion with that of other pupils. A framework that adopted an alternative perspective might attempt to inspect schools using criteria that were tailored to the needs of individual schools. However, this alternative framework might be criticised as unable to show how a school was faring in comparison with others.

Richmond (2000) has outlined the OFSTED school inspection framework as it operated in 1999, and offered an account of some of the implications of this for special provision in schools:

> **The Framework for the Inspection of Schools (OFSTED 1995b) is a statutory framework and applies equally to all nursery, primary, middle, secondary and special schools. Whatever the population of the school the same test of the quality of education provided by a school is applied. The OFSTED inspection process is in effect organisational research**

(Shaw 1982). It uses a planning model, a statutory framework for the inspection of schools. Planning models can be useful for researching organizations but they also have serious weaknesses in that a fixed set of relationships are suggested. The model adopted for the framework for the Inspection of Schools (OFSTED 1995b) has three components:

- the context of the school

- the outcomes of the school

- the contributory factors to those outcomes.

The framework and schedule make the assumption that there is fixed causal relationship between specified contributory factors and the outcomes it specifies. The specified outcomes are the:

- attitudes, behaviour and personal development of the pupils

- attendance of the pupils

- attainment and progress of the pupils.

Richmond notes that, in practice, pupil attainment is the dominant outcome. Registered inspectors are reminded, (OFSTED, 1998a):

In all that you (inspectors) do when inspecting schools, you should be evaluating:

- **what is achieved and in particular: attainment – educational standards and whether they are high enough**

- **and progress – whether pupils are learning well enough**

- **how well the school promotes pupils' achievements, particularly through the quality of teaching.**

(op cit. p. 9)

The framework and schedule specify the factors which are assumed to promote or inhibit attainment or progress in a school under two main headings:

- provision made by the school

- management of the school.

The sub components of these two factors are further specified. The central and dominant contributory factor determined by the Framework is the teaching of lessons.

(Richmond, op cit.)

Commenting on the framework, Richmond makes a number of specific criticisms. For example, there is a rigid assumption that the quality of pedagogy influences the attitudes, behaviour, development, attendance and progress of pupils in a simplistic cause-and-effect manner: the higher the pupils' academic attainment, the better must have been the pedagogy. He feels that it is unfair to use comparative attainment data to measure the effectiveness of a given school because like is obviously not compared with like. Different schools serve different populations and the existing arrangements for comparison across schools do not allow for this. It simply cannot be the case that all schools are capable of achieving to the same standard as the highest attaining schools if only teachers made the necessary effort.

In addition, if progress is poor, teaching cannot be graded as satisfactory. Registered Inspectors are criticised if grades for progress differ significantly from the teaching grade.

There is a very narrow view of achievement:

> **The standards are attainments of pupils in the subjects of the National Curriculum, particularly in the core subjects of English, mathematics and science. The standards of any particular school are judged against Key Indicators: the expected attainments of children at a given age as identified by level statements in the National Curriculum programmes of Study and particularly comparative attainment data (OFSTED 1995,c,d,e). In practice the quality of the education provided by a school has to be judged against the actual average attainments of children of the same age as measured by the national Standard Assessment Tasks (SATs) at the end of the year in which children are 9, 11 and 14 years of age and the actual attainments of children in the year in which they are 16 in the General Certificate of Secondary Education (GCSE), (OFSTED 1998a). The key statistic for secondary schools is the proportion of children attaining five A* to C grades. Some Registered Inspectors will refer to the comparative proportion of pupils attaining A* to G grades as a measure of the success of the school for pupils with learning difficulties.**

(Richmond, op cit.)

Attainment in the subjects of the National Curriculum and religious education is a relevant but limited view of the outcomes of schooling on which to judge the effectiveness of schools. Attainment data in the form of test and examination scores are easy to obtained and for this reason are used to make judgments about the school standards. However, they offer a limited view of what children can do. In addition, the underlying assumptions of the tests may be questionable as may the manner of their administration. The data is made available in comparative form about individual schools in the pre-inspection and contextual school indicator reports (PICSI) received by schools and Registered Inspectors before an inspection. OFSTED (1998a) claims that this data provides:

an increasingly secure picture of the past standards achieved by the school.

(page 9)

Furthermore, the requirement to judge pupils' progress ('rate of learning') offers inadequate definition of what constitutes a particular 'rate'.

... data does not exist about the progress: (defined by OFSTED as the rate of learning), 'expected' of individual or groups of children. It has not been established what learning 'as well as expected' or 'well enough' actually means. The expectations of the National Curriculum programmes of study for any given age are merely expectations and have no foundation in the actual progress that any children make over a given period of time or over a key stage.

(Richmond, op cit.)

Having said this, Richmond also points to the advice given to inspectors to use documentation relating to Statements and IEPs to judge whether progress is being made by identified pupils. However, if the purpose of talking with pupils during school inspections is 'in honestly gathering, representing and understanding the learner's perspective' (Richmond, op cit.), there is little guidance to inspectors on how to engage with learners' views on their education.

There is no statutory requirement to report the attainments of children assessed as having special educational needs. Richmond notes that Registered Inspectors can choose not to judge or report on attainment for such pupils. Major emphasis is then given to progress in relation to prior attainment (OFSTED 1995e). A special school inspection report usually contains wording to the effect that:

It is inappropriate to judge the attainment of pupils for whom this school provides against age related national expectations or averages. The report does, however, give examples of what pupils know, understand and can do. Judgements about progress, and references to attainment, take account of information contained in pupils' statements (of special educational needs) and annual reviews.

(OFSTED 1996 p. 21)

Richmond (op cit.) feels that:

... if it is inappropriate to assess the attainments of some children with special needs against the average attainments of children of the same age

as a measure of the quality of the education they receive then it must be inappropriate to do this for all children. But OFSTED does not recognise that what sensibly applies to children with special needs applies equally to all children.

(Richmond, op cit.)

In judging the quality of education on offer in a school, little account is taken of the extent to which a school provides for the whole diversity of pupils' needs:

> … All those Code of Practice (DfEE 1994) guidance things: a staged register of children with special needs, keeping meticulous records, individual education plans, parental contacts and so on or a show piece learning support base are similarly only of value in that they also are perceived to have an impact on the progress made by the children.

(Ibid)

The major contributory factor to pupil learning is assumed to be the quality of teaching in lessons, (OFSTED 1998b). However, the criteria against which the quality of teaching is judged are ill-defined:

> … at the core of the inspection process are high stakes judgements about teaching quality which are based on snap shots of evidence … which take no account of the composition and attitude of classes at any one time … lessons observed by inspectors are atypical, the quality of which are influenced by whether teachers can rise to the occasion to give demonstration lessons … (consequently) inspectors are in no position to evaluate the quality of teaching taking place in normal circumstances.

(NUT 1998, para. 21)

Richmond comments on the fact that the PICSI report for the school means that the inspectors know the comparative attainment of the school and therefore what they are guided to say about it. Additionally, the OFSTED criteria on which teaching is to be judged 'are not informed by any of the research into effective lessons let alone the features associated with effective teachers'.

Revisions to the OFSTED Framework

Since Richmond's article was written a new inspection framework, *Inspecting Schools* (OFSTED, 2000) has been compiled, to take effect from January 2000. As the new framework points out, school inspections 'are governed by the School Inspections Act 1996' which requires inspectors to report on the same four issues as the previous framework, that is schools' 'educational standards', the 'quality of education' provided, whether resources 'are managed efficiently', and the 'spiritual, moral, social and cultural development of pupils' (ibid, p. 4). Inspectors are required to answer the central question 'How well is the school doing, and why?' (ibid, p. 34). This question is to be addressed through seven subsidiary questions covering much the same ground as before. The evaluation schedule attached to the new OFSTED Framework is 'not radically different' from the previous one but has been 'strengthened in areas closely associated with standards, notably pupils' achievement, teaching and learning, and leadership and management' (Tomlinson, 1999). In terms of 'standards' and 'teaching and learning' there are two questions to be answered:

- 'How high are standards?', which is subdivided into two parts. First is 'the school's results and achievements'. Second is 'pupils' attitudes, values and personal development'. Subsumed within the first of these are academic results, the school's progress towards its own targets and 'how well pupils achieve, taking account of the progress they have made'. The emphasis here appears to be on pupil achievement rather than progress *per se*, thus responding to some extent to criticism of the use of the term 'progress' by such as Richmond (above). However, in the same section (OFSTED, op cit., p. 36), inspectors are required to consider the extent to which pupils identified as having special needs 'are making good progress'. There remains the difficulty implicit in defining what constitutes 'good progress'.

- 'How well are pupils or students taught?', again, subdivided into two parts. First is 'the quality of teaching', to be evaluated, as previously, in terms of its 'impact on pupils' learning and what makes it successful or not'. Second is 'how well pupils learn and make progress' (ibid, p.38).

Preparing for inspection of special educational provision in schools

Whatever the nature of the critique that might be offered of OFSTED inspection criteria, inspection is a reality for schools, careful preparation for which is vital. Richmond (op cit.) points to issues that must be taken into careful consideration prior to such inspection if effective provision to support the progress of pupils who have special learning needs is to be demonstrated. His advice to special needs co-ordonators whose schools are about to be inspected was written against the Framework in operation prior to January 2000. However, it contains many points which are important to the new Framework and Evaluation Schedule also, given that the 'progress' of pupils 'with special educational needs' remains a central focus of the inspection. For that reason it is quoted verbatim below:

When inspection is a practical reality, the sensible school will recognise that education reform legislation clearly states the requirements of schools. The OFSTED Framework is a test of the effectiveness of the school in implementing those requirements. Personal views about what is important for the education of children with special needs, or for that matter what school inspections ought to be, are irrelevant to the reality of an inspection under the current regulations. The requirements for an effective education for children with special needs are those requirements established by the government and it is those requirements on which the quality of education provided for pupils with special needs will be judged. It is in the interests of children with special needs that the school responds well to those requirements.

The special needs coordinator who manages the process of the inspection effectively and confidently will be anticipatory, proactive rather than reactive. However, the rewriting of policy documents smacks of panic whilst the maintenance of clear and consistent records of pupils' progress and teachers' practice is more considered. In any test knowledge about the test: the nature of the test, the scope of the test, the rules of the test and the criteria to be applied is essential for a successful response.

In the present arrangements for the inspection of schools, as has been discussed, the central outcome on which provision for special educational needs will be judged is the progress made by pupils identified as having special educational needs. Effective provision will include monitoring the progress of the pupils across the curriculum. The prepared SENCO along with class or subject teachers will therefore:

- have some good reliable and clear evidence of pupils' progress recorded

- will ensure inspectors see this

- will produce examples for inspectors.

The evidence about that progress will be drawn from:

- responses of pupils in subject lessons

- written work in subject lessons and any special teaching arrangements

- what pupils and their parents say about their learning across the curriculum.

The evidence will be recorded in writing and might include:

- contents of statements of special educational needs

- detailed curriculum planning in individual education plans

- reviews of progress meetings

- informed test results

- relevant samples of work including work from subject lessons.

(The records will include parents' and pupils' views)

The quality of the provision for pupils with special needs and the management of that provision is not of importance in itself, only in that the quality is associated with the judgements made about the progress of the pupils. Governors are required to inform parents about the success of the special educational needs policy in their annual report. The effective school will be regularly monitoring the effectiveness of the special needs provision as it impacts on pupils' progress. Inspectors will seek causes of the progress or lack of progress made by pupils in the quality of the provision for:

- the curriculum: access, entitlement, teaching/timetable arrangements, provision for specific needs, the use of assessment for example

- teaching: (the major factor to be associated with the progress made by pupils) planning for differentiation, use of support staff, use of resources and special equipment, assessment against learning targets for example

- support and guidance: pastoral support including that for pupils with emotional and behavioural, difficulties, medical supervision, therapy, liaison with support agencies for example

- partnership with parents: that parents are properly informed and involved in the educational planning for their children for example.

and the quality of the management of arrangements for:

- leadership and management: for example: of statutory responsibilities and the CoP, policy, provision, funding, staffing, identification and assessment, reviews of progress, that school staff work closely with SENCO and are aware of procedures, parents know the point of contact and outside support is well managed

- staffing, accommodation and resources: for example additional support for statements, the level of any designated unit staffing, that support staff work with teachers planning and recording progress, the appropriateness of staff training and experience, adaptions to accommodation for physical and sensory needs, ensuring the adequacy of technological communication aids

- efficiency of provision: use of, for example, funds made available for SEN, any LEA devolved funding, specific grants and the deployment of support staff.

Verbal feedback is very likely to be offered to the special needs coordinator at the end of the inspection. This might take the form of a report under each of the relevant aspects of the framework. The effective special needs coordinator will, during the course of the inspection have developed a professional dialogue with the inspectors and particularly the lead inspector for special educational needs. If this dialogue and the provision of additional supporting evidence has been successful there should be no serious surprises in the verbal report. However, the verbal report does not have to be a passive activity. Asking for further explanation of unclear points is acceptable. All the judgements by inspectors must be based on reliable evidence and if points made are not genuinely considered a fair reflection of the school then the alert SENCO will be asking for the evidence on which particular judgements are based, perhaps even challenging that evidence if appropriate. In the written inspection report the quality of education for pupils with special needs and the contributory factors will not be in a separate section but be under the appropriate headings in the inspection report.

Summary

Pupils have a statutory entitlement to having their 'special educational needs' identified, assessed and met in an individualised way. This is the way in which attempts are made to put the principle of universal education into practice and recognition given to the fact that some pupils experience difficulty in coping with the regular curriculum. Whatever views any individual may hold, the current system is underpinned by law and reinforced by inspection procedures, and therefore must be respected by professionals associated with schools.

Suggested Activities: Reflection and discussion

1. Preparing for an OFSTED inspection

Those with responsibilities in the co-ordination of special educational provision in schools who also have to consider the requirements of an OFSTED inspection might:

(Cont...)

- obtain a copy of the Inspection Framework and Evaluation Schedule either directly from OFSTED, or from the OFSTED website;

- use Richmond's checklist in the chapter above to help with their planning and preparation.

2. In-school needs analysis: reviewing school policy documents

For those with an interest in reviewing a school special educational needs policy document it would be useful to remind themselves of the required format for, and content of, schools' special needs policies in the *Code of Practice* (DfEE, 1994) in England and Wales or in Northern Ireland, the Code of Practice (DENI, 1998).

Then collect together the school policy documents on special educational needs. With colleagues, discuss the detail of the policy against

- the requirements as laid down in the Code of Practice.

- the guidelines offered by Tarr and Thomas in this chapter.

Complete Needs Assessment 2 Whole-school needs assessment: school special needs policy documents in the Appendix.

List, in order of priority, areas for improvement in the paperwork.

6 Special learning needs in the school context

For a number of reasons it is essential that special educational needs co-ordinators and others are aware of both the features in schools that facilitate the learning of all pupils, including those who experience difficulties, and also the features that predispose to creating barriers to learning. Firstly, one of the changes proposed for the revised National Curriculum for 2000 (QCA, 2000) is a new statutory statement on 'providing effective learning opportunities for all pupils' which is to replace the current statutory access statements. The *General Statement on Inclusion* (ibid) sets out three 'key principles for inclusion'. These are:

- Setting suitable learning challenges

- Responding to pupils' diverse learning needs

- Overcoming potential barriers to learning and assessment for individuals and groups of pupils

Schools are enjoined to 'take action at all levels' to ensure that provision meets learning needs and that all pupils have 'the relevant opportunities' to enable them to make progress.

Secondly, those responsible for making special provision for pupils are charged with securing that those pupils engage in school activities together with peers subject to three provisos relating to the use of resources, education of peers and receipt of the specified special provision. There is also an expectation in the Code of Practice that all teachers should take responsibility for the progress of pupils who experience difficulty in learning. Translating the ideology of inclusion into practice is unlikely without this awareness. Furthermore, assessment and planning for individual pupils identified as having special learning needs must take place within the context of whole-school policies and procedures. Sensitive, flexible provision resulting from this process implies a thorough grasp and understanding of this context.

The inclusivity of schools

Salmon (1998) feels that a number of factors make schools as institutions incapable of responding to the learning needs of all pupils. These can be categorised as arising from school and educational systems, external constraints and expectations and government regulations:

Below is a table of the factors she has identified:

Factors arising from: School and educational systems	External constraints/ expectations	Government regulations
Regimentation of pupils	Local relations between races, social groups and genders	Strictly governed schedules, e.g. national curriculum, standardised testing
Lack of individuality and personal recognition	Parental expectations	Emphasis on performance and results: league tables
Chronological age grouping		
Inappropriate model of child-as-learner		
Within-school power relationships		

Authoritarianism

How far there is common agreement that all these factors necessarily operate to exclude some pupils is a matter for debate. What is in the interests of some children may militate against the interests of others. Some of these factors, for example those relating to the National Curriculum, are deliberate government initiatives. This same initiative can be viewed as both causing difficulties in learning and ameliorating them. Those who view the National Curriculum as inclusive feel it acts to raise standards and offers a general framework within which to conceptualise education for all pupils. Others perceive the National Curriculum operates to exclude pupils with particular learning needs because they cannot be adequately accommodated within it.

Any student's difficulties can be seen to arise at the point of interaction between the learner and the context in which she or he finds her or himself as a result of the mismatch between what she or he brings to the situation and the expectations of the teacher and the provision available. Whether a child needs 'special provision' to meet his or her learning requirements depends, to some extent, on what kind of arrangements operate in a school as a 'normal' part of its organisation. In some schools, for example, extra supportive programmes for developing reading are already organised through peer tutoring or paired reading with adult volunteers (Merrett, 1998). It may be that in such schools fewer pupils may be seen to have 'special needs' in the area of literacy than in schools where no such provision normally exists. By implication, therefore, schools need to re-evaluate provision regularly to reduce the possibility that barriers may be created to students' learning in the first place. However, current statutory requirements which focus on an individualised approach to meeting learning needs may militate aginst whole-school practices of this sort.

Inclusive policies are based on a notion of all children having the same general learning needs and entitlements. Below is the outlines of a policy initiative in a secondary school which has been proactive in attempting an integrated whole-school approach to raising the standard of achievement, expectations and self esteem of all pupils. It illustrates how successful implementation of policy initiatives in a school is dependent on common ownership of them.

Clark, Dyson, Millward and Skidmore (1997) document attempts to realise principles of participation and values of equity at 'Downland', an urban comprehensive school created from the merger of two single-sex schools. In a deliberate effort to avoid the traditional terminology and practices of special education, a metaphor of 'energy' was adopted, the term 'children who challenge the curriculum' replaced 'pupils with special educational needs' and curriculum development and innovative approaches to teaching and learning were promoted as the appropriate response to difficulties in learning, rather than the creation of a special system. Forms of provision in which pupils were withdrawn from regular classrooms were outlawed as exclusionary and an extensive support system concerned with working with the class teacher and the whole group was developed. A new teaching and learning co-ordinator with a background as a mainstream subject teacher rather than a special educator was appointed to observe and report on any aspect of pedagogy or learning, and difficulties arising at any level. However, a number of problems became apparent which thwarted the school's approach to inclusion and led to some incoherence in direction and resistance from staff working at different levels in the school. Two of the most serious factors in contributing to the lack of cohesion were

- the failure of the senior management team to consult adequately with, and take account of the feelings and perceptions of, the whole staff during the process of curriculum innovation

- pressure from parents to ensure that their own children should receive their statutory entitlement to individual support for their learning rather than that this support should be embedded in the whole-school support system.

One might reflect on the extent to which any artificially-imposed change of terminology which does not arise spontaneously from, or reflect, changed circumstances could affect change in attitude towards particular pupils. The initiative had been introduced by the head teacher with the support of his senior management team. When the anticipated change failed to be as effective as had been hoped, certain staff who had been openly sceptical of the projected changes were conceptualised as 'unreconstituted' and saddled with the role of 'institutional scapegoats'.

The role and function of the teaching and learning co-ordinator at Downland might well have been interpreted very differently by staff who were broadly in favour of the move towards inclusion as opposed to those who were sceptical of this move. The extent to which one individual is in sympathy with another will have a great deal of influence over how actions are interpreted. Behaviour which seems to be supportive to one person may feel intrusive and threatening to another. The presence in a classroom of a senior member of staff may be experienced as supportive and facilitative or as inspectorial, for example.

One of the issues which was particularly contentious was that of whether withdrawal from class was always to be viewed in a negative light as exclusionary. There are institutions where small groups of pupils are withdrawn from class groups for all sorts of reasons, from specialist music lessons, to special enrichment activities to individual tuition in literacy. How far withdrawal appears to be exclusionary and potentially damaging to the pupils may depend on the status attributed to the particular activity. In the end, this particular school was forced to recreate special forms of provision for some pupils as a result of pressure from parents of those with Statements who regarded generalised in-class support as insufficient to meet specific needs.

Criticism of anyone is always easy after the event, particularly where, as here, the vision of a few people in positions of authority in a school is not entirely shared by everyone else. However, it may have been that greater sharing of understandings and a willingness to share perspectives might have been possible at an earlier stage.

School priorities

The National Curriculum

The imposition of the National Curriculum with its prescription of subjects, programmes of study and assessment arrangements may be seen as overly constraining and inflexible. Dyson (1997) comments that the establishment of a National Curriculum as a 'curriculum for all' (NCC, 1989b) conveyed a rhetoric of 'breadth, balance, relevance and differentiation' In reality, however, the academic demands it made on pupils were exclusive and inaccessible to some. Pupil entitlement, therefore, was to a 'confinement within a rigid and inappropriate hierarchy of knowledge' rather than to experiences in which all children could meaningfully participate.

> **The dilemma facing special education professionals and commentators is summed up in the elaborate disapplication procedures in the 1988 Act and the injunctions not to use them in NCC (National Curriculum Council) circulars (NCC, 1989a) and elsewhere. On the one hand, the**

curriculum was palpably inappropriate for large numbers of children; on the other, special education professionals could not reject it without at the same time resegregating children with special educational needs.

(Dyson, op cit.)

Dyson goes on to note that, unsurprisingly, most of the effort of professionals with regard to the National Curriculum was 'focused on the logistics of access and differentiation', rather than re-thinking curriculum issues in a fundamental way.

It also has to be said, however, that many of those working in the Special Needs field see it as supportive of the notion of a common curriculum framework and entitlement for all. The dissatisfaction with the way in which the programmes of study and assessment arrangements have been enacted cannot detract from this principle, even though there are issues concerned with the application of this principle to the education of all young people.

Meeting National Curriculum Requirements

There may be problems in implementing certain areas of the National Curriculum in relation to the needs of some pupils identified as experiencing difficulties in learning. If so, it is essential to consider both what it is about the aspect of the curriculum that is inappropriate, and also what the pupils bring to the situation that makes the issue problematic.

Whatever alterations teachers make to enable the pupils to engage more fully in this aspect of the curriculum might solve some problems but create others (Norwich, 1996). Solutions commonly adopted include:

- reducing the content coverage of the curriculum so that some young people have more time to reinforce their learning of key areas of the curriculum

- enabling some pupils with sensory impairments to access the curriculum through alternative means, for example particular kinds of switch access to computers, use of special talking word-processing software

- providing different teaching approaches, materials or settings for some pupils.

In addition to statutory requirements which affect the education of all young people, there are regulations which relate specifically to the needs of those deemed to have 'special educational needs'. Teachers have to consider very carefully the basis on which they make decisions, whom to consult, and how to conceptualise pupils' 'best interests'. If they choose to reduce coverage of the curriculum for a child, for example, there must be a very clear rationale for deciding what to omit.

National targets

The government has established a set of standards in the areas of literacy and numeracy. By the year 2002:

- 80 per cent of 11 year olds leaving primary school will be expected to reach the standards expected for their age in literacy.

- 75 per cent of 11 year olds will be expected to reach the expected standard for their age in numeracy.

Whilst, on the surface, aiming at high percentages of pupils achieving the designated level is laudable, there are also features of this that must be of concern to those involved in the area of special educational needs. These 'standards' refer to only a section of the pupil population. It is noticeable that the same percentage, 20 per cent, is used as the proportion expected not to achieve the expected standard in literacy, with a slightly higher proportion in numeracy, as the expected proportion of pupils who, it is anticipated, will 'have special educational needs' at some stage in their schooling. There appears to be a worrying disregard for this group of pupils. Applying 'standards' to the majority does not explain how progress should be conceptualised for the remaining pupils.

One very serious issue that must be of great concern to all those considering the needs of students who experience difficulties in learning is the extent to which the focus on achieving targets related to national norms together with the added pressure of competition to achieve a high position on the academic league tables, will function to squeeze these pupils out of the system. It is difficult to see the attraction of students who will never reach the national norm to schools anxious to raise their overall standing.

Pressure for a school to achieve well on the league tables may result in young people who experience difficulties being given more work in those areas which are reported and less work on other aspects of the curriculum, a situation which is clearly unacceptable from a consideration both of maintaining balance in the curriculum and in maintaining young people's enthusiasm and interest.

Time constraints

The amount of curriculum time that is already taken up with compulsory elements of the curriculum has recently been increased by the introduction of the "literacy hour", leaving many schools finding it difficult to ensure the necessary curriculum breadth. A study by Mortimore et al. (1988) found that actual teaching time in London junior schools amounted to approximately five hours per day and of this 17 per cent (Tizard et al., 1988) is taken up with non work-related activities such as tidying up and registration. Lewis (1995) offers two possible alternatives for increasing time available for learning: increasing the length of the school day and using current curriculum time more effectively. Some schools have already introduced the first where a comparatively minor alteration has been made to current arrangements, but if additional time were to be introduced nationally it should involve proper negotiations with teachers and their representatives. The annual conferences of the national teachers' unions are often concerned with the degree of work overload already felt by teachers without adding to this further by increasing the length of the school day, (National Union of Teachers Annual Conference, 1998). Alternatively, many schools have found ways of creating additional teaching time in the current structure. Flexibility over break times which allows young people to continue working during these periods and sharing the supervision of classes, structuring break time activities to include reinforcement of number or language skills through the use of rhymes, singing games and competitions, turning the playground into a richer learning environment by marking out hopscotch grids or organising garden areas. Careful consideration of grouping arrangements in class may also have considerable bearing on the time young people spend on-task.

Classroom pedagogy

The extent to which any school is able to facilitate the learning of any child is largely the function of classroom practice. Richmond (2000) notes that, for pupils with special needs (OFSTED 1995c, d, e) inspectors are directed to look for evidence in lessons that:

- work is well matched to pupils needs

- appropriate resources and special equipment is available and in use

- pupils' work is assessed against any individual learning targets

- teachers plan and manage the work of support assistants in the lesson.

In 1995 the annual report of the Chief Inspector of Schools (OFSTED 1995a) reported broad features of good and poor lessons frequently identified by inspectors in lessons observed in special schools.

The features of good lessons were:

- careful lesson planning that took account of individual needs

- skilful questioning

- a balance of individual and group work

- pupils challenged by the activities

- pupils working co-operatively and assuming some personal responsibility for their own learning.

The features of poor lessons were:

- failure to ensure effective deployment of support staff in lessons
- little consideration to matching tasks to pupils' abilities and learning needs; insufficient opportunity for pupils to take a degree of responsibility for their own learning
- pupils required to listen for unduly long periods and offered too few opportunities to demonstrate their knowledge and understanding.

A preoccupation with the presence or otherwise of a limited set of observed events in lessons can be a distraction from what it is to be an effective teacher responding to the diversity of educational needs (Florian, 2000). Powell (1985b) after observing many teachers at work in Scottish primary school classrooms, claimed that:

> ... good teaching practices cannot be had 'off the shelf': they arise from analysis of needs, from the monitoring of effects, and from imaginative and insightful attempts to meet ever changing and complex requirements.

> *(Powell, 1985b, p. 36)*

Commenting on how misleading appearances could be he, (Powell 1985a) commented that:

> ... there were at least some grounds for thinking that what the teacher does may be less important than the way he does it.

> *(op cit., p. 6)*

In a conclusion consistent with O'Brien's (1985) notion of 'communal learning needs', the DES (1985) in a study of good teachers, concluded that the educational development of pupils is dependent on:

> ... the respect which (teachers) show for their pupils, their genuine interests and curiosity about what pupils say and think and the quality of their professional concern for individuals.

> *(DES, 1985, p. 3)*

Many studies of inclusive education have been focused on the level of the school and only indirectly on classroom practice (Florian, in press). There has been very little direct research on effective teaching in inclusive classrooms. However, there is a growing awareness of the importance of the quality of children's classroom experiences. Simply including pupils by admitting them into the school or a classroom is not enough. There have been a number of attempts to describe teaching and learning in inclusive schools (Ainscow, 1991; Thomas, Walker & Webb, 1998; Tilstone, Florian & Rose, 1998; Sebba & Sachdev, 1997). A review of these reveals remarkable consensus on the tools and strategies available to educators wishing to create more inclusive schools and classrooms. Co-operative learning, peer mediated instructional approaches, multi-age grouping, and team teaching are all suggested 'best practice' for inclusive education. However, little is known about the parameters of these techniques as teaching tools for supporting learning in classrooms which include children of widely varying abilities.

Florian (op cit.) has outlined new research on classroom practice being carried out at the University of Cambridge (UDIS, 1998). This research aimed to identify and evaluate the classroom strategies and techniques in use in four secondary schools which described themselves as inclusive. As part of the data gathering, volunteer teachers kept 'inclusion journals' in which to record their thoughts and feelings about their practice. The guidelines instructed them to consider how the nature of the subject area informed their teaching practices, how they took account of individual differences between pupils, and what they felt was successful in the way in which their department approached the National Curriculum and prepared pupils for the GCSE examinations. One English teacher recorded her experience with a year 9 group as follows:

November 4th

Year 9 are starting *The Outsiders* by S.E. Hinton. I have three concerns about reading this text with the group. One is to do with the two students who will understand little if any of it. Louise can read fluently and write neatly, but what she reads makes no sense to her and what she writes makes little sense to me. She is statemented but I do not think the summary of her needs quite covers her problems. I don't know how to put it myself but I would say that her conceptual awareness is extremely limited. She was also very withdrawn and shy and in her primary school spent much of the time in tears. The group is supportive of her and I have never seen her cry. She also takes part in drama and discussion activities, largely because others in the class strive to involve her.

The other student who worries me is David who just returned from an extended (several months) stay in Guyana. He is completely illiterate – last year he struggled to read the word 'the' and I would have him 'reading' my son's baby books to me. Yet, he is a bright little thing; listens intently when not distracted; and takes part happily in drama and discussion activities. He also speaks a Guayanese Creole which has been an asset in the past when we have discussed languages and dialects.

Luckily I am supported by teaching staff for all 4 Year 9 periods so there is help in the classroom for David and Louise. However, Louise seems shy and wary of the male support teacher who is with us for two periods a week and he now feels happier supporting others in the class. Perhaps David will strike up a rapport with him.

The second concern is to do with the very able students in this group. Will I allow them to read on if they want to? This will allow a lot of preparation to provide different tasks for different people. However, my main worry is a boy who, I have discovered, has already read *The Outsiders*. Clearly, I can't just demand that he trudges through the book again, even if he wanted to.

Luckily, for me, he was absent today. I approached the novel through well-tried methods: predictions re: the title, put a spidergram on the board; reading and discussion of the blurb; reading of the first page with focus questions. Each time questions were set I allowed the groups to discuss possible answers and then directly asked people for responses. In this way everyone could answer a question.

November 5th

Year 9 again. I have re-arranged the groups today. I like them all to sit with different people every half-term. By chance a few people were absent and I joined two groups. Thus, David and Louise, the two 'weakest' children in the class were seated together at the same table. This may be no bad thing. The support teacher sat with them and helped them both. Coincidentally, the third child at the table (the room is oddly arranged, with small and round tables which accommodate only 3 at a time) also needs support for a variety of reasons. However, I do worry that this is merely setting within the classroom. I'll discuss it with the two support teachers and perhaps change the seating next week.

Today we re-capped what we had learned about Ponyboy, the main characters in *The Outsiders*. I wrote the question on the board and drew 5 arrows from it, asking each group to think of 5 things to say for two minutes. I then stopped the discussion and picked on people for answers, again asking everyone and everyone was able to give a response which I could put on the board. This is an inclusive technique which works well, I find. It takes longer than 'hands up' but it means each child can feel he or she has contributed something and it stops the 'brighter' children and stronger characters – in this class mainly boys – from dominating such sessions.

I wanted them to write a paragraph or two on Ponyboy using the notes on the board. We discussed how best to use the notes and one child – of 'average' ability – suggested putting them into categories. Excellent, I thought – just what I wanted. They then suggested three categories: family, appearance and character. After that they wrote the paragraphs in groups, either just giving each other ideas or writing the same thing exactly. I stopped them after 10 minutes and asked one boy to read his out. (I had gone round and seen his was one of the best). I have found this method of collaborative writing also very useful; particularly with regard to different forms such as 'lit-crit' essays.

We then read aloud for 10 minutes – the narrative involved action and dialogue here so the boy who had read the book acted as narrator and the other students 'played' different characters.

(Florian, in press)

These two journal entries give an idea of how an experienced teacher copes with the complex issues of a mixed attainment group and the wide diversity of pupil learning needs.

One of the many emerging findings from the Cambridge study (Florian & Rouse, in press) is a clear picture of the shift in teachers' concerns as pupil progress shifts as pupils get older and move through the key stages of the National Curriculum. This 'shift' is from a 'concern with individual pupils' progression through the curriculum to a preoccupation with preparing all pupils to achieve the highest possible GSCE grade in as many subjects as possible' (ibid). Teachers commonly view the examination as something that must be made accessible to pupils. Consequently, increasing amounts of time are devoted to talking about the examination process, demystifying it and preparing for it as pupils grow older.

Pupil grouping arrangements

There is no single clear-cut way of ensuring the meaningful inclusion in the classroom of pupils who experience difficulties in learning, are non-English speakers, and/or have physical disabilities. The demands placed on teachers of mixed attainment groups will vary according to the characteristics of the particular teacher and the size and complexity of the group. Teachers have different levels of understanding of the ways in which pupils learn, and of pupil diversity. They also have different levels of comfort and experience in working with other adults in the classroom. One comment from the above journal entry that related to in-class grouping arrangements:

I do worry that this is merely setting within the classroom...I'll discuss it with the two support teachers and perhaps change the seating next week ...

underscores the importance of creating opportunities for teachers to talk with colleagues about their concerns. It is extremely important that priority is given to teachers meeting to discuss concerns with colleagues and work out ideas for practice (Florian, op cit.).

Setting, streaming and withdrawal groups

In many schools there has been debate around appropriate grouping arrangements for delivering the formal curriculum for a number of years now. A consistent finding in research into streaming of students by level of measured attainment is that it tends to demoralise those placed in lower academic streams (Hallam, 1996). Slavin's (1987) conclusion from a review of American studies which investigated the effects of streaming, setting across classes for individual subject areas and grouping by attainment within individual classrooms was that:

- for the majority of the time pupils should be taught in mixed attainment classes

- grouping should be by attainment within specific subject areas, not by general overall attainment

- grouping arrangements should be flexible and open to amendment

- grouping arangements should be enough for the teacher to be able adapt his or her teaching approach appropriately for each one.

Lewis (1995) notes that the withdrawal group work focused on the teaching of specific skills for pupils who experienced difficulties in certain areas that was common practice in the 1970s and early 1980s has now largely fallen into disfavour because:

- apparent gains made in the small group situation could not be sustained and/or generalised in the context of the classroom

- students lose the continuity of classroom activity and instruction while they are withdrawn

- the teaching methods used in the withdrawal groups may conflict with those in the main classroom

- when the onus for supporting students fell on the support teacher who was working outside the class, there was less incentive or need for class teachers to take an interest in examining how teaching for all pupils might be improved.

It is hardly surprising, however, that many primary teachers would still support withdrawal group work, given the pressure of time on normal classroom activities (Gipps, 1987). Moss and Reason (1998), for example, note that in-class support is often used to facilitate access to the curriculum and, as a result, the explicit teaching of reading to those pupils experiencing difficulties in literacy development may have suffered. They describe a 10-week programme with four groups of Year 1 children. In this programme, sixteen pupils altogether were selected because they were making the slowest progress in developing literacy skills in a school in a 'relatively unprosperous' area. This programme incorporated 'interactive group work', shared activities which involved the children in listening to each other and turn-taking in reading and writing guided by the teacher. The aim was to encourage fluency in word recognition and reproduction, competency in phonics and the comprehension of text. At the end of the ten weeks ten children had achieved the criteria for success in this programme. It has to be said that these groups were very small and consisted of pupils with a very narrow range of overall literacy achievement. The factors that the researchers felt were conducive to the success of this project were that:

- the researcher was highly knowledgeable in the area of literacy development and so could draw on a range of strategies

- there was adequate time for joint planning between the researcher and the class teacher of the activities for pupils

- the activities were designed to engage the pupils' attention and to be enjoyable as well as to focus on particular skills.

Despite the best endeavours of the researcher, however, it is noteworthy that some pupils still failed to make acceptable progress within the group and would need additional individual attention. It may be that there is room for intensive specialist work in particular areas but, if this is the case the central issues revolve around ensuring the quality of the special programme, finding the time for liaison work between the classroom teacher and the organiser of the groupwork, maintaining continuity for these pupils and minimising the risk of stigma attached to this form of additional support for learning.

Collaborative group work

There is a large body of research on the relative effects of co-operative, competitive and individualistic goal structures on student outcomes (Fraser and Walberg, 1984; Johnson et al., 1976). The generally positive effect of co-operative learning approaches on student achievement is illustrated by Johnson et al's (1981) study, but even so 'is not totally conclusive and generalisable' (Fraser, 1986). For example, a large proportion of these studies involved group outcomes and tells us nothing necessarily about the individual student outcome. Slavin's (1983) review of cognitive achievement in 41 studies in primary and secondary schools illuminates some of the conditions under which co-operative learning was most effective. He found little evidence to support the view that working in small groups is more effective that studying individually except under certain conditions: group rewards had to be provided based on group members' achievement; there had to be individual accountability. He concluded that the effects of co-operative learning on achievement are primarily motivational. The impact of co-operative learning strategies on non-cognitive outcomes include enhanced self-esteem, peer support for achievement, greater internal locus of control, more time spent on task, greater liking of class and classmates, and more co-operativeness (Slavin, 1983).

Collaboration between peers is often recommended as one way in which pupils who experience some kind of difficulty in learning in a mainstream class might be included without risking being stigmatised for being different from others. We might readily appreciate the logic behind assuming that a more competent peer might be able to 'scaffold', offer support to, another learner who is experiencing difficulty (Bruner, 1985). We might also agree with the view that having to explain ideas to a peer helps to clarify thinking. Recent research has, however, provided mixed support for the assumption that collaborative grouping arrangements between pupils is always and necessarily valuable. Mercer (1995), examined how pupils construct knowledge in classrooms through talk in joint activities. Those groups where most learning seemed to take place tended to be those where:

- pupils have to use language to make plans explicit, make decisions and interpret feedback

- decision-making is shared between partners rather than where one partner is dominant

- there is the opportunity for open-ended discussion and argument outside the visible control of the teacher

- opinions are clearly explained and examined critically. Talk which merely rehearses 'unexamined platitudes' does not enhance understanding

- pupils have a common understanding of what is relevant to the discussion and of what constitutes an appropriate outcome of it

- learners are paired with friends

- the activity is designed to encourage co-operation rather than competition between group members;

He concluded that what pupils were expected to do in such groupwork was not always obvious to them. From the factors teased out above it was possible to work out ways in which pupils could be explicitly taught the ground rules for collaborative activity in the classroom.

Peer tutoring

A special kind of grouping that is adopted in some schools as a means of matching different kinds of teaching expertise to particular learning needs is that of peer tutoring in reading. In his review of a number of studies of the 'Pause, Prompt and Praise' procedures (Glynn and McNaughton, 1985), Merrett (1998) notes that three important elements must be supplied by the organiser of any paired reading project: the reading level of the child, a means of monitoring progress and positive feedback. He notes also that peer tutoring is seen as enhancing the function of the teacher as facilitator and developer of the whole initiative, rather than detracting from the teacher's role. This strategy is intended only for those students who have acquired some skill in reading, not for those who have not yet begun, and must be carried out on a regular daily basis. It is an approach that assumes that students learn to read by reading complete texts, not by learning separate sub skills such as phonics or individual whole words. It is not therefore proposed as a whole reading scheme. In some schools parents of the tutors object to their children being used as the teachers of other students. However, Merrett feels that pupil-tutors improve their own reading skills as they engage in teaching others.

Summary

Florian, (in press) notes Powell's conclusion (1985a) that 'there are many ways of being a good teacher and that rigidity of mind was the enemy of good teaching'. Certainly. those responsible for overseeing any kind of special programme for individual pupils within a school require flexibility of mind to understand and take account of the individual school context and priorities in addition to colleagues' preferred practices and statutory demands, when the make decisions on behalf of, and with, individual pupils and parents.

Unless the learning needs of certain children are to be viewed as totally different from those of everyone else, it is very difficult to separate them from those of other children. The issue of how the institution of school can simultaneously respond to sameness and diversity is clearly show here to be problematic, however. A right to be registered at a particular school does not guarantee that a pupil will be included and will thrive.

Suggested Activities: Reflection and discussion

1. Reflecting on developments at Downland

Clark, Dyson and Millward and Skidmore (1997) discussed developments towards an inclusive approach at Downland. Reflect on:

- the extent to which you feel a label such as 'children who challenge the curriculum' is likely to confront within-child notions of special needs

- your reflections on whether withdrawal from class is always 'exclusionary'

- possible interpretations that might be placed on the role and function of the teaching and learning co-ordinator at Downland if you were:

(Cont...)

- ◆ broadly in favour of the move towards inclusion

- ◆ sceptical of this move

- what you feel might have contributed to a more satisfactory outcome?

- possible ways to avoid the danger of 'unreconstituted' members of staff becoming the 'institutional scapegoats' if a school fails to change in a particular direction.

2. Individual school priorities in pupil grouping arrangements

Anyone interested in reviewing a school's priorities in relation to pupil grouping might find it useful to note down responses to the following questions:

How do the school's priorities in relation to pupil grouping impact on provision for pupils who experience difficulties in learning?

If you have noted any negative effects, what might be done to mitigate these:

- in the short term

- in the medium term

- in the long term?

3. Consideration of the inclusivity of schools

With colleagues discuss how far the factors related to the inhospitality of schools in relation to some pupils that have been identified by Salmon (above) exist and serve to exclude pupils at your school. Then note down what might be done at school level to ameliorate these factors

- in the short term

- in the medium term

- in the long term.

What kind of resistance to your proposals might you meet in the context of a school with which you are familiar?

In-school needs analysis

Those with an interest in, and/or responsibility for, staff development in relation to special educational needs in schools might wish to complete *Whole-school Needs Assessment 3: Staff development* that is included in the Appendix.

7 Users' Perspectives: pupils, parents and carers

One of the major challenges facing those with responsibilities for co-ordinating special educational provision in schools is that of engaging with the perspectives of the users of the system, pupils, parents and carers, in a positive and meaningful way. On the one hand there is an expectation that pupils', parents' and carers' views will be sought over provision made for the child and that teachers as well as pupils, parents and carers will be willing and able to engage in this activity, however much their interests may be in conflict. On the other hand, traditional school structures and bureaucracy often present barriers to the expression of pupil opinion particularly, but also, sometimes, of parent opinion as well. Avenues for participation need to be established before proper account can be taken (Florian, 2000) and institutionalised resistance to change is a well known problem in schools (Hopkins, 1991).

Learners' Views

Issues of access to, and the validity of, pupils' own accounts of experiences and personal viewpoints

The Code of Practice encourages the participation of pupils in decision-making. It advises schools to consider how they:

- involve pupils in decision-making processes

- determine the pupil's level of participation, taking into account suitability for age and experience

- record the pupil's views

- involve pupils in implementing Individual Education Plans (IEPs).

(DfEE, 1994, 2:37)

However, it does not provide guidance on how this should be achieved, leaving questions about access to, and the validity of, pupils' personal viewpoints unanswered. In the absence of guidelines, many teachers, sensitive to the vulnerability of children, may feel reluctant to engage in practice which they do not feel qualified to undertake. Moreover, the assumption that 'teachers know best' can become a barrier to participation. Research (Wade & Moore, 1993) suggests that some teachers believe pupil consultation is time-consuming and of little value; that decisions are made at a higher level and preclude consultation;

that even if given the opportunity for participation, pupils would not take the task seriously; and that the range of perspectives within a given group would not be coherent.

Garner and Sandow (1995) have identified philosophical and practical problems surrounding advocacy and self-advocacy which impinge upon the child, teacher, parent and law-maker. Some professionals associated with schools may feel that some of their arguments are not those that they would wish to entertain. On the other hand, they may feel that they are pragmatically sensible and address the reality of many school-leavers' worlds:

- The complexity of the law relating to special education means that many people rely on legal advocates to access their rights, particularly as regards the statementing procedure. There is a view (Wolfensberger, 1989) that advocacy relies for its existence on the continued dependency of its clients and therefore it is in the interests of advocates to seek to create further dependants. Use of legal advocates may be seen to encourage an adversarial situation of parents or carers fighting their way through the system opposed by local authority bureaucrats whose job it is to defend the public purse.

- Advocacy by teachers also depends upon the continuance of the client group. It may undermine the confidence of the client-group in self-advocacy whilst serving the vested interests of the professionals (Tomlinson, 1982). To avoid the suspicion of self-interest, the teacher must work to do him or herself out of a job.

- Teacher-advocates are often marginalised and/or poorly regarded by other teachers and senior managers, thus reducing their potential to promote the interests of the client group.

- The model of pupil as participant and self-directed learner rather than empty vessel to be filled implies that the traditional role of the teacher as purveyor of wisdom and transmitter of knowledge must change to that of facilitator. This development in the teacher's role may be uncomfortable and not always welcome.

- Some pupils may be seen as undeserving of the right to self-advocacy, for example those whose behaviour is seen as disruptive. Others may be perceived as incapable of contributing rationally to decisions about their own lives, for example those identified as experiencing severe difficulties in learning:

The dilemma for the teacher is thus to decide whether to extend to such children the same rights to self-representation as are afforded to others, or whether to act instead as a guardian, protecting the child from the world and the world from the child.

(Op cit., p. 20)

- Traditionally society takes the view that rights and responsibilities are age-related, with the very young seen as incompetent to judge, and those under 10 incapable of bearing criminal responsibility for their own actions. No account is taken of individual differences. However, it is clear that those as young as nursery-age are able to engage properly in decision-making about their activities. There is an obvious tension here between lowering the age at which children are assumed to have rights and rational views at the risk of exposing them to failure, and raising it for the sake of prolonging the possibility of legal protection.

- It may be that not all children wish to be self-advocates and that choosing not to engage with the decision-making process may be a valid choice in itself. It may also be the case that forcing children to make their own choices where the learning goals do not seem relevant to the individual is counter-productive.

- There is a view that self-advocacy skills and independent thinking may not be appropriate to permanent employment in situations which school-leavers may commonly experience.

- Self-advocacy may be viewed as a threat to the existing order and may therefore be unpopular with some teachers. Pupils may openly verbally challenge teachers' authority as well as the structure and organisation of the school. In addition self-advocacy involves a transfer of power from teacher to pupil in the degree of legitimacy accorded to pupils' opinions.

- Self-advocacy may appear to run contrary to the traditional behaviourist model of learning adopted in some schools which rely, at a very basic level, on learning programmes designed to reinforce desired behaviour and inhibit undesired behaviour.

- The time-constraints operating on schools through the demands of the National Curriculum have resulted in a reduction of opportunities to promote self-advocacy in lessons planned to develop skills of speaking and listening. The recent introduction of the Literacy and Numeracy Hours have reduced the time available for activities seen by some as optional extras.

Legal considerations

The notion of self-advocacy is supported by international law, and by one piece of British legislation. In the United Nations Convention on the Rights of the Child (1989) Article 12 states:

(1) Parties shall assure to the child who is capable of forming his or her own views the right to express those views freely in all matters affecting

the child, the views of the child being given due weight in accordance with the age and maturity of the child.

(2) For this purpose the child shall in particular be provided the opportunity to be heard in any judicial or administrative proceedings affecting the child, either directly or through a representative or an appropriate body, in a manner consistent with the procedural rules of national law.

Article 13 (1) states:

The child shall have the right to freedom of expression; this right shall include the freedom to seek, receive and impart information and ideas of all kinds, regardless of all frontiers, either orally or in print, in the form of art or any other medium of the child's choice.

There is conflict between these rights and practice in many schools, however, since:

- within schools teachers are regarded legally as 'in *loco parentis*' and therefore participation by children is more in terms of an indulgence that may be granted

- pupils have no right to see their files until they are 16

- they cannot appeal directly against exclusions but must rely on parents or carers to do so

- they have no automatic right to be present at appeals against exclusions.

In the domain of child welfare, the 1989 Children Act represents the first attempt to take the views of children into account in decisions about their future. Children's views must be ascertained in any proceedings. In courts a 'guardian *ad litem*' and a solicitor must be appointed to look after their interests. However, children rarely address the court directly and the guardian's account of the child's view may be distorted through his or her own particular lenses.

The value of the learner's perspective

Gersch (2000) notes that although, over the past 20 years, there has been progress in involving children more actively in their education, 'such progress as has occurred has been patchy, unsystematic and slow'. In his opinion, this is a matter of regret because, in listening to what children say about their education and their needs there remains a 'wealth of untapped resource for teachers, schools and other professionals'. Awaiting discovery there is a 'gold mine of ideas, views, feedback, information and motivational energy'.

Research was conducted at the Bolton Institute in 1998 into the views of 2,527 pupils in primary and secondary schools in one Education Authority located in the North West of England in response to four open-ended questions (Whittaker, Kenworthy and Crabtree, 1998). The purpose of the study was to investigate factors conducive to happiness and unhappiness among pupils, and pupils' constructions of good and bad teachers. The responses represented a wide range of views.

The most significant factor conducive to happiness was 'friendship', (63 per cent), followed by particular subjects (25 per cent), with only 1 per cent indicating rewards. The most significant factor conducive to unhappiness was bullying (33 per cent), then involvement in particular subjects (25 per cent), and 'unfairness' (16 per cent). The descriptors of a 'good' teacher most commonly identified were 'happy, kind and understanding' (54 per cent), 'respectful and fair' (27 per cent). The most common descriptors of a 'bad' teacher were 'shouting and bad tempered' (44 per cent), 'too strict and unfair' (27 per cent) 'disrespectful', (13 per cent).

Often teachers and pupils have very different understandings of classroom processes and events. The authors of this report appear to take a stance on the importance of listening to pupils' views which is based on both moral and pragmatic considerations. They note that:

- pupils are often capable of articulating their views and have the right to be heard on issues that concern themselves

- the pupils surveyed appeared to be pleased to be keen to offer their views, given that not one questionnaire had been 'spoilt'

- listening to pupils will enable professionals better to understand and reduce the barriers to their learning

- pupils attach far more significance to personal relationships at school than professionals

- engaging with pupils' views in this way can help teachers and policy-makers to consider more effective solutions for halting the increasing numbers of pupil exclusions from school.

There is now evidence from schemes based on collaborative learning, for example paired reading and peer tutoring, to indicate that teacher-pupil collaboration will enhance the performance of pupils generally. From a social constructivist view, dialogue between teacher and learner is important because the process of cognitive development involves internalising social interactions. Concepts, language, voluntary attention and memory are mental functions which come from the society into which the child is born. They appear twice in a child's development: first as shared between the child and the adult (social) and then as internalised within the child's own thought processes. The child has a zone of proximal development (in other words the next step in development), which is achievable only with the help and support of an adult.

Engaging with challenging views

There are certain situations in which a teacher may feel particular challenges in engaging with pupils' perspectives. One of these might be where disaffected pupils express views which can be perceived as threatening to the school system and the authority of the professionals working within it.

Cooper (1993), in his review of the effectiveness of engaging with pupils' perspectives, states his view that behaviour seen as disruptive and challenging to the teacher's authority is often embedded in pupils' self perceptions. Change in behaviour can begin with the verbal expression of these perceptions. Traditional medical and the psychological models used to explain this kind of behaviour ignore the possibility that behaviour labelled 'EBD' might be a rational reaction to stressful circumstances. Given this, pupils may well perceive themselves to be acting perfectly reasonably. If we assume that children actively engage in construing themselves and learning about the world through social interaction we should be far more concerned about what they themselves make of the circumstance in which they find themselves and their own position in relation to it. 'All actions serve some useful purpose for the actor' (Ravenette, 1984). The challenge for those concerned with supporting children is to discover what this purpose is. Pupils may experience 'competing values and expectations stemming from internal idiosyncratic processes or from differing family and sub-cultural values' (Ravenette, op cit.) which lead them to rejection of everything associated with school. In the past what has often been missing from any analysis of pupils' 'problems' is their perspective, sometimes with disastrous consequences.

In a recent interview (Wearmouth, 1997) Jack, for example, described how, after his parents divorced and he was left in the care of a sister, he was categorised as 'maladjusted' at the age of six and then placed in a special school for 'maladjusted' pupils until he was 15. Finally, he was allowed into a mainstream secondary school and his perception of himself as capable of high achievement if only he were allowed access to 'good', traditional education was put to the test. He was presented with a teacher of English from an ethnic minority group. Jack appears to have considered that 'proper' English is taught by the English and construed this teacher as 'bad' because he could not speak it in an English accent and therefore violated his sense of the 'normal' and 'good'. He did not therefore, in Jack's view, have command of his own subject, but was presenting 'rubbish' to the pupils of the sort that Jack considered he had already been subjected to in his previous special schools for the 'maladjusted'. The teacher did not have long enough to show whether he was good or bad in any other terms before Jack walked out of the classroom.

> I went to a school in L where they had an English teacher who was *** (from an ethnic minority), and I didn't even understand what he said. I was only there for about two weeks ... I got kicked out of there because I didn't want a *** English teacher. Totally disgusting that a *** who couldn't even speak my language was trying to teach me English.

It may be naïve to assume that engaging with Jack's perspective at the time would have achieved any positive outcome and, if mishandled, may have inflamed the situation. On the other hand simply expelling Jack was no adequate solution either, and he still feels that he was badly let down. He ended his educational career in secure accommodation. In the interview he expressed his view that questioning authority is acceptable, indeed is necessary, when the questioner is reasonable and the authority is misdirected. Over the past few years schools have operated within a national context of competition, a drive to demonstrate accountability for the use of public money in education, and recourse to the law by parents dissatisfied with the provision on offer to their children. Pupils such as Jack are not popular in the system. Few interest groups exist to support their needs. From a human rights perspective it is even more important to attempt to engage with pupils' perspectives in this kind of situation.

Pupils are now encouraged to express their own views during the assessment process to ascertain their 'special educational needs'. The rationale given for this in the Code of Practice is seen in part as a disclosure of information from child to professional, in part as enlisting the support of the child for the programme that is devised, and in part as a matter of human rights:

The benefits are:

- practical – children have important and relevant information. Their support is crucial to the effective implementation of any individual education programmes

- principle – children have a right to be heard. They should be encouraged to participate in decision-making to meet their special educational needs.

(DfEE, 1994, 2:35)

However, the list of benefits above begs the question of the willingness of pupils to participate positively in a process if, as is the case of a boy such as Jack, it constructs a socially unacceptable identity such as 'maladjusted' (which more recently would be termed 'emotional and behavioural difficulties).

Including pupils whose behaviour seems threatening to the system is not easy. Pupils who require additional resources are not popular in schools and exclusionary pressures resulting from the current competitive climate are very strong. Assuming an interactive view of the child's learning implies an approach which is time-consuming in the short term and requires the co-ordination of views from a number of different sources. Ravenette (1984) offers three principles from a constructivist perspective which may lead to an understanding of the child that is rigorous in its approach yet moves away from the need to label:

- Behaviour is perceived as challenging in varying degrees, according to how closely the professional is involved in interactions with the child and under what circumstances. Professionals therefore need to accept that others' views of the child are equally valid.

- Everyone both creates his or her own world and is created by it and by others around. Account needs to be taken of how children make sense of their own circumstances and what impression is conveyed to children of others' constructions of them.

- All actions serve a purpose for the actor. It is important therefore to find out what purpose is served by the behaviour that poses the threat to the system and/or others around and how this purpose might be fulfilled in a manner that is more acceptable socially.

Action based on this understanding is more likely to fit the pupil than that which depends on a model which fails to take into account the child's agency and alternative view of the self.

Cooper & McIntyre (1996) studied what teachers and students understand by 'effective teaching'. Some of their conclusions might be seen as particularly relevant to considerations of how to engage with disaffected pupils. They found, for example, that student involvement and participation in lessons was a vital component for effectiveness; students showed a preference for active rather than passive involvement in lessons. Teachers were most effective when they showed sensitivity to individual variations in students' cognitive style and matched their teaching strategies with students' preferred learning strategies. Effective teacher-student relationships were marked by collaboration, co-operation and co-option rather than coercion.

Affective considerations

One of the issues facing those responsible for special provision is that, despite the evidence demonstrating the crucial importance of the quality of teacher-pupil relationships in promoting pupil learning, relationships with teachers and fellow pupils are conventionally viewed as largely irrelevant to education:

The organisation of the school regime makes no room for these features. ... Despite all this, the personal encounters that young people have with each other, and with their teachers, often have a momentous significance ...

(Salmon, 1998, p. 12)

There is an irony in the fact that classroom order in activities which harness the energies and interests of pupils depends on how far a negotiation of power has been successful between teacher and learners. Teachers have to be consistent and fair in their dealings with pupils. These qualities are prized highly. Commenting on research at Highfield School (Highfield Junior School, 1997), Salmon (1998) notes:

Classroom learning proceeds best when pupils are granted personal acknowledgement and respect, and a recognition of their competence, resourcefulness and responsibility.

(Salmon, 1998, p. 41)

In a study of the views of boys in two residential schools for 'disaffected' pupils, Cooper (1993) also showed that boys in these two schools identified a number of positive personal outcomes related to relationships with teachers and peers in the school, which have a therapeutic and supportive effect. He concludes that disaffection from school may have stronger links with the effects of particular schools on particular pupils than it is to do with the individual's rejection of schools. Cooper discusses how many of those in his sample come from 'disadvantaged' backgrounds and therefore represent a critical group because they are pupils for whom particular mainstream schools have found themselves unable to cater. These boys broadly agreed with the school effectiveness researchers that individual schools make a difference. He concludes that:

This focus on the pupils' perceptions of effectiveness is vitally important. It is only by trying to develop a construction of the school environment through the eyes of pupils that we can begin to understand the ways in which aspects of that environment impinge upon them. By learning about what matters to pupils in their schools, we can start to understand the mechanisms for producing and reducing disaffection, and then employ this understanding in the development of a whole-school approach.

(pp. 155–6)

Ways of reducing pupil disaffection

Gersch (2000) has reported on two projects which aimed to increase the active participation in school of disaffected pupils, but were designed to involve everyone. The first of these took place in a junior school:

On a visit to a junior school, my advice was sought about a particular 10-year-old child. The teacher wished to explore ways of motivating him to complete work, stay on task and of course make faster progress with his schoolwork. We began considering ways of enhancing this child's motivation. During our deliberations, however, it became clear that there would be major benefits in planning a whole class system rather than just for one child.

A system was devised which involved every child being given a list of 15 tasks to complete on a "To Do List" for the day. Other columns were "work completed" which the child had to tick when the task was done, self graded score (which the child had to rate from A to D, from excellent effort, to good effort, to satisfactory effort, to not very good effort).

Finally there appeared a column for the teacher to add in her grades of the child's efforts. The teacher's grade was then converted to points (A=3 points, B=2 points and C=1 point) and the points totalled weekly. Points were exchanged for rewards such as free time, choice of work on a Friday, going to help in another younger class, on the basis of one point for one minute earned.

The sheet was signed at the end of each week by the child, the teacher and the head teacher, and sent home for the parents to see and sign.

The sheet was eventually evaluated at the end of the year, with feedback being sought from the children, the parents, the teacher and the head teacher. The key findings were that the system had been enjoyed by more than 90% of the pupils in the class, 56% of the children said they were working harder. All of the children enjoyed receiving rewards listing their preferred options as playing, watching TV or video, drawing, chalking on the board, chatting and, interestingly, helping out in another class with younger children.

Only a few parents responded to the evaluation questionnaire, but those who replied did so in favour of the system. Other responses, together with those from the children suggested a finer grading scale to a 5 point one, which was subsequently developed.

The teacher felt that the system was very useful, if tiring and drew attention to important discussion between herself and children regarding the gradings. Pupils often under-estimated their performance and effort. She reported that children seemed to develop greater self-discipline, their effort had improved, and she certainly wished to continue with the system.

Gersch comments on several features of the system that are especially worth highlighting (Gersch 1987):

(a) It encourages children to develop organizational and study skills

(b) It encourages children to assess their own efforts

(c) It encourages frequent and specific feedback from teacher to pupil

(d) It encourages greater responsibility in children about their work

(e) Work tasks are broken down into small, manageable chunks

(f) The process encourages two way understanding between teacher and learner; children begin to predict their teacher's views and the teacher may learn much about the child's self image

As adults, do we not find the 'To Do list' motivating when faced with large projects?

The second project related to a group of Year 11 pupils in a secondary school:

One secondary school approached the educational psychology service expressing concern about disaffection and poor attendance in a group of Year 11 students. A steering group was set up and ways explored of organizing a whole school systems project.

The particular school already had in place relatively elaborate decision making machinery, including departmental and full staff meetings at which vital decisions were debated, proposed and decided upon. It was therefore agreed that we would set up 5 small groups to investigate the causes of disaffection and to make recommendations to the staff meeting.

The innovative element of the working parties was the involvement of students, and indeed those who were particularly disaffected or not attending school. Interestingly, these young people were very happy to attend school regularly for this purpose, which itself shows how much students want to talk about their school and education.

Each of the five working groups comprised 2 teachers, 2 students and an external consultant. The consultant came from outside the school and was either an educational psychologist or specialist teacher engaged in a local project to combat truancy in the area. The consultants met regularly to discuss progress and to receive support from the principal educational psychologist.

Each working group met weekly for about an hour and a half, over the course of a term, and was given three main questions to address:

1. What do you think are the causes of the disaffection and truancy in the school?

2. What could the school do to improve the situation?

3. Prioritize three main proposals to take to the full staff meeting for decision.

It was very evident that the groups worked hard in a focused way to produce many positive, constructive and intelligent ideas. Students reported that they enjoyed the meetings, which were conducted in an informal and relaxed way, and of course implicitly acknowledged the importance of student views.

The end result was the production of a number of creative proposals ranging from improved work areas, feedback about work, staff-student communication, assessment, a pupil council, a newsletter and use of school for activities beyond the school day.

Many of these ideas were implemented and in a subsequent evaluation a year later there was evidence of some (slight) improvement in attendance but a reported improvement in the communication and relationships between staff and students.

The author comments on the significance of fostering a sense of ownership among pupils for new initiatives in schools:

This project highlights the point that there is merit in involving students actively in whole school developments as well as in respect of individual programmes. Such initiatives are likely to create a shared feeling of ownership amongst young people, enhance their feelings of responsibility and moreover elicit some creative and productive ideas in respect of school improvement.

Identifying, and coping with, the dilemmas

Gersch lists a number of dilemmas encountered during the development of the initiatives he outlines.

- How does one deal with other colleagues who might feel that children should be seen and not heard?

- Are some children not mature or capable enough to participate? (In the author's experience even very young children and students with severe learning difficulties can make some choices about their educational programmes.)

- How does one deal with parent-child dislike?

- What about scope needed for children to negotiate, try things and change their minds?

- **How do adults distinguish what a child needs from what he or she prefers or wants?**

- **What if the SENCO comes into conflict with their head teacher over ways of meeting a child's needs? What then happens to the child's views?**

Clearly there are no easy solutions to these dilemmas which represent, essentially, conflict between the roles of the participants. The nearest Gersch himself comes to offering an answer is to point to the 'the importance of a trusting, listening, open, non-judgmental relationship' between teacher and pupil that he feels must exist if a positive way forward is to be found.

Parents' and carers' perspectives

Issues related to the development of parent partnerships

There is overt acknowledgement in the Code (paragraphs 2.28–2.32) of the supreme importance of effective and positive working relationships with parents: 'partnership' with parents. Teachers are enjoined to 'take account of the wishes, feelings and knowledge of parents at all stages' of the 'carefully planned and recorded actions' (op cit. para 2.28) taken in response to a child's difficulties. In addition to the Code itself, the Department for Education, then the DES, has produced a document in the 'Citizen's Charter' series: 'Children with special needs. A guide for parents', first published in 1992, supporting the rights of parents to be involved in decisions about their children's education.

The ways in which families are viewed is very important in parent-professional partnerships. Turnbull & Turnbull (1990, p. vii–viii) have articulated a set of values which offers a positive perspective on the sense of ownership which many families need over issues affecting their own lives:

- Individual differences enrich families, communities and society. People with disabilities therefore contribute positively to their families.

- Families sometimes need a new vision of what life can be as well and support to fulfil these dreams and expectations.

- Families should have choice to direct their own lives. Supporting families to work towards their own preferences is building from a position of strength.

- Positive relationships within the family and community are crucial. Members of families need connections with each other and with friends outside.

- People with disabilities and their families are entitled to be considered as full citizens with a right of full participation in society.

- Inherent strengths – Families are inherently strong, although at times they need support from outside agencies to realise their expectations.

Florian (in press) notes Turnbull & Turnbull's report (op cit.) that families with members who have disabilities often experience increased stress. Major areas of family functioning include: economic, daily care, recreation, socialization, and affection. The areas are interrelated and often a problem in one area can have an impact on another area. For example, there are often increased costs associated with having a child with a disability. The demands of daily care may be greater and increased demands in these areas will have an effect upon the other areas. Turnbull & Turnbull note that there is a higher rate of marital problems among families of children with disabilities than other families. In addition to the added pressures on family functioning associated with having a child with a disability, it has historically fallen upon parents to also serve as advocates in paving the way for participation.

Parental choice: the case of the SEN Register

One of the underlying, quite clearly stated, intentions of the Code, is that parents are to be full partners in the process of the education of their children with Special Needs. There is evidence to indicate that insufficient note of the wishes of parents in the way in which the some of the Code's recommendations is put into practice in schools. For example, it appears that advice given in the Code to maintain the school Register of Special Needs, is, in practice, accepted as a given rather than simply as guidance. No account seems to have been taken of the fact that parents might have very good reasons for not wishing their child's name to be recorded on a Register and what the consequences should be if this is the case.

The results of a recent (1996) small-scale study in a mixed comprehensive upper school appear to indicate that maintaining a Register of identified pupils is not necessarily compatible with the ability to sustain positive working relationships with parents (Wearmouth, 1997). Parents of pupils who had been identified as experiencing difficulties in learning were asked whether they would have any reservations about their children's names being included in the school's Register of Special Needs. Of those replying to the letter sent home, a number expressed serious deeply-felt concerns with regard to issues of stigma, confidentiality, segregation and labelling, and withheld their permission to 'register' their children.

A cross-section of 42 parents had been contacted, and, of these, 27 sent replies:

- 16 parents said that they had no objections

- 9 said that they would not wish their child's name to be included on an SEN Register

- 2 signed the slip at the bottom of the form to indicate that they had received the letter, but did not indicate their feelings.

Out of the 16 parents with no objections, some added further comments which expressed a perception that the registration of the needs of their child on an official document would act as a 'guarantee' of continuing extra provision:

- **It will guarantee my son the necessary extra resources.**

- **I think it is a shame that children can go through Lower School and Middle School without any special needs being given and have to wait until XXX School for anything to be done - as is the case with my son.**

- **I have no objection as long as A. is not singled out in any way. At the moment he is happy to do his extra (literacy/curriculum support) lessons and is not made to feel inferior or stupid where friends are concerned. I mention this because this is how he was made to feel at lower school. He was always being told he was lazy and stupid and that when he got to middle school they would send him back to lower school. Of course this didn't happen but we had a dreadful 6 weeks with a child who, according to the doctors, was having what would be classed as a nervous breakdown in an adult. I wouldn't want to have to cope with this again.**

Comments from the 9 parents with objections, who comprised 33 per cent of those who responded, between them summarised all the concerns associated with public identification of 'difference' – issues of confidentiality, stigma, labelling. categorisation and segregation:

- **I have no problem with you giving the government a head count of pupils with Special Needs, but for reasons stated on the phone to you, I would be unhappy with names being given to 'Big Brother'. (This parent requested immediate contact by telephone on receipt of the letter. He asked for details about the Register itself, who would have access to it, and what would happen to his son's records in the future. He also asked that all reference to his son's needs should be deleted from his records before he left school so that nothing would come back to 'bite him' in the future.)**

- **We feel there is no benefit at all for our child to have his name put on this register. The very good Special Needs teacher and the school itself must already keep some sort of record and we think that should be enough.**

- **I can't understand what such a register would be used for and why exactly it is necessary. (This parent also requested telephone contact to** explain her view that under no circumstance did she want her son's name on the Register.)

- We feel it's not necessary for J. at this stage of his education to be put on a register. At Lower or Middle School – yes – so that it can be passed on to the next school.

- I have reservations about a list of Special Needs pupils.

- One cannot guarantee the confidentiality of such a register.

- It would not be in the best interests of my son, as the present help available to him will remain unchanged at the moment.

- We do not like the idea of our son's name being put on a Special Needs Register, which may then be kept into the foreseeable future. If this becomes compulsory he will leave Special Needs. P is still 13 and young for his age. We feel he will catch up given time and support, like his sister and brother. His elder brother and sister are both late developers.

- Monitoring of a pupil's progress is already of a high standard. I'm sorry, but we do not believe in the categorisation of children into certain groups. We feel that segregation of children's names on a Special Needs Register will be of no beneficial use. The class in itself (a curriculum support group) is a necessary backup for children who need extra help. It is very well run and our daughter has gained enormously. In our opinion this document would be labelling children who may lack confidence in certain subjects.

(Wearmouth, 1997)

The solution reached in this school was to set out clearly what forms of provision were being made which necessitated higher levels of staffing and resourcing, and the names of the pupils in each group, in the same way in which lists of pupils in option groups were published. This solution does not, however, really address any of the parents' concerns. The staff were left asking themselves whether there really was ever any real intention of involving parents as *partners* in their children's education – partners with any real say, that is - and what rights parents actually have in this particular situation. Very little, was their conclusion. The research raised serious questions about what parents are to make of the 'recommended', but in much of the documentation assumed as mandatory, practice of keeping a Register of their children's names, confidentiality not guaranteed, readership unknown, purpose unspecified in the Code. What are parents to make of the 'recommended', but in much of the documentation assumed as mandatory, practice of keeping a Register of their children's names, confidentiality not guaranteed, readership unknown, purpose unspecified in the Code? And, perhaps as importantly, if the Register is important, not mentioned at all in the Parents' Guide.

Lady Blatch (op cit.) has asserted that the Code is part of a 'system which protects the children with special needs' and 'gives new rights to parents'. It is difficult to see how a school Register of Special Needs, open to view 'and available as needed' to anyone who can claim a legitimate purpose can give parents new rights.

Parent power

The power of parents to influence the organisation of a school, especially when supported by the force of law, is illustrated by the way in which teachers at 'Downland', a secondary school attempting to adopt an inclusive approach to pupil learning, were forced to re-structure its overall curriculum response to meeting the diversity of pupil learning needs:

> **In Downland there were a number of pupils with statements of special educational needs, largely for specific learning difficulties. These statements had included reference to individual non-specialist support. This was at odds with the ethos of inclusion and non-withdrawal from the mainstream classroom. Initially, the response of the school had been to provide non-specialist support in the context of the classroom, but this had been challenged by the parents of the statemented pupils who demanded that the requirements of the statement were fulfilled. The response of the school was to set up an alternative system in which the statemented pupils were to become the responsibility of a former member of the girls' school and to receive the 'entitlement' of their statement through her specialist teaching … The solution was in effect to 'hive off' a small sub-group of pupils in an effort to retain the liberal values of the school for the overwhelming majority by leaving the existing system intact.**

> *(Clark, Dyson, Millward and Skidmore, 1997, p. 65)*

In the face of well-organised pressure groups lobbying for individualised special provision the rhetoric of liberal values may be insufficient to protect more generalised and inclusive curriculum approaches designed to ensure equal opportunities and participation for all pupils in a school. The researchers point out the significance of the alliance between parents and psychologists in the emergence of the category 'specific learning difficulties'.

> **… psychologists employed by, for example, the Dyslexia Institute, appear to play a key role in helping parents secure resources and provision for their 'dyslexic' children, often in the face of opposition from professional educators and educational administrators.**

> *(Clark, Dyson, Millward and Skidmore, 1997, p. 110)*

There are many debates around the cause of the difficulty and appropriate forms of curriculum differentiation or intervention. Often the pupil him or herself is ashamed of his or her inability to learn to read properly. The pupil's family may feel guilty that they have not been able to help him or her more. Whatever the cause, it remains the case that attributing a pupil's problems to a sensory, neurological or psycho-linguistic impairment is one way to absolve the pupil and his or her family from blame for lack of progress.

Throughout the 1980s and 1990s there has been a series of initiatives designed to support parents in exercising their rights. However, exercising rights requires a high level of motivation and determination as well as, sometimes, access to legal representation and financial resources. The inevitable consequence of this is that some parents will be better able to exercise their rights than others. The law in relation to 'special educational needs' is concerned with meeting an individual need that has been assessed, not with what local authorities decide they can afford or what they and/or schools think is desirable. The basis of special education legislation is that of entitlement for individual learners. Gross (1996) concludes that resources are unfairly allocated to children whose parents are more literate, persistent and articulate and supports the notion of formula funding in the interests of 'fairness' for all children. Making the same point about unfairness, the Audit Commission (1992) observed:

> **LEAs admitted that factors which had no bearing on the level of need of a child were influential in the decision to issue a statement. The most significant factors were the level of determination of the school or the parent and whether the parent was represented by a lawyer or voluntary organisation.**

(para 22)

However, as Simmons (1996) points out:

> **Those who support the case for formula funding in the interests of 'fairness' must be prepared to acknowledge that they support the dismantling of entitlement. Seen in that light, how many professionals or voluntary agencies would say publicly that they were in favour of removing entitlement from the most vulnerable sector of the educational community? Are they really willing to support restructuring which would give disabled children only what local politicians had determined was available rather than what was needed?**

(p. 107)

She concludes that the solution to the problem is not to remove entitlement from learners, but to persuade local authorities to fulfil their obligations towards every child. Even if the local authority does meet its resource obligations, however, there is still no guarantee that the child will accepted by the school as a fully participant member and his or her needs met appropriately across the curriculum.

There is a big difference between what is perceived as fair and necessary by different groups of parents whose perceptions may be viewed as neatly encapsulating many of the issues and tensions inherent in Special Education, with particular regard to separation and inclusion. The extent to which competing or conflicting parents' voices can be reconciled within the walls of one school is questionable. Some pupils are not popular with other pupils' parents. In response to the government Green Paper one parent of a child with Down's Syndrome wrote:

We had a particularly bruising and discriminating experience by other parents at a mainstream primary school with our son who has Down's Syndrome. We have now moved him to an MLD where he feels wanted and has settled well.

Adopting particular perspectives on specific issues will be advantageous to individual interest groups ('stakeholders') in society. A good example of the different perspectives taken on policy in the area of special educational needs, according to the differing interests of the groups concerned, is that of the responses made to the recent government Green Paper *Excellence for All Children* (DfEE, 1997). Currently the law distinguishes two types of special educational needs: those that can be met within the existing resources available within the school and those for whom the local authority must make provision because the resources are not available within the school. To safeguard the latter a Statement of needs is written for the individual pupil. Whether or not Statements are regarded as a positive way of looking at pupils' learning requirements tends to depend on their effect on the central concerns of the group concerned. Parents often have very different views from local education authorities on this issue:

- local authorities have a statutory obligation for ensuring effective education for all the young people of school age in their own geographical areas. They tend to view Statements as inequitable because they draw resources away from the common pool intended for all pupils towards a minority assessed as 'having a special educational need'

- many parents see Statements as the only way of securing a legal entitlement to the resources needed to support their own children's education

- central government is concerned about the cost of the whole referral and assessment process and in the Green Paper proposed cutting the number of Statements to 2 per cent of the total pupil population.

It is clearly the case that some parents or carers are unable, or unwilling, to support the progress of their child through school. In a recent interview (Wearmouth, in press), an inmate of one of Her Majesty's prisons whom I interviewed recently related the following experience from his childhood:

> ... when I was seven years old, my Mum was killed in a car crash and this seemed to devastate our family you know. My Dad turned to drink and I had a sister, a year old sister and up until then it was kind of a normal happy life really, you know. I remember before then I was just a normal child, you know. ... Fairly soon my Dad met another woman and we moved in with her. She had two kids, and we kind of moved in with the kids and everything but he wasn't very happy at all - always drank pints. ... She didn't like me very much this lady and I was relegated really ... She would compare us, me and the oldest son who was going to grow up to be a lady killer, but I was an ugly bastard. It was quite cruel stuff. ... We ... lived in her house but occasionally they would argue and fight and he would, you know ... real physical violence, and she would throw my Dad out! So, he would take me and my sister down to the local Police Station.

Summary

Engaging with pupils' and parents' views is now an expectation of all teachers generally, as a regular part of a child's education. In the context of special educational needs there can be particular challenges in this regard. Teachers are professionals in the education industry. It is their role to make informed decisions based on their knowledge and experience. In many school staffrooms, attempting to claim the high moral ground by appealing to colleagues to respect the rights of the individual child is insufficient to justify pupil participation in decision-making processes. It is important, therefore, that a greater degree of pupil participation can clearly be justified.

There is considerable evidence to support the conclusion that taking seriously the views of the users of the system is part of a process of developing an ethos which is supportive of learning and of positive reciprocal working relationships. The Elton Report (DES, 1989), for example, reflects other research discussed in this chapter which characterises the inclusive school as one where 'teachers treat pupils courteously, respect their ideas, value their individuality, and listen carefully to what they have to say.' This is perceived as promoting a context where pupils are 'much more likely to respect teachers and behave considerately and sensibly themselves' (DES, op cit.), thus serving the interests of the whole school.

The Scottish Council notes how important it is to 'effective' teaching to take pupils' views seriously:

Effective teaching means avoiding the abuse of authority, leading without dominating and not being remote and aloof. When teachers trust and respect young people as learners and thinkers and as people, and let them see this, they are much more likely to receive trust and respect in return ... Knowing what kind of people your learners are, and having some understanding of what they are thinking is essential for effective teaching

(pp. 16–17)

In the parent professional relationship it is important to keep in mind what parents expect and professionals aspire to. Parents involved in focus groups managed by Supportive Parents for Special Children (SPSC, 1996) revealed that they expected professionals to be experts; they want continuity and co-ordination of services; a satisfactory relationship and recognition that they are experts too. Professionals in the same sessions stated that they aspired to meet the needs of families, to cope with all of the demands placed on their time and the courage to speak openly.

In a recent interview (Wearmouth, 2000) Sally Capper a lawyer with a great deal of experience in advising parents or carers who have not been satisfied with the provision made for their child, offered some advice about ways to support the development of mutual understanding between school and home. This advice addresses many of the issues raised in this chapter. In order to tap into parents or carers' expertise to shed light on the child's learning in the school context, she advised the use of non-teaching assistants to talk with parents, setting aside prescribed times for meetings and/or telephone calls, a non-patronising attitude and the use of a home-school liaison book. In addition, she suggested that SENCOs should establish clear lines of communication with parents or carers, honesty and openness and early warning of the kinds of difficulties experienced by pupils.

Suggested Activities: Reflection and discussion

1. Encouraging a listening ethos

For those with an interest in promoting the active involvement of pupils in a school it might be useful to reflect on:

- the extent to which the school affords authentic space to pupils to compile their own formal or informal, written or verbal, reports that expresses their own views and perspectives

- how far Gersch's 'To Do List' would have value in the school

(Cont...)

- how far there is scope at your school for setting up working groups of both staff and pupils to sort out issues of real concern, such as poor attendance.

2. Providing for parents' needs

Read the following suggestions for professionals dealing with parents and for parents dealing with professionals, which have been adapted from Friend & Cook, 1996, p. 232). With colleagues discuss how practicable they are, and how closely they parallel provision with which you are familiar.

Suggestions for schools:

- create an environment that is welcoming
- schedule the meeting at the convenience of the parent
- provide an advance summary of the topics to be covered and a list of questions the parent might want to ask
- suggest they bring to school copies of work the child has done at home
- let the parent be seated at the meeting table first
- provide the parent with a file folder containing copies of the information the professionals have in their folders
- use your communication skills to structure the meeting so the parent has opportunities to provide input throughout the meeting.

Suggestions for parents:

- review records on past meetings
- talk with other family members and friends about what questions to ask and what information to share
- make a list of questions to ask
- make a list of information to share
- ask another person to go to the meeting with you
- take all relevant records to the meeting
- bring a pencil and paper
- check the time and place of the conference

3. Engagement with challenging opinions

(Cont...)

It might be useful for those with an interest in the education of pupils who are disaffected from school to reflect on the following questions:

- do you have experience of trying to engage with the views of pupils who are clearly disaffected from school? If so, how did you cope with this?

- what kinds of explanations might you yourself give for pupil behaviour which displays overt pupil disaffection from school?

- how far might these explanations lead to a positive way forward for these pupils?

In-School Needs Analyses

1. Those interested in evaluating the extent to which a school engages fully with pupil perspectives might complete *Whole-school Needs Assessment 4: Pupil Involvement* that is to be found in the Appendix.

2. Those with an interest in evaluating a school's engagement with parent perspectives might complete *Whole-school Needs Assessment 5: Parental involvement* in the Appendix.

8 Assessment Issues

All pupils have a statutory right to having their 'special educational needs' identified and met. Identification of the barriers to pupils' learning and assessment of special learning requirements is crucial to the role of the special needs co-ordinator. In many schools it will be the special needs co-ordinator who plays the major role in information gathering and assessment, and in planning intervention aimed at reducing the barriers to learning experienced by such pupils. It is obviously very important that SENCOs have a firm grasp of the stages of assessment outlined in The Code of Practice, because, as discussed already, this is used as a shared text during school inspections. However, a clear understanding of broader issues particularly relevant to assessment of individual learning needs is essential because approaches to identification and assessment have an important influence on how a school constructs its special needs policies and provision.

Assessing individual learning needs

The five stages of assessment in the Code

OFSTED (1996) reminds us that assessment in relation to curriculum planning for individual learners should be:

- embedded within whole-school procedures and policies

- linked to purpose, i.e. to record concerns, ways in which the learning environment facilitates or causes barriers to learning, pupil strengths and weaknesses, strategies, targets and progress

- evaluated in a way which informs the next stage.

Whether or not assessment leads to the issuing of a 'Statement of special educational need', it must have regard to the five-stage model of assessment outlined in the Code of Practice.

The summary of the five-stage model below is drawn from paragraphs 1:4 and 2:65 to 2:68 of the Code of Practice (DfEE, 1994):

Stage 1: The class teacher, subject teacher or year tutor identifies the student's 'special educational need', consults the learning support co-ordinator, the parents and the student. The learning support co-ordinator records the student's 'need' on a register. The class teacher has responsibility for matching or differentiating the curriculum to correspond to the student's present attainments and interests and then reviews the student's progress.

Stage 2: The school's learning support co-ordinator takes lead responsibility in producing an individual education plan (IEP) and in reviewing the student's progress.

Stage 3: Class and subject teachers and the learning support co-ordinator are advised by specialists from outside the school on developing the IEP and in reviewing the progress of students.

Stage 4: LEA officers consider the need for formal assessment, working co-operatively with the student's school and parents, and others as appropriate, and arrange for it to be carried out if they find it to be necessary.

Stage 5: LEA officers consider the need for 'a statement of special educational needs', draw one up if they find it necessary, then monitor and review the provision.

Stage 1 represents an expression of concern about a student's learning by a teacher which might be resolved in collaboration with colleagues and parents. Movement through the stages implies that the considered suggestions attempted at a particular stage are unsuccessful and that progressively greater levels of expertise are required.

Every mainstream school has an element in its budget specifically for overcoming difficulties in learning. The five-stage model might be seen as a resource model which is also a model for the categorization of students. Stages 1 to 3 are concerned with using the existing material and human resources of the mainstream school to overcome difficulties in learning, with the addition of external advice at stage 3. Stages 4 and 5 are for students who are seen to have more intractable difficulties, those who require more expensive intervention and those for whom the appropriateness of the location in which they are currently being educated may be considered questionable.

The five stages do not have to be treated as a single inflexible sequence and it is important to recognize the different purposes of stages 1–3 and 4–5 if resources are not to be expended needlessly on paperwork. If a blind child is about to enter a school, the school may need particular pieces of additional equipment straight away. If a child is distraught because of the death of a parent then perhaps some extra support may be required at the school for a while. The system ought to be adaptable to the lives of children.

The five stages are concerned with children who are already in school. Before school age, children may be assessed as needing support and become the subject of statements or records and usually this will be because they are thought to require some long-standing support for their learning. Hence some students under five may enter school already at stage 5 in the proposed assessment process.

One of the changes proposed for the revised Code is that of reducing the number of school-based stages to two – School Support and Support Plus.

Issues in the assessment of 'special educational needs'

A number of fundamental issues make the assessment of individual pupils' learning needs problematic in some respects. These include the very basic question of test validity, differences in the underlying assumptions and consequences of the various psychological models of pupil learning commonly used to assess barriers to learning and design interventions, factors related to formative and summative assessment, norm-referenced assessment, assessment used to confirm prior perceptions, the level at which it is appropriate to assess: the learner, the task or the environment, the issue of funding-led assessment and provision, questions of accountability for resources, the constraints of the national assessment framework, and the principle of harnessing assessment techniques in the classroom to enhance the learning of all pupils.

Test validity

Test validity is concerned with the question of whether a test assesses what it claims to test. A major distinction between what reading tests are designed to assess, for example, is that between comprehension and accuracy of reading. In this case it is clearly very important to consider the context within which meaning is framed in the text when assessing the level of reading comprehension of all children, but particularly of those whose culture is different from that of the dominant group, in terms of class, race or gender. In the area of reading generally, there are still in use in schools tests which are many years out of date, in particular some of those of word reading.

Psychological perspectives on the development of special provision

It is important for those assessing pupils to be able to engage with psychological discourse on the difficulties in learning faced by pupils and the kinds of special provision that are made so that to adopt a personal position on it. Those working within the field of psychology have had a very strong influence on the special sector in education. Educational psychologists are crucial to the formal process of identification and assessment of pupils' special learning needs in schools and teachers are likely to encounter a number of different psychological perspectives among those with whom they work. Below I outline very briefly the range traditionally associated with provision for pupils identified as 'having' special learning needs.

Behaviourism

Probably the most significant influence in special education over the past quarter of a century has been that of behaviourism.

The notion that anything that was not "observable, measurable and repeatable" was not relevant or testable in education became the catch cry of the behavioural movement.

(Bailey, 1998)

Behaviour modification techniques became very popular in classroom practice and are still widely used to control undesirable behaviours and in schools for pupils who experience severe difficulties in learning. This technique relies strongly on operant conditioning principles. Desired behaviours are encouraged through 'reinforcement', which can be concrete rewards, like toys, money or sweets, or intangible, such as praise, approval or affection. Reinforcement is used to increase the likelihood of a behaviour being repeated; lack of reinforcement is expected to lead to a behaviour decreasing in frequency and being eliminated or 'extinguished'. Traditionally, behaviourism has led to a view of the young person as a passive recipient of environmental influences.

In special education behaviour modification extended into the realm of curriculum and pedagogy. Influenced by behaviourism, sometimes in a modified form which recognises the power of human cognitive processes, those involved in special education were motivated to view with scepticism any approach which relied simply on intuition for curriculum planning and pedagogy. Behaviourist principles were seen as key in techniques designed to 'prevent' pupil failure in the classroom by some authors (Ainscow and Tweddle, 1979). 'Direct Instruction', a strongly behavioural method of instruction, employing, for example, "Distar" materials in mathematics, reading and writing, is still commonly used in classrooms.

An ecosystemic approach

A more recent ecosystemic approach in psychology assumes that students belong to, and learn to play a role in, a number of different systems, for example the family, the school, society in general and their peer group. Bronfenbrenner (1979) suggests that there are four levels that influence student outcomes:

I. **microsystem,** the immediate context of the student – school, classrooms, home, neighbourhood

II. **mesosystem,** the links between two microsystems, e.g. home-school relationships

III. **exosystem**, "outside demands/influences in adults" lives that affect young learners

IV. **macrosystem**, cultural beliefs/patterns or institutional policies that affect individuals" behaviour.

This approach indicates that students may fail to thrive, show poor achievement and/or behave 'badly' when the relationship between these systems is dysfunctional. An educational psychologist working with this model is likely to look to how a school's system operates to include or exclude a student, how the group dynamics in class operate to maintain his or her behaviour or how family processes operate to maintain the status quo in his or her behaviour.

Constructivism

In some ways constructivist approaches have led to a re-examination particularly of the behaviourist perspective. From a constructivist orientation, students actively engage in construing themselves and learning about the world through social interaction which itself shapes the structure and pattern of their cognitions. Piaget, for example, believed that the child plays an active role in developmental change by deriving information from the environment and using it to modify existing cognitions. She or he is independent, learning through discovery.

Constructivism is concerned with what individuals make of the circumstance in which they find themselves and their own position in relation to it. 'All actions serve some useful purpose for the actor' (Ravenette, 1984). In the area of special needs the current emphasis on eliciting learners' views on their own behaviour and learning can be seen, in part, as a reflection of a constructivist approach.

Social constructivism

Social constructivism is barely reflected in the area of special educational needs. However, it is currently commonly used as a conceptual framework by researchers investigating children's learning in contexts which tend to be mainstream rather than special. I am outlining the approach here because I feel it has much to contribute to an understanding of all students' learning and I will make further reference to it later.

The seminal figure in the area is the Russian psychologist, Lev S. Vygotsky (1896–1934). From a social constructivist viewpoint, society is essential to human cognitive development, beginning with interaction between the child and another person. Like Piaget, Vygotsky saw children as active organisers of their own knowledge, who used sign systems in a continuous interaction with the social world. The process of cognitive development involves internalising social interactions. What begins as a social function becomes internalised, so that it occurs within the child. Concepts, language, voluntary attention and memory are mental functions which come from the society into which the child is born. They appear twice in a child's development: first as shared between the child and the adult (social) and then as internalised within the child's own thought processes.

Vygotsky argued that although children might develop some concepts on their own through everyday experience, they would not develop purely abstract modes of thought without instruction and support to develop the abstract sign systems of the culture. The child has a zone of proximal development (i.e. the next step in development), which is achievable only with the help and support of an adult. A social constructivist perspective stresses the importance of participation in activities which is guided and supported through 'scaffolding' (Bruner, 1996), shared problem-solving, and the interdependence of the student with adults and one student with other students.

The limitations of a single perspective

One drawback of using a single perspective on young people's learning is to exaggerate its explanatory power. Inevitably, behaviour and experience are the outcome of many factors. Whilst one perspective may provide a plausible account of one or two factors, any perspective is based on a metaphorical representation of reality, not reality itself, and therefore has explanatory power only within the domain of that metaphor. A mechanical metaphor can only explain factors within the domain of mechanics. A narrow over-emphasis on any one perspective may preclude the consideration of other significant factors, particularly where these factors are interactive.

Distinguishing between formative and summative assessment

Since the inception of the Code of Practice, the Individual Education Plan has become a major tool for planning individual pupil's programmes of study. Tod, Castle and Blamires (1998) make the point that the term 'Individual Education Plan' refers both to the process of planning the next steps in a pupil's learning programme on the basis of an analysis of pupil needs and the summative document.DfEEThe assessment process can therefore be regarded as both formative and summative. Formative assessment is an on-going process that can be carried out both formally and informally to collect information and evidence about a pupil's learning and used to plan the next step in his or her learning. In contrast, summative assessment is intended to provide a global picture of the learner's progress to date without the addition of too much detail. Harlen and James (1997) discuss differences and relationships between formative and summative assessment. They argue that formative and summative assessment are different in kind as well as in purpose and note the main distinctions between them. Formative assessment:

- is concerned with information about ideas and skills that can be developed in certain activities, and so is important for everyday teaching

- is carried out by teachers

- combines criterion-referenced tests, which are concerned with assessing the skills required for specific tasks, and pupil-referenced (ipsative) techniques where the same pupil's progress is tracked across time

- can be contradictory as pupils' performance can be inconsistent – such differences can be used diagnostically

- places more significance on validity and usefulness than on reliability

- should involve the student.

Summative assessment:

- is concerned with the bigger picture of progress, across several activities perhaps

- takes place at certain intervals when achievement has to be recorded

- may involve a combination of different types of assessment, for example the measurement of individual pupil progression in learning against public criteria

- requires a high degree of reliability, and therefore involves some quality assurance procedures.

Issues related to norm-referencing: segregation as a result of apparent difference

As we saw in Chapter 1, assessment has played a pivotal role in the development of special education. Dockrell and McShane (1993) note that norm-referenced methodology still 'characterizes most of special education assessment'. Norm-referenced tests are frequently based on the notion of measurable intelligence (IQ), which give information about a pupil's ability or attainment relative to his or her peers, and typically produce measures in terms of standards or ranks, for example standardised reading scores. Statements about a child's potential should not be made on the basis of a single test score, nor should IQ scores be viewed as measures of intellectual potential. Norm-referencing is designed solely to indicate a learner's achievement in comparison with others:

Some of these tests have a value as a first line method in identifying the existence of a problem. However, they do not provide a direct link to intervention since the scores do not provide details of what the child knows or does not know, nor do they elucidate the processes that are involved in the child's difficulty.

(Dockrell and McShane, 1993, p. 34)

Historically, this task was directed towards categorising and segregating children with disabilities and learning difficulties in order to identify and label children who would not benefit from mainstream schooling. Various tests and screening procedures, such as IQ tests, were developed for this purpose enabling decisions about placement and provision to be made for 'special children'.

The purpose of such assessment was to determine eligibility for special education. These approaches were concerned with looking for deficits in children and they emphasised the difference between the so-called special and normal populations.

> … special educators have come to be very sensitive about the use of tests. There are good reasons for our sensitivity. With tests, children were segregated from their peers. With tests, they would be labelled ESN or maladjusted. With tests, they would have all sorts of scientific-sounding syndromes like 'minimal brain damage' used to explain away their difficulties. We have every right to be circumspect about tests: the children about whom we are concerned have not fared well from their use….
>
> In the mainstream also, they have come to be associated with the separation of the sheep from the goats; they have come to be associated with children failing, with loss of confidence, with a stilted test-led or exam-led curriculum….

(Simmons and Thomas, 1988, p. 145)

Some writers have commented on the way in which assessment can perpetuate social inequalities and be used to establish social control. The following is illustrative of such a perspective:

> … the proliferating division of labour that the process of industrialization increasingly required posed quite novel problems of social control concerning how the allocation of such new roles and indeed the management of the state as a whole might be regulated and legitimated, and that it was formal assessment techniques within the educational process that provided the solution to this problem….

The provision of a competition which is apparently open and fair suggests that those who are not successful in achieving their aspirations will accept the rational selection criteria being applied and, hence, their own failure. In so doing they acquiesce not only in their own defeat but in the legitimacy of the prevailing social order. To this extent the provision of an apparently fair competition controls the build-up of frustration and resentment among the least privileged.

(Broadfoot, 1996, pp. 9–10)

Assessment is undeniably linked with differential opportunities throughout life. For example, those with few qualifications may have more limited employment opportunities than those with nationally recognised qualifications.

Over time, the negative consequences of ability testing and the limitations of certain diagnostic procedures became apparent. This growing awareness resulted in dissatisfaction with traditional views of assessment and with the consequences of such approaches.

Confirmation of prior perceptions

There are negative consequences of assessment of which the assessor should be aware. Assessment may be used simply to confirm what a teacher suspects. Dockrell and McShane criticise assessments that serve only:

to confirm the obvious, that the child has learning problems – and do not indicate the specific curriculum and behavioural changes that would lead to a more successful educational experience for the child.

(Dockrell and McShane, 1993, p. 53)

Such a confirmatory use of assessment, what has been called 'rubber-stamping the teacher's own opinion' (Dockrell and McShane, 1993, p. 53), can be questioned. There is a danger that relying on formal testing can undermine the professional's own judgement and integrity.

Implicit model of learning

There is a great deal more to teaching and learning than resources and funding. Real attention to provision for all pupils must pay attention to the model of learning underpinning assessments, and consider whether or not this is at odds with what goes on in the classroom.

Conceptualising learning difficulties in the context of the Code of Practice

It is important not to accept documents such as the Code of Practice (DfEE) 1994) as 'givens' that cannot be questioned. It will be useful to reflect on how difficulties in learning have been conceptualized and whose interests might be furthered by the use of one model rather than another.

The five stages of assessment and the framework for the Individual Education Plan in the Code, imply that special needs are something that children or students 'have'; that learning difficulties are seen as problems of students rather than arising in a relationship between students, curricula, teachers and other human and material resources, including the cultures of school and home. However, at a number of places in the Code, a more sophisticated view of the origin of difficulties in learning is suggested. For example, in paragraph 2:19 it is argued that 'schools should not automatically assume that children's learning difficulties always result solely or even mainly from problems within the child'. Paragraph 3:50 suggests that 'a child's apparently weak performance may, on examination of the evidence, be attributable to factors in the school's organization'. Paragraph 3:65 asserts that 'emotional and behavioural difficulties may arise from or be exacerbated by circumstances within the school environment'. Yet, as Booth (1996) notes, these occasional acknowledgements of an alternative model are set alongside the principal medical model running through the Code whereby students' difficulties arise because of their deficiencies and are to be resolved by specific action directed at them rather than the total learning environment. It is also clear that the Code defines learning difficulties almost invariably as about 'low attainment' or 'difficult behaviour' rather than about difficulties in learning that can affect any student. But the presence of conflicting models within the Code does mean that we can 'have regard to the Code' and adopt, consistently, an interactive and social model of difficulties in learning which applies to all students.

The terminological confusion in Section 3 of the Code suggests the following types of learning difficulty:

- learning difficulties
- specific learning difficulties (for example Dyslexia)
- emotional and behavioural difficulties (EBD)
- physical disabilities
- sensory impairments: hearing difficulties; visual difficulties
- speech and language difficulties
- medical conditions.

However, in this Section the Code also uses the term 'learning difficulty' in reference to pupils who have a low level of academic attainment. The Code therefore fails to distinguish between a concept of 'learning difficulty' as a 'failure to learn' without specifying any particular cause, and 'learning difficulty' with a specific causation (Booth, op cit.). This distinction is clearly important in considering, for example, how the way in which students behave relates to the difficulty that they might experience in learning. It is also important in explaining why 'failure to learn' is often seen as an area of concern which should be addressed by the special needs co-ordinator, but 'difficult behaviour' is the concern of pastoral staff.

Requesting money from the LEA to buy the 'treatment' for pupils' difficulties in learning is an incentive for schools to use the medical perspective to conceptualise pupils' difficulties as an innate deficiency which can be measured and remedied. However, 'treating' the individual student may well do nothing to influence the context which itself may have contributed to those difficulties.

Whether the individual student benefits from the attribution of a problem and the treatment that may follow will depend on how stigmatising is the problem, how advantageous are the additional resources and what perception the student, his or her peers, teachers and parents has of it.

The following extracts from various assessments concerning sixteen-year-old Joseph's transition to a local college of Further Education reflect the discussion above on the use of labels and the implied model of Joseph as a learner:

Extract 1: Report from local careers service to the Further Education Funding Council 1996/7, supporting a recommendation for funding for a special residential placement

'Joseph has significant and complex learning difficulties: his levels of Literacy and Numeracy are below average; he has poor short term memory and weak perceptual and visuo motor skills; ... Joseph's speech is dysarthric and not fluent. He is unable to function independently in the community. He can be excessively anxious....'

Medical condition: 'Perinatal oxygen starvation causing neurological difficulties in speech and language and learning.'

Extract 2: Assessment from the City Children's Disability Team, August 1996

'Joseph was statemented at age 13 from which time he attended as a boarder at a special school, residential Mon-Thurs, for children with moderate learning difficulties and often emotional and/or behavioural problems. He was then offered a place at a local college but his mother was unhappy with this, believing the environment 'too open and unprotected' for someone with autism or Asperger's. She and his father therefore desired that he should be placed at a residential school out-county to continue his further education. I am not clear why Joseph went to Winterborn School ... as his learning difficulties seem very mild and not within the remit of Winterborn. Also, he does not appear to have the behavioural problems I associate with pupils offered residential care there.... [More residential arrangements] would have the effect of *dis*abling Joseph, lowering his self-esteem and causing him to distrust his abilities, just when he should be enjoying adolescence and the rights and responsibilities it brings. What Joseph lacks is confidence: confidence in himself and the confidence from the people closest to him that what he has to offer is valuable.'

Extract 3: Report by the local college of FE, following Joseph's attendance on a 'Link' programme, June 1996

'Joseph presented as enthusiastic/motivated; relaxed and confident; relating well with peer group; contributing well in group discussion; able to converse with staff; able to cope well in social settings, and in his ability to move around the campus.'

(Rustemier, in press)

Rustemier herself feel that these extracts illustrate clearly the issues discussed above. The difference a label might make is important in Joseph's mother's opinion (though, in fact, Joseph has never been 'officially' diagnosed as having autism or Asperger's syndrome). The very existence of the reports is intricately bound up with resources and an application for additional funding to support and out-county special placement. Furthermore, very different models of learning may be detected – contrast the focus on cognitive factors in the report by the careers service with that on social factors in the college's report. The extracts may also be seen as highlighting the influence of philosophical positions on integration and inclusion, and the view taken on segregated/discrete provision for young people with Statements: therefore, the question of who is involved in the assessment process is a critical one.

Funding and resources

A major issue associated with the formulation of assessments for statutory purposes is that it has been provision-led (Cline, 1992), that is that available resources have dictated the provision made for individual pupils. I discuss below how some local authorities might use a reading quotient of 70 as the cut-off point for additional resources for supporting learning if they have assumed additional funding for, in the region of, 2 per cent of their pupil population. It is in the procurement of 'necessary' educational resources for pupils experiencing difficulties in learning that assessment of SEN is most often justified. However, this linking of resources to individual need raises fundamental questions discussed elsewhere in this book: the labelling of the individual learner, the implied focus on the individual as the source of the 'problem' rather than the learning environment and the potential for an over-reliance on norm-referenced tests of doubtful validity.

Assessing the learner, the learning task, or the learning environment

Cline (1992) notes that assessment focused on the learner makes certain assumptions not necessarily justified by the evidence. Among them are that:

- traits and abilities are fairly permanent

- normative tests can reveal pattern of a child's strengths and weaknesses

- this pattern is causally related to child's classroom performance

- teaching programmes which build on strengths and remediate weaknesses will lead to improvements in performance

- categorisation and then placement in provision for children so categorised is an appropriate response.

In contrast, approaches which analyse the task have the following advantages:

- assessment is classroom based and by the teacher, not an expert outsider

- information is specific with direct implications for planning

- sequences of objectives can be used to facilitate continuous assessment and review

- pupils can progress at their own rate

- they are more optimistic because failure in learning is assumed to be due to a flaw in the plan rather than in the child.

There are, however, some limitations. For example:

- a focus on narrow skills could be encouraged because some aspects of the curriculum are not easily accessible to systematic observation

- the focus on constructing individual programmes may be at the expense of other important contextual factors, e.g. general curriculum, classroom organisation, interpersonal relationships

- a largely passive role of the pupil in learning situations is implied.

Cline (op cit.) discusses additional problematic assumptions associated with an approach to assessment that focuses on the teaching programme. The assumptions he challenges are that:

- the school curriculum can be analysed into tasks which can be expressed as behavioural objectives

- these tasks an be arranged into pedagogically viable sequences

- noting a child's attainments within one of these sequences can help in matching teaching closely to the learning stage of the child

- through teacher controlled instruction a child can acquire, maintain, transfer and adapt new skills.

Students with special needs and national assessment

Dearing reiterated the view that the national curriculum is an entitlement for all children and therefore implies that, to the maximum extent possible, children with special needs must participate in this national educational and assessment framework. Evidence suggests that few children have been 'disapplied from' the requirements of the National Curriculum (Lewis and Halpin, 1994). SENCOS and other teachers seem to have been using their professional judgement to adapt the curriculum to individual children's learning needs (Lewis, 1995).

Although recent policy developments have been couched in more inclusive language, there is an intrinsic contradiction relating to the assessment of students with special needs. On the one hand, certain forms of assessment are used to identify some students who are different so that they can receive something additional or special. Indeed, special education depends on such approaches to decide who is eligible for these additional services. On the other hand there is the drive to create universal high standards together with a common system of assessment that can recognise the learning of all students. If such systems are to be inclusive then they will need to be criterion-based, using task analysis, and result in such measures as developmental profiles and checklists. This is because there is an inherent problem for students with special educational needs with systems of assessment that are predicated on comparisons with others:

> **(Criterion-referenced) tests help identify whether or not an individual possesses some particular skill or competence and may allow for the analysis of error patterns. ... These tests are not designed to discriminate among individuals in the same way that norm-referenced tests do. Rather, they are designed to provide a clear indication of what a child**

can and cannot do and thereby are a guide to what skills should be taught next.

(Dockrell and McShane, 1993, p. 35)

The strength of such an approach is that it allows conceptual analysis of errors and thus helps to target intervention. However, identification of what needs to be measured is not simple. Beard (1990) notes a fundamental issue which must be addressed in criterion-referenced assessment, and that is the particular aspect of the reading process or practice to which the test criteria apply. He notes that some aspects of the reading process, and therefore the tasks which need to be performed to achieve mastery over them, are easier to define than others. Not every aspect of the reading process lends itself to assessment through specific teaching objectives. It may be possible to break the development of awareness of sound-letter correspondence down into measurable objectives, for example. However, enjoyment of reading and aspects related to the finer points of the meaning of text are much more problematic.

Despite the disadvantages inherent in norm-referenced tests, there are a number of reasons why teachers might decide to use a norm-referenced test of reading which is designed to compare the performance of one learner with other learners of the same age. It might be important to have some idea of the reading level of a whole year group on entry to a school to establish a rough baseline for the purpose of 'value-added' or as a preliminary way of identifying pupils who are experiencing difficulties in reading development. Or it may be necessary to show that an individual pupil appears to experience significant difficulty in reading development in comparison with peers for the purpose of justifying a request for additional resourcing for him or her. Beard (op cit.) discusses the notion of 'reading quotients' and notes that the statistical manipulation of the figures results in 2.14 per cent of the total population of pupils scoring below 70. Some local authorities anticipate that additional funding may be needed to support the special learning needs of 2 per cent of the pupil population in their areas. A teacher may be required to show that a pupil's reading quotient is lower than 70, in other words falls within the lowest 2.14 per cent of the school population. Local authority officers also have to justify to the elected representatives their reasons for the allocation of additional funds and insisting that a reading quotient is below 70 may be one way to approach this.

It is obvious that norm-referenced tests of ability and attainment make it extremely difficult for some children to demonstrate progress because of the assumptions that underpin this psychometric view of the world. Indeed normative assumptions in education and assessment carry the power 'to determine selectively the way in which issues are discussed and solutions proposed', (Broadfoot, 1996). In other words, the influence of psychometric thinking leads to deterministic views of ability and achievement which not only limit what we expect from certain students, but also restricts developments in education and assessment.

Ainscow argues:

> **... what is needed more than anything else is an attitude of mind. The key to effective assessment is not in the adoption of new techniques from courses or text-books, but in the realisation of the importance of learning from the experience of working with pupils in the classroom.**
>
> *(Ainscow, 1988, p. 152)*

Dissatisfaction with conventional methods of assessment coincided with the growing recognition that contextual factors, such as the quality of teaching and the curriculum, have a major impact on learning. As a consequence, commentators called for the assessment of the characteristics of the child and the child's total environment (Ainscow, 1988). This view holds that, since the child's learning takes place in a particular context, assessment should not be devoid of that context and its influence on the child. It adopts an 'ecological perspective' which recognises that features of the learning context such as the curriculum, the teaching, the organisation of the classroom and other school variables, as essential factors that influence learning. Teachers are encouraged to be aware of various aspects of classroom life and to account for these factors during assessment. Such interactive, or ecological, explanations became an essential feature of the concept of special educational needs that emerged from the Warnock enquiry in England and Wales (DES, 1978) (see Chapter 1).

An example of assessment which takes account of these contextual factors is that of the 'teach-test-teach' model which can be carried out in the classroom and falls in the general category of 'teaching experiments' closely linked to careful observation of the learner and the context.

Observational procedures and teaching experiments

Classroom activities based around models such as the teach-test-teach model may be used 'as a means of gauging an individual's ability to retain the content of the material and to transfer the principles learned to new tasks' (Dockrell and McShane, 1993, p. 38). We might categorise the kind of 'dynamic' assessment as discussed by Lunt (1993) under the general heading of 'teaching experiment'. Lunt explores the notion of dynamic assessment and its relation to Vygotskyan theories of learning. Assessment focused on the zone of proximal development as discussed by Lunt, assumes that:

- traditional methods underestimate ability because they ignore emerging skills and understanding

- it is more helpful to base teaching on what a child can achieve with help than by reference to a sequence based on what he or she can do unaided

- a child has different zones of proximal development for different tasks – assessment relates solely to particular objectives being assessed.

Lunt notes two fundamental differences between dynamic and static methods of assessment, concerning the actual test situation, and what is being measured. Static tests (such as psychometric assessment and curriculum-based assessment), prohibit interaction between the child and the tester, and emphasise discovering what the child can do unaided. The focus here is the product of learning, what the child knows. Conversely, in dynamic assessment, interaction between the child and the tester is integral to the learning situation, the emphasis is on how the child learns (the process rather than the product), and the focus is on what the child can do with support (the zone of proximal development). In practice, dynamic assessment can be of two kinds: (i) methods which focus on the psychological processes involved in change, and (ii) those focusing on the individual's potential for change. These represent two ends of a continuum rather than discrete approaches, and each is based on a different interpretation of Vygotsky's theory:

a) Those focusing on the processes involved in learning are qualitatively oriented, e.g. looking for an improvement in score using a test-teach-retest model, and the interaction between tester and child is structured and standardised. An example of such an approach is the Learning Potential and Educability Program (Budoff).

b) Those focusing on the potential for change are quantitatively oriented, and the interaction between tester and child is flexible, unstructured and clinical. An example of this approach is the Learning Potential Assessment Device and Instrumental Enrichment programme (Feuerstein).

Summary

Those responsible for assessing the difficulties experienced by pupils would be well advised to familiarise themselves with the staged approach recommended by The Code of Practice (DfEE, 1994). It is important, however to be aware of fundamental issues which make the assessment of individual needs problematic in some respects. Among these are the assumptions and consequences of the various models of learning which underpin approaches to assessment, the nature and types of assessment in common use and issues of funding-led assessment and provision.

Suggested Activities: Reflection and Discussion

1. Assessing individual pupils

It may be appropriate at this point to engage in the following activity. Think of an individual pupil in your school in whose assessment you have been involved and make notes on the following questions.

- What was the purpose of the assessment?

- How was it carried out, and who decided on the method(s) to be used?

- What was your role?

- What model(s) of learning was/were implied by this particular assessment, do you feel?

- What was the result of the assessment?

- How did the assessment affect the educational provision for this child (consider both intended and unintended outcomes)?

2. Issues relating to the assessment of special educatuional needs

Consider the extent to which any of the issues raised in this chapter in relation to the assessment of special educational needs areb problematice in your own context. What action might be take to address the problems you have identified:

- in the short term

- in the medium term

- in the long term?

In-School Needs Analysis

Those with a responsibility for any form of assessment in a school might choose to complete *Whole-school Needs Assessment 6: Assessment and planning.*

9 Planning provision to meet individual learning needs

Planning a curriculum to meet the particular learning needs of individual pupils must take account of any formal and informal individual assessment of pupil learning that has taken place, and this must include statutory requirements. In addition it should take place within the context of the same overall curriculum structure that relate to teaching and learning for all pupils in a school (OFST-ED, 1996). It is therefore very important for those planning programmes for individual pupils to take considerations relating to curriculum differentiation and equal opportunities into account. Furthermore, there are a number of issues in the planning process that need to be teased out in relation to planning a programme for any individual pupil:

- long-, medium- and short-term plans

- requirements of Individual Education Plans and Statements of Special Educational Needs

- ways of embedding individual plans into the mainstream curriculum

- approaches to coping with the bureaucratic demands of the IEP process

- target setting

- opportunities for formative assessment in the classroom.

Issues of differentiation

From one perspective meeting individual young people's learning needs in school is a straightforward question of enabling access to the broad balanced curriculum through a process of 'differentiation'. Two important points to consider in any discussion of the notion of 'differentiation' are that:

- the term implies a pedagogy which assumes that teaching and learning occurs in groups and that students can accommodate to the teacher's and the school's conventional approach. We all know, however, that every learner is different and that effective teaching must take account of this diversity in terms of the way in which students learn and also the level they have achieved at any one time. When students experience barriers to their learning the teacher needs to be able to see the task and learning situation through their eyes

- in thinking about which strategy to adopt, it is essential to consider what assumptions about the learner and the nature of the subject material might underpin each one.

Hart (1995) raises a very important question of how we reach views about the nature of the differences between young people which have relevance for teaching and learning. Teachers' perceptions of young people are coloured by their experience of the way in which young people behave in interaction with the school environment. It is important not to treat the 'differences' which emerge between young people in school as 'given'.

Limiting by label

An example of the way in which a student may be stereotyped by a label attached to him or her through an assessment of difficulties in learning has been described by Mehan (1996). Using an ethnographic approach to his investigation, Mehan described the processes by which a pupil, seen by his teacher as having trouble applying himself to his work in the classroom, rapidly acquires the identity of 'learning disabled student' through the formal processes of referral and assessment. Reports based on the pupil's social interaction in one context became divorced from the setting in which they were created and were transformed into recommendations for the 'treatment' of an 'educational handicap' as they moved through the system. The child became the object of this process, and both parents' and class teacher's perceptions of the child were gradually sidelined as the psychologist's opinion, expressed in quasi scientific terminology, was given precedence. Hart (1994) concluded that there are two essential questions that need to be asked when addressing the question of how to to take better account of student diversity in order to respond appropriately and sensitively to his or her learning needs:

- How do school and classroom processes help to shape pupils' responses and therefore our own perceptions of their 'abilities, aptitudes and needs'?

- How do the particular resources which we bring to the interpretative task help to shape our perceptions of these 'abilities, aptitudes and needs'?

In relation to pupils with physical disabilities, Pickles (2000), comments:

> Every child is an individual … Disability affects people in different ways and it is dangerous and impossible to predict the intellectual abilities, emotional needs, outcome of different physical disabilities and the level of independence a child may attain.

> The implication of this view, as applied to all pupils, is that sensitivity of approach is essential if provision is to be responsive to pupils.

Equal opportunities' issues

Every young person has an entitlement to having his or her 'special educational needs' identified. assessed and provided for. However, there is a serious dilemma between supporting pupils' entitlements to a common programme, and offering alternative provision to accommodate a diversity of needs and interests.

Many of those teaching young people who experience barriers to their learning at school feel that attaining specific subject targets is less important than developing other skills that they may need later on in life, for example intelligible speech patterns, or personal attributes such as self confidence, awareness of others' needs, and interest and enthusiasm for learning. In the past, the emphasis given to literacy and numeracy to the exclusion of most other areas has led to a great deal of repetitive practice for pupils who already have a history of failure, whilst that on everyday skills has predisposed to spending school time on activities such as catching buses or shopping (Lewis, 1995).

Diversity and equal opportunities

Norwich (1994) has examined the issue of differentiating the curriculum from the perspective of resolving tensions between diverse personal values in a pluralist society. If, from a belief in equality for all pupils, the intention is to treat all young people in fundamentally the same way, there is a clear implication of differentiation through encouraging a diversity of means of access to the same task. The corollary of theoretical work linking knowledge to power and control in society (Foucault, 1980, Tomlinson, 1982, Armstrong, 1995) is that denying access to the same forms of knowledge means excluding individuals from potential access to power and decision-making processes in society. Any other form of differentiation is seen from this standpoint as discrimination and exclusion.

In examining the issue of why teachers do not differentiate more in class to meet pupils' needs I concluded that it may be because it is costly in both time and resources (Wearmouth, 1997). However, there could also be an additional reason: teacher discomfort arising from unexpected pupil achievement (Rosenthal and Jacobson, 1968). 'Over-achievement' of 'low' achievers challenges the stratified model of pupils' 'abilities' which is still the prevailing paradigm in many schools, reflecting both the beliefs and anticipations of many teachers and also schools as institutions.

Planning for learning: long-, medium- and short-term planning

Curriculum planning for any learner or group needs to incorporate an overall long-term plan based on a global view of the learner and an awareness of the context (see Chapter 8) within which the plan must take effect. From this long-term plan it is possible to draw up medium- and short-term plans. A flowchart can show how both an initial assessment of the difficulties experienced by the learner and the context of the whole-school curriculum might, together, lead to long-term, medium- and short-term planning. This chart takes into account some of the principles described in the work of Tod, Castle and Blamires (1998):

Account taken of contextual factors related to the whole-school curriculum:	Assessment of the strengths and difficulties experienced by the learner based on:
• national requirements • school priorities • school grouping arrangements for pupils' learnin • approaches to diversity and equal opportunities • issues of differentiation.	• teachers' assessments • SAT results • prior records/reports • assessment by outside agencies • the pupil's views • the parents'/carers' perspectives.

Long-term plan for learner based on aspirations and strengths with provision for access to the whole curriculum

Medium-term plan outlined in the Individual Education Plan document which must:

• reflect strategies appropriate to the context and the individualism of the learner

• incorporate termly and yearly achievable targets designed to lead to the learner's long-term goal

• reflect the Key Stage and associated programmes of study

• offer regular assessment opportunities.

Short-term, day-to-day planning which must:

• incorporate medium-term targets

• offer opportunities for daily, formative assessment.

Long-term planning

Planning for the long-term might imply taking a view about the pupil's future over the next few years. This will depend on the age of the learner, the degree and type of need, and the length of time during which an individual plan has been structured for him or her.

Tod, Castle and Blamires (1998), however, suggest that 'long-term' might be a year. This equates with the cycle of annual reviews. At the annual review a considerable amount of revision and amendment to a pupil's programme might be needed in the light of progress and personal development as well as changes in the learning environment and the stage reached in the National Curriculum. This yearly cycle does not detract from the need to think about possible routes for learners over a much longer period than this. A longer term vision of a range of possibilities for a learner that can be shared between the learner, the parent or carer and the professionals is important to give a sense of direction to the whole planning process. Having said this, however, it is very important to retain flexibility of thinking so that the planning process is facilitative of learning rather than restrictive. Individuals' needs change over time.

In the case of pupils with severe motor difficulties, for example, individual children:

> ... may have difficulties affecting some or all of their limbs, limited hand function, fine and gross motor difficulties and sometimes difficulties with speech and language. Most, though not all pupils will have a medical diagnosis. A diagnosis may have been given at birth, at about the age of two or a later date, though deteriorating conditions such as muscular dystrophy may not be diagnosed until the child attends school. Some children may have physical difficulties as a result of an accident or illness, which can happen at any age. It must be remembered that, in the same way as other children, they may also have learning difficulties, dyslexia, dyspraxia, asthma, epilepsy, vision and hearing difficulties or hidden handicaps affecting their visual/auditory perception or eye/hand co-ordination etc.

(Pickles, 2000)

A long-term plan for these pupils would take into account 'dignity and emotional needs ... especially in positioning, toileting and transfers ... to enable pupils to be as independent as possible ... recognising that teaching methods may need to vary as needs change is all part of inclusion' (Pickles, op cit.). It would also need to include:

- views of the student as a person, with hopes, expectations and rights, every other student

- considerations of physical access to the school environment

- ways in which the needs of the family and the student's place within it can be taken into account by the school

- in-school factors that support, or militate against, the student's inclusion

- the role of the support assistant(s) and the kind of relationship that might be established with the student and the family, and any issues this raises

- the role and function of information and communications technology

- the role and function of any other appropriate technological aids

- professional development and awareness raising of teachers and other staff in the school

- awareness-raising among peers, if appropriate

- the place of therapy in the student's curriculum.

Medium-term and short-term planning

Medium- and short-term planning should be seen to flow logically from the long-term plan for the learner.

```
┌────────────────────────────────────────────────────────────────────┐
│ Long-term plan for learner based on aspirations and strengths with   │
│ provision for access to the whole curriculum                         │
└────────────────────────────────────────────────────────────────────┘
```

```
┌────────────────────────────────────────────────────────────────────┐
│ Medium-term plan outlined on the IEP document which must:            │
│                                                                      │
│ • reflect strategies appropriate to the context and the individualism│
│   of the learner                                                     │
│ • incorporate termly and yearly achievable targets designed to lead  │
│   to the learner's long-term goal                                    │
│ • reflect the Key Stage and associated programmes of study           │
│ • offer regular assessment opportunities                             │
└────────────────────────────────────────────────────────────────────┘
```

```
┌────────────────────────────────────────────────────────────────────┐
│ Short-term, day-to-day planning which must:                          │
│                                                                      │
│ • incorporate medium-term targets                                    │
│ • offer opportunities for daily, formative assessment.               │
└────────────────────────────────────────────────────────────────────┘
```

For example, as in the case of pupils with severe motor difficulties described by Pickles (above and below):

A life skill, long-term physical target might be for the pupil to stand and walk with a walker. The long-term target might be for the pupil to stand and weight bear. The short-term target might be for the pupil to use a prone stander in a low angle position, twice daily for 20-minute sessions, in class, taking some weight on the body and raising the angle of the stander by a few degrees with success.

Any specific equipment should also be noted at this point, detailing where, when, how and why it should be used.

The Individual Education Plan

The Code (DfEE, 1994) advises that Individual Education Plans should be constructed through Stages 2 to 5 of the staged process of assessment discussed above in Chapter 2. An IEP at Stage 2 should set out the:

- nature of child's learning difficulties
- special educational provision
- school staff involved including frequency and timing
- specific programmes, activities, materials, and/or equipment
- help from parents at home
- targets to be achieved in a specified time
- pastoral or medical requirements
- monitoring and assessment arrangements
- review arrangements and date.

At Stage 3 information about the external specialists involved, including frequency and timing, should also be included. Stages 4 and 5 relate to assessment associated with the process of drawing up a statement of special educational needs.

Tod, Castle and Blamires (1998) make the point that the term 'Individual Education Plan' refers both to the on-going formative process of planning the next steps in a pupil's learning programme on the basis of an analysis of pupil needs and the summative document. The formative process should be carried out formally and informally to collect evidence about a pupil's learning and used to plan the next step in his or her learning. The summative document provides a summary outline picture of the learner's progress to date.

The review process

It is essential that Individual Education Plans are reviewed regularly and, as Cowne (1998) notes, 'a planned timetable for IEP reviews is needed for every school'. Decisions must be taken about the review and planning process itself: who should be involved, who should receive information and how the whole system of record-keeping and transmission of information should be managed.

At Stage 2, the SENCO, class and subject teachers will need to be involved, together with the Head of Year, or pastoral head, the parents or carers and the pupil herself or himself. If the decision is taken at the Stage 2 review meeting that a pupil should move to Stage 3 because she or he is not making the progress anticipated by the provision that is already being made, outside agencies will be called in to add their views and assessments of the pupil. Subsequently, if the pupil continues to experience very severe difficulties which are persistent, and if the required resources are not available, after consultation with the support services and the parent or carer, the head teacher or parent may consider requesting a formal multi-disciplinary assessment of difficulties in learning from the local education authority. The school, probably in the person of the SENCO, will then have the responsibility of collecting and collating formal school-based evidence to support the request. The circumstances under which the formal assessment process may be requested is discussed more fully in Chapter 2.

Stage 4: the school's advice – Appendix D

When a request is made for a formal assesment at Stage 4, 'the critical question for an LEA will be whether there is convincing evidence that, despite the school taking relevant and purposeful action to meet the child's learning difficulties, with the help of external specialists, those difficulties remain or have not been remediated sufficiently and may require the LEA to determine the child's special provision' (DfEE, 1994, 3:39). The LEA will always, therefore, 'wish to see evidence of the school's assesment of the child's learning difficulties and will wish to establish what action the school has taken to meet those difficulties. They will always wish … to secure evidence of the child's academic attainment in the school and to ask questions of that evidence in order to understand why the child has achieved the levels shown. Beyond that the evidence authorities should seek will vary … according to the child's age and the nature of his or her learning difficulty' (ibid). The implication of this for the school is that the SENCO, or other nominated person, must first ensure that she or he is familiar with the kinds of assessments expected by the local education authority in addition to those that she or he feels are appropriate. Second, that she or he must keep a meticulous file of records of all IEPs, reviews and their outcomes, and any special programmes that have been devised for a pupil in order to have the necessary evidence to pass on to the LEA when required.

Annual reviews

The local education authority has the statutory duty to initiate a review of the statement within 12 months of its issue and then annually thereafter. The purpose of the review is to assess the child's progress towards meeting the objectives specified on the statement and towards the annually agreed targets, to review the special provision that has been organised, to consider the appropriateness of the statement and to set new targets for the forthcoming year. The head teacher (or a teacher appointed by the head) must convene the meeting. She or he should request advice in writing from the pupil's parents or carers, the people specified by the local education authority, those people he or she thinks appropriate, for example class or subject teachers, pastoral staff, support teachers or outside agencies. The head teacher should ensure that this written advice is sent to all those invited to attend. A representative of the LEA should be present at the meeting.

Following the meeting the head teacher is responsible for preparing a report which summarises the decisions made and sets out the targets for the following year. She or he must then circulate this report to all those concerned. The LEA must decide whether or not to amend the statement as a result of the review, and must send copies of its recommendations to all parties involved. The appeals procedure open to parents wishing to appeal against local authority decisions is described in Chapter 2.

The Transition Plan

Regulations require that a *Transition Plan* is drawn up at the review following a young person's fourteenth birthday. The LEA should convene this meeting, unlike other annual reviews, and should invite the pupil, the parents, teachers, the careers service, social services and other professionals, as appropriate. The transition plan is intended to ensure coherent provision to smooth the student's transition from school to adult life, including college and employment.

Questions to be addressed in the Transition Plan are laid out in detail in the Code, paragraph 6:46 (DfEE, 1994). They address issues related to:

- the school: ways in which the curriculum can support the young person to play a role in the community and curriculum needs during transition

- the professionals: ways to develop collaborative working arrangements to ensure effective transition plans, transfer and exchange of information between services, the existence of appropriate training arrangements for any new technological aids

- the family: its expectations for the student, support that can be contributed by, and should be offered to, the family

- the young person: information needed to make informed choices, local arrangements to support self advocacy, arrangements relating to the location of support services for a young person living away from home or in residential care, hopes and aspirations for the future.

The outcomes of previous annual reviews, including the targets set, should contribute to the Transition Plan which should 'focus on strengths and weaknesses and cover all aspects of the young person's development, allocating clear responsibility for different aspects of development to specific agencies and professionals' (DfEE, 1994, 6:47). Social Services, Health and Careers Services 'should be actively involved in the Plan' (ibid).

Embedding IEPs into the mainstream curriculum

Cowne (2000) makes the point that targets for Individual Education Plans need to be embedded in the regular cycle of classroom activity married together with the learning experience offered to the child through the curriculum. In lesson planning, teachers and classroom assistants need to be aware of which pupils have IEPs and be conversant with their content so that they can take adequate account of individual pupils' needs. Cowne advises that teachers must have a very clear grasp of eight issues when planning lessons that take IEPs for individual pupils into account:

1. how the principal curriculum objectives and key concepts for the lesson relate to the overall schemes for the school

2. the way in which the principal objectives and key concepts are to be assessed, the criteria which indicate a satisfactory level of skills and understanding of key concepts, ways in which the assessment process might be differentiated and the means by which the outcome of the assessment is to be recorded as part of the IEP

3. the prerequisite skills for the principal objectives, and the prior level of knowledge required to understand key concepts

4. the extent to which all pupils in the classroom, including those identified as having special learning needs, have the prerequisite skills and prior knowledge in order that any 'pre-teaching', or a different resource to assist access to information, might be arranged

5. relevant skills and knowledge that might be cross-referenced from another curriculum area

6. ways in which various kinds of group work, with or without additional assistance from adults, might assist learning in the particular lesson

7. the extent to those pupils with the greatest needs might be expected to fulfil the principal objectives and grasp all key concepts

8. whether an alternative set of objectives will be needed for any children.

Cowne's views imply a flexibility of approach which demands a thorough grasp of, and familiarity with, the National Curriculum structure and its underlying principles in addition to the strengths and needs of individual pupils.

Pickles (op cit.) discusses how targets for pupils with complex physical difficulties might be integrated in a practical way into lesson planning for all pupils:

> **Children with severe motor difficulties may not have been able to internalise concepts such as direction, shape, size, height and weight, because of their inability to explore the environment and objects. They often require adult facilitation, making them more likely to be passive learners, lacking independence and unable to consolidate learning in the same way as the majority of pupils. Pupils in this situation are likely to switch off.**
>
> **It is vital for teachers to devise activities to enable consolidation and repetition, using a multi-sensory approach, utilising the pupil's auditory, visual, tactile and sensory skills. These activities will also enable the pupil to internalise a wide range of general concepts such as perception, distance, depth, weight etc. Thinking laterally to plan activities to meet the greatest needs, as well as majority needs, is cost effective in time and energy. Activities or games with learning and therapeutic targets using real objects and utensils, ensure that therapeutic targets are used functionally, included into everyday learning and accessible to all.**
>
> **Although some games may have therapy targets for specific pupils they remain extremely good to teach all pupils, because the learning targets remain the same. It is how the games are played, which enables different therapeutic targets to be incorporated. Multi sensory games are particularly useful to teach children with any kind of special need as learning is positively reinforced through the senses.**

Streamlining the bureaucratic demands of the IEP process

The pressure on SENCOs to comply with the procedures relating to IEPs as outlined in the Code, in particular the heavy demands on time, have been well documented (OFSTED, 1997). It is important therefore for SENCOs, with the support of the school staff, to develop ways of working which keep this pressure to a minimum whilst at the same time considering how to develop systems for ensuring that the learning programme is carried out, monitored and evaluated.

Tod, Castle and Blamires (1998) note that attempts to reduce the bureaucratic demands on SENCOs of the IEP process have included:

- allocating the meeting arrangements and collation and distribution of information to clerical staff

- using in-service training to encourage class teachers and form teachers to prepare IEPs at Stage 2 and to support all those involved in the education of pupils with IEPs to monitor progress

- delegating responsibility for IEPs to one person in each subject area for overseeing the progress of all pupils experiencing difficulties in learning

- the use of electronic means of communication which has become increasingly common in schools for generating reports for all pupils from, for example, banks of comments pre-existing in a data bank. Many of the issues relating to the use of pre-specified comments for all pupils apply equally to the use of computerised files of comments for the specific purpose of generating IEP documents, in particular that of time efficiency versus individuality of approach

- training classroom assistants in aspects of the process

- organising group learning plans which incorporate the monitoring of individual pupil progress

- increasing the involvement of parents or carers which can result in a higher degree of 'fit' for the individual pupil.

Pickles (op cit.) offers an example of an efficient, time-saving way to ensure that where a pupil is supported by a team of adults, every member of that team is aware of others' work. She advises:

> **Information recorded by the support team needs to be easily accessible. One simple way is for every member of the team to record their visits on the same liaison form, which can then be copied for filing and sent home to parents. These can be filed in an A4 ring binder for each child with up-to-date information and liaison forms, reports, individual therapy advice, the IEP, information on specialist equipment, medication and feeding etc. Older pupils might use a ring binder the size of a small filofax or passport.**

> **It should be remembered that this is an open file and should not contain anything which cannot be shared.**

> **Parents, pupils and members of the support team and school staff should agree the presentation and use of the file. It should then be the responsibility of each team member to communicate with the rest of the team via the file, meetings and phone calls.**

However demanding on time, in the current climate of increasing accountability, teachers must recognise the importance of maintaining recording systems which are effective and efficient. In order to sustain continuity of provision and a sensitivity to individuality, clear records, with supporting evidence, must be passed to the next class or phase.

Target setting

In some schools there appears to be confusion over the level of detail required for the targets that are set for pupils. This may be resolved by considering the purpose of the IEP and the nature of the assessment it reflects. Cowne (op cit.) notes the different types of target that may be set for different purposes.

> Some are short term and 'SMART' (Specific, Manageable, Achievable, Relevant and Timed) with definite measurable outcomes. Some are experiential, longer term or without measurable outcomes. Some targets relate to skills, some to conceptual understanding, some to self awareness. Others relate to increased self confidence and self esteem.

> Behavioural targets are typically set by teachers and imposed on pupils. There are other targets which children can choose for themselves with support. Achieving self determined targets strengthens pupils' coping ability. The first sign of progress may be an increase in confidence and a willingness to take charge of their own learning. Some individual targets will be necessary as will group targets, but the SEN Co-ordinator needs to continually check that target setting is not narrowing the curriculum and limiting progress or demotivating pupils.

OFSTED (1997) notes that the purpose of IEPs is to facilitate pupil learning by means of the effective planning of learning goals. Lessons may be planned to facilitate understanding of content, develop concepts or skills, practise problem-solving or encourage pupils' personal interests. Sometimes it happens that barriers are created to children's learning simply by the way in which material based on the same underlying concept is presented in particular ways. If a pupil is experiencing difficulty it is essential to tease out whether the problem lies at the level of conceptual understanding or is the result of the mode of communication, especially that which is reliant on text. We might take the example (Lewis, 1995) of the different ways in which it is possible to express in writing the same piece of mathematical knowledge. It may well be that some pupils can recognise some of these expressions and not others. The barrier to the child's understanding then is the mode of expression, not the level of conceptual understanding of number:

- two and five make (…)

- two plus five equal (…)

- a 2p coin and a 5p coin make (…)

- a 2m piece of wood added to a 5m piece of wood gives me a piece of wood (…) m long

- $2 + 5 =$

- $5 + 2 =$

- $(2,5)$

- $2 + 5$

- $2 + 5 = {}^*$

- $2 +$

  5

  $=$

- $2p + 5p =$

- $2kg + 5\ kg =$

The effectiveness of educational targets rests on their design and selection, as well as a shared belief of those involved that the targets are realistic and worthwhile (Tod et al., 1998). There is a variety of ways in which target setting can be conceptualised. Similar issues arise in relation to target setting for IEPs as those relating to the notion of targets within the national context. The strength of targets may be that they provide a focus for the combined efforts of all those concerned to support a learner's progress and highlight the need to link planning and provision. This is the reason why it is crucial that all those involved in teaching a pupil for whom an IEP has been designed must be fully conversant with its contents.

There are, however, reasons why any assumption that all targets must be measurable and quantified in order to achieve clarity is questionable if we try to apply it to every aspect of the curriculum and every aspect of learners' development. Firstly, the setting of measurable targets is closely associated with a behaviourist perspective. It is possible to view a school curriculum as a ladder of progression from rung to rung of which it is feasible to set learning goals which can be assessed. An inherent difficulty in this view, however, is that not all children learn the same way, so setting targets which follow in a similar sequence for all pupils is not necessarily appropriate. Dockrell and McShane elaborate on the problems of this approach:

One of the major criticisms of task analysis and learning objectives is the conceptualization of the learning process. There may be a number of routes by which a child can acquire mastery, rather than a single instructional hierarchy that is common to all children. When a task analysis is being performed, it is assumed that each child will learn the task components in the same order, because the task is analysed and not the learning processes or the learning context. An over-reliance on task components can lead to a rigid application of prescriptive teaching, which takes no account of the knowledge a child brings to any given task or the specific strategies that a child utilizes.

(Dockrell and McShane, 1993, p. 51)

Secondly, there are areas of the curriculum where it is problematic to conceptualise measurable targets, for example, those that involve the emotions and creativity. One reason why designing IEPs relating to pupil behaviour is often seen as challenging (Tod et al., op cit.) is that they are seen to draw on the affective aspect of the curriculum.

It is clear that some areas lend themselves to a target-setting approach more easily than others. If we examine the series of activities designed by Lewis (1995) to encourage children's early reading it will be clear why it is problematic to assume that every area of the curriculum can lend itself easily to quantifiable objectives:

- watching another child, or an adult, looking at a book
- sharing a book with an adult
- sharing a book with another child
- sharing a book to look at from a classroom book area
- hearing print in a familiar context, e.g. from a known story
- hearing print in an unfamiliar context, e.g. from a birthday card
- activities linking the written symbols with meaningful messages, e.g. counting from a written list of names the numbers of children having school dinner
- collecting a variety of printed media (e.g. music scores, birthday cards, bottle labels) that convey information
- 'reading' a book in role play (later recognising rules concerning the direction of print)
- letter/word games, e.g. finding the first letter of the child's name in other contexts (e.g. on road signs, in a teacher's name), at first with adult help then independently

- decoding some basic sight vocabulary words from the daily environment (e.g. classroom, street, home)

- 'playing' with rhyming words

- games involving recognising individual letter sounds in different contexts

- games involving identifying individual letter sounds in different contexts

- games involving matching individual letter sounds with their written symbols (and vice versa)

- retelling to an adult, with some prompting, incidents from (and later the main story-line) of a story, film or event

- retelling, without any adult prompting, a sequence of events

- inventing own stories stimulated by a variety of media (pictures, events, objects, dramatic play, etc.)

- making own story and reading books using words/sentences written by an adult but dictated by the child (building up from single word to simple sentences, and beyond).

It is obvious that this list cannot be used as a linear sequence of teaching activities, nor as a set of tasks that can be broken down easily into teaching objectives which together would add up to the goal of reading.

Drawing up behavioural IEPs

Aa already noted, areas which involve creativity or the emotions cannot offer targets which are readily measurable. Cornwall and Tod (1998) identify a number of reasons why 'behavioural' IEPs cause concern to teachers:

- **situations regularly challenge the competencies and knowledge of the adults involved**

- **personal relationships cause problems and the skills to handle these effectively are not always to hand**

- **classroom management and group dynamics often provide a challenge, particularly to less experienced teachers (though not exclusively)**

- **there is fear involved – fear of losing control, of taking action that damages their professional standing or of the consequences of failure to themselves and to their pupils.**

(Cornwall and Tod, 1998, p. 3)

The level of explanation adopted for any behaviour in the classroom is clearly extremely important in formulating programmes for any learner. Different psychological perspectives on pupils' learning and development offer different explanatory models for behaviour perceived as 'difficult'. The kind of targets which are appropriate from one perspective may well be inappropriate from another.

From a behavioural perspective the following interventions are appropriate:

- detailed observation of antecedents, behaviour, consequences behaviour management programme

- teacher-consistency

- explicitness of rules.

From a psychodynamic perspective, 'difficult' behaviour assumed to originate from the child's unconscious mind might be approached through:

- therapy used by a professional in the area, exploring unspoken feelings or using careful listening

- counselling – reflective listening, offering feedback and empathy (Lawrence, 1971–4)

- teaching all pupils to give positive feedback where warranted.

An ecosystemic approach might predispose to addressing 'bad' behaviour by attempting to achieve:

- greater compatibility between the systems of which the pupil is a member, for example home and school

- emphasis on the whole-school system. Schools make a difference (Mortimore et al., 1988) Schools with 'better' behaviour are:

  - proactive in recognising and taking steps to prevent 'difficult' behaviour at whole-school, classroom and pupil level

  - community-focused, i.e. pay attention to student affiliation with the school and encourage teacher-pupil contact outside the classroom

  - characterised by teacher-collaboration

  - concerned with promoting pupil autonomy.

From a constructivist approach it may be important to:

- find out what purpose is served by the behaviour that poses the threat to the system and/or others around. Work out how this purpose might be fulfilled in a manner that is more acceptable in class.

A medical model might assume that behaviour perceived, for example, as 'disruptive' is caused by AD/HD or brain damage. These 'conditions' might warrant medical diagnosis and treatment.

Approaches to behavioural interventions

An Open University student on a teachers' professional development course described a curriculum intervention designed to address both the emotional needs of a pupil, 'Jake', who had recently suffered a family bereavement, and the concerns of those who taught him (Wearmouth, 1999). His extremely aggressive behaviour towards other pupils had drawn him to everyone's attention.

In her initial assessment of the difficulties 'Jake' appeared to be experiencing she noted that he was resistant to direct help. It was important therefore to design an approach which would take account of his sensitivities, would fit in with the curriculum offered to his peers, and also 'be compatible with the school's philosophy and mission statements concerning the personal well being and development of the students'. During further informal assessment through small-group discussion in which peers participated on equal terms, 'Jake' was encouraged to express his feelings about what was important to him and what he found hardest in school. It appeared that two issues were causing 'Jake' anxiety and upset: lack of friends and the fact that he hurt peers and did not understand his own actions in doing so.

'Jake's' assessment was discussed with his parents, and, with his particular needs in mind, 'Circle Time' (Mosley, 1993) was introduced as the major part of the Personal and Social Education curriculum. A nine-week programme was designed for the whole class, in three main topic areas: friends, recognition and expression of feelings, and bereavement and grief. These topics lent themselves very appropriately to follow-up discussion and written work in English lessons. The targets set for Jake were not easy to specify in the detail which would be required for exact measurement, as is common in the area of behaviour. They centred around developing and maintaining positive relationships with peers and teachers, and were negotiated between the teacher, Jake and his parents. These targets were also seen as appropriate for other pupils in the classroom and included listening carefully to others, taking turns, being polite, concentrating on the work in hand and looking out for ways to help other people. New routines were introduced to support the development of these relationships: a 'magic shell' in 'Circle Time' which bestowed permission to speak solely on the person holding it, personal confidential notebooks to draw, write about or use symbols to describe thoughts, feelings and 'new' behaviour, and play activities designed to build co-operation and mutual trust between the children.

A close record kept of 'Jake's' behaviour by means of what he chose to disclose from his notebook and through the teacher's own observation showed a significant improvement in the areas which had been causing concern to her and his parents as well as to the pupil himself. During this time there were 'no major incidents … no aggression' and only one occasion when 'Jake' 'felt the need to storm off' after an argument. At the same time he appeared to be responding much more positively to his family.

The teacher herself, reflecting on this intervention, was left wondering whether the improvement in 'Jake's' behaviour was the result of the plan drawn up for him, of the closer, happier relationship within his family, of both of these, or of time and added maturity. One of the issues in the area of behaviour programmes often is that we cannot be sure of the reason for change in behaviour. However, this should not detract from clarity of thinking about what might or might not contribute to pupil behaviour which is causing concern or from attempts to understand a situation from the pupil's perspective.

This intervention appeared to meet the expectation that a plan for a pupil should be embedded into the school curriculum, be based on an appropriate, sensitive assessment of need, be well focused even if the targets do not lend themselves easily to clear measurement, and should take both pupil and parent views into account. However, this example is not intended to be interpreted as specific advice on particular ways of approaching the question of approaches to pupil behaviour which is viewed as the cause of concern. It is intended as a reflection of the particular teacher's perspective on children as learners and her view of the nature of emotional development. She adopted an approach which attempted to take account of Jake's grief and anxieties and used positive feedback from pupils.

Summary

Planning an individual programme for a pupil must take account of evidence from assessment of pupil learning and advice offered in the Code of Practice (DfEE, 1994) as well as statutory requirements. Additionally, it should take place within the same overall curriculum structure that relates to every other pupil in a school. Particular challenges facing teachers in this process are issues of curriculum differentiation and equal opportunities, ways in which IEPs can be embedded into the mainstream curriculum, streamlining the bureaucratic processes and setting appropriate targets in relation both to an individual pupil's needs and to the particular curriculum area.

Suggested Activities: Reflection and Discussion

1. Integrating individual targets into regular classroom activities

It might be appropriate for those with a responsibility for monitoring individual education plans to consider how far, in their own institutions:

- general classroom practice takes account of individual pupils' needs

- how it might be improved

- what scope there might be for disseminating through the school the kind of practice advocated by Cowne in the above chapter?

2. Keeping records and disseminating information

It is in the interests of individual pupils identified as experiencing particular difficulties that records of any assessments made are clear, relevant, and useful to the process of planning ways to reduce barriers to learning. They must be accessible to those who need to know about the difficulties facing these pupils, but must also pay regard to confidentiality and pupils' sensitivities. Reflect on the extent to which the records maintained in the area of special educational needs in a school with which you are familiar are:

- clear relevant and useful

- sensitive to pupils' needs and individuality

- maintain confidentiality as far as possible

- accessible to the appropriate teaching staff

- reviewed and updated regularly.

What improvements might be made to the system of record-keeping:

- in the short term

- in the medium term

- in the long term?

In-School Needs Analysis

Those interested in reviewing practice in relation to Individual Education Plans might choose to complete *Whole-school needs assessment 7: Individual Education Plans* which is included in the Appendix.

10 Managing staff support for learning

The use of support staff in the classroom to assist pupils who experience some kind of difficulty in learning or physical disability is common practice in many schools these days. Official sources have openly condoned the use of support staff as a strategy in helping pupils in class, but are less than specific in identifying exactly how it should be used, or of what it should consist. For example, the Code of Practice, paragraph 2:58: 'SEN support services can play an important part in helping schools … make provision for children with SEN.' A report from the Scottish Office Education Department (1993) mentioned the presence of support staff in the classroom as a 'potent' factor in relation to pupils' achievement, without actually specifying the nature of this potency. Teachers' perception of the effectivess of support teaching 'all too often is reduced to judgements about personalities or vague notions of rapport' (Allan, 1995).

Funding in-class support is an expensive option for schools and colleges. It is inevitable that the outcomes of this kind of provision will come under great scrutiny as demands for accountability in education grow. For a number of reasons, therefore, it is probably time for a re-appraisal of what classroom support for pupils both is and could be. Among these are: to explore ways in which institutions can set up systems which are clearly designed to include all students from the outset, and to address issues of accountability for additional resources.

Issues in the management of support staff in schools

Support teaching

There are a number of different ways of conceptualising the role of support teachers which in fact indicate the need to consider very carefully the aim of this kind of provision. Clark, Dyson, Millward and Skidmore (1997) outline three functions:

- provision of sufficient support to individual pupils to enable them to engage with their learning in classrooms where otherwise the curriculum would be inaccessible

- assistance in the management of behaviour of pupils who would otherwise be experienced as challenging to the class teacher

- support in the development of differentiated curricular approaches appropriate to meet the diversity of pupils' learning styles and needs.

Allan (op cit.) has identified four aspects of support teaching concerned with raising the performance of individual pupils, providing coping strategies for pupils, and alleviating demands on teachers which indicate effectiveness:

- resolving individual pupils' difficulties

- correcting pupils' mistakes at an early stage

- clarifying concepts and cajoling pupils to produce more work

- reducing the pressure on the class teacher to interact with the target pupils and preventing disruption from some pupils.

The role of support teachers and classroom assistants

Schools employ a variety of adults to support pupils in the classroom: support teachers, classroom assistants, teachers and care staff. Whereas there is often a clear delineation of role for care staff whose responsibility lies in the area of the physical well-being of the child, in practice there is often much less clarity in role-difference between support teacher and classroom assistant. For the purpose of this discussion support teachers are defined as those staff with qualified teacher status (QTS), with or without additional specialist qualifications, who are employed as teachers by schools or local education authorities to teach individual pupils or groups either in the classroom or in a withdrawal situation. Classroom assistants do not have the authority or status of fully qualified teachers in the role which they perform, and are employed as 'assistants' under the direction of the class teacher. Typically, infant and primary schools employ their own classroom assistants and enjoy the services of specialist support teachers from external support services. In the past, secondary schools have tended to employ their own support teachers, for example to work with pupils who have a Statement, and use staff from the local support service in addition. More recently. however, it seems that secondary schools have increasingly begun to employ classroom assistants for in-class support activities.

The support teacher

The conventional model of the role of the support teacher is that of the external specialist engaged in the process of 'integrating' the child 'with' difficulties into the mainstream class. The professional autonomy of this teacher is guaranteed by a supposed mastery of the field of his or her specialised knowledge. There is still a mandatory qualification for support teachers employed to work with students with sensory impairments. More recently, however, in recognition of the fact that there is no hard and fast line between pupils who experience difficulties in learning and those who do not, there has been a growing tendency to employ classroom assistants in secondary as well as primary schools to support any child in the classroom who appears to need help, or who asks for it. Dessent (1987) in Duffield (1995) spoke of the emergence of an 'anti-expert trend' away from the traditional basic tuition skills of the remedial teacher. However, one might well ask what support teachers have to offer, if not expertise in something.

Whilst in theory it is possible to draw different role models for the support teacher in the classroom, in practice there seems to be inadequate consensus among teachers, parents and pupils about what exactly is the role, let alone what it ought to be. It seems to be the case that in-class support is often very much a 'bolt-on job', something imposed on the class teacher from without to accompany the 'integration' of pupils 'with' difficulties; therefore accounts are written from the point of view of the support teacher and reflect that perception, for example the accounts of frustrations and misunderstandings written by Best (1991) and Thomas (1992a and b), or are written from some ideal model of what an 'other' person thinks should exist, rather than reflecting the concerns of both the class teacher and the pupils in the classroom. A summary (Lovey, 1995) of the aim of secondary support exemplifies this lack of agreed definition of role. The aim stated here is simply that of the support teacher herself, and by no means one that has been negotiated with class teachers or students: to provide an advocate and easy access to help in the classroom for the pupil who is experiencing difficulty; to build up a child's self esteem, quietly to defuse potential confrontations, and to provide more attention for all the children. Lovey concludes that probably the most important function of a support teacher is to develop a pupil's self esteem by listening to stressed pupils, helping them complete work which otherwise would have added to the pile of unfinished bits, and often just by getting to know the pupils as individuals.

Much has been written about an ideal support model which encompasses regular liaison and joint planning of lessons between class and support teachers, a co-operative partnership of professionals of equal status in the classroom sharing the lead role (Bibby, 1990). It is clear, however, (Lovey, ibid) that much support teaching in fact operates within an authoritarian, single-teacher-controlling didactic framework. There are obvious contradictions and potential clashes inherent in a situation where, traditionally and conventionally, one professional has been seen to be in control by him or herself, but suddenly a situation occurs where two professionals appear in the same place at the same time. One is obviously in charge and therefore has a legitimate role, and the other one can have nothing other than a subsidiary role. Bowers (1989) and Thomas (1992) highlight sensitivity about the relative status of the class teacher and the learning support teacher as presenting problems in the move towards co-operative teaching. There is the important issue of who is in charge in the classroom. If the two teachers are not in close agreement, or do not get on, pupils will play one off against another. In the traditional, authoritarian, expert-teacher, apprentice-learner model of the classroom, one must be in charge, unless the support teacher is also an 'expert' in that subject area. Support teachers often lack status in the eyes of staff and pupils, lack authority and lack subject specific knowledge. In this context, even the best qualified, most experienced teacher in the support role can be humiliated by lack of definition of role, being treated like one of the pupils, and not being able to act in the familiar capacity of authoritative adult.

Many studies have shown little evidence of joint planning and team-teaching on the part of class and support staff:

> **This small piece of research offered little evidence of explicit professional collaboration between mainstream and learning support teachers ... One notable absence from the teachers' outcomes is professional development as a result of "collaboration" ... Another omission is a consideration of how the children perceive co-operative teaching.**

(Allan, 1995)

As in so much of this area of work, implicit in the aim of improving the quality of pupils' learning experiences through the use of support staff are contradictions. If a support teacher's role is basically seen as managing the behaviour of 'difficult' pupils there is little incentive to consider changes in pedagogy designed to include all pupils in the first place. Often, support teachers find themselves propping up the system by helping pupils through inappropriate lessons, thus, unwittingly, contributing to pupils' problems in the long run, rather than alleviating them:

> **Learning support teachers commonly reported finding the target pupils unable to cope with work which over-estimated their likely attainments (usually, they said, this work had been set by the mainstream teacher). After one such instance, a learning support teacher said she had simply been telling the pupils what to write, otherwise they would have failed to complete any of the work.**

(Ibid)

'Cajoling an unmotivated pupil' itself can be both good and bad simultaneously. It certainly can obscure inadequate teaching. On the other hand some pupils come to school carrying a lot of personal concerns which the support teacher can help to defuse. In addition:

> **Teachers commented on the difficulties that arose when the pupils reached secondary school age because they became more self-conscious and reluctant to be in close contact with the learning support teacher.**

(Ibid)

Allan puts this down to the issue of labelling, but it is just as likely that pupils are much more inclined to compare themselves with peers and find themselves wanting.

Despite the drawbacks, attaching individual support teachers to individual pupils is a form of provision which serves two very important purposes. These will have to be taken seriously when faced with the decision of how to organise this particular form of additional provision for pupils:

- it reduces the threat to the dominance and authority of the traditional role of the class teacher and therefore is likely to be seen as an attractive option in schools

- it constitutes an easily identifiable arrangement and can be more readily justified as a discrete form of provision for pupils with statements if parents have recourse to the law.

In their discussion of forms of pedagogy which can respond to a range of differences in learning, attainment, aptitude and style, Clark et al. (1997) discuss the trend, in some schools, towards a much more flexible and creative use of support teaching. For example, individual teachers and/or groups or subject departments might be asked to put in a bid for in-class support for the purpose of developing differentiated strategies and schemes of work differentiated for all pupils. Alternatively, partnerships might drawn up as formal arrangements, requiring class and support teachers to plan lessons together. Support teachers might also be regarded as full members of a department of year group, involved in any relevant planning.

The classroom assistant

Susan is a support assistant employed for 25 hours per week in a secondary comprehensive school to support six pupils who have all been identified as 'slower' to learn than most of the other pupils and as finding difficulty in reading text and in writing coherently. Among these pupils was 'Dean'. She is employed on classroom assistant rates but is a graduate herself. Some of the experiences she described in an interview (Wearmouth, in press) exemplify potentially useful functions of a classroom assistant that should be recognised in any evaluation of that role: facilitation of learning, close observation of behaviour, collection of evidence for an evaluation of pupil progress. However, they also exemplify concerns that need to be addressed if classroom assistants are to be used to maximum advantage: a sense of inadequacy generated by the class teacher, inferior status made apparent to pupils, inappropriate use of the assistant as disciplinarian. Her words are quoted here verbatim:

> **... there was a meeting of teachers recently where everybody got together and discussed what they thought ought to happen with Dean and really I**

was the only one who knew much about him. I was a bit upset because I had not been invited to the meeting originally and I heard about it when other people were talking about it, and I really do think I should have been invited. I think the invitation should have come from the deputy head but nobody seems to have thought about me even though I was the one who seemed to have the most information about him. ... If I had not been there a lot of information about Dean just would not have been there. From that meeting a lot of positive things were worked out for him. In a lesson I would say about 60 per cent of my time is given to Dean. ... even though there are several other pupils in the class who are statemented whom I am supposed to be supporting. ... The kind of things I do with him are to stand over him quite a lot of the time because he has got great avoidance tactics, he just does not like the idea of being the last to do things, he knows he can't keep up with the pace that everyone else does. Some days he will work really hard and do his best but other days he will think well, I can't do this, I can't do this and you give him a pen and he just pulls it apart and sometimes he refuses to bring a pen because it is just an avoidance tactic. ... If he works very hard occasionally he can keep up with the rest of the class. Sometimes he surprises me. He can write things down quite quickly if he wants to. Again, he has not got very good joined up writing or anything but he can work at a pace that he wants to sometimes, depending on the other kids he is with. If he feels pressurized to keep up with them, he will keep up with them. Other times you have to sit by him just to get him started. He is very slow at getting started, 20 minutes to write the title of something and things like this, but once you get him interested he can get involved, but still the writing down is a problem. He would rather talk about it.

He is expected to do pretty much the same level of work as everybody else in the class in some lessons. Sometimes there is some differentiation in the work between him and other pupils but in general terms he is expected to do exactly the same as everybody else, exactly the same as those who find it very easy to write things down and very easy to understand things quickly. If I had not been there in the last year he would not be turning up at all at school. He just would not be there because he could not cope. ... I really think he should have more individual targeted help ... but the English teacher said, 'Well, I would rather he stayed with the class' because they had just started Romeo and Juliet at the time. ... 'I really do think that he can cope with it like everybody else in the class because he can understand the story', and in actual fact he has got a lot out of being there with the drama and the acting and all that and he does really well. He has a part and it is good to see him working with the others understanding the story, watching what the others are doing. It probably was better that he was in that class actually with the others. Now they have got to do an essay on the parents of Romeo and Juliet but it's pointless giving him something like that, but he will still have to do it. That's the writing side and I will just have to dictate in the end what he does because otherwise he can't cope. He just will not be able to do it. He just won't be able to go away and do it on his own.

The teachers never ever ask me for suggestions about what I think he could be doing in the time ... she is aware of the level that he is at but it is just a case of me making sure that he just does something, she just wants him to produce something whatever it is, however long it is does not matter. She is very adamant about the fact that it does not matter how much he produces as long as he produces something it is okay.

I think there actually is a big place for negotiating more with support teachers appropriate tasks for particular children to do because the support teachers know those children very well, definitely. I feel I know a lot more about the children that I'm with than a lot of the teachers. ... The trouble is I'm not qualified really to talk, you know, they don't think I'm qualified really to talk about it at all, you know. ... The other thing is if he is coming out of ordinary lessons he is getting further and further and further behind. It's just so difficult. He has got no incentive either if he is always miles behind. He has got no incentive to try.

There was a discussion at the meeting and it was just decided that he was taken out of lessons and because he was doing the reading programme he needed to go home and relax. I never got a chance at that meeting to say what I thought about that, not really. I did not have the status or the position. I felt out of my league there anyway. ... A lot of these things you just don't know do you until you try it with him really. I would have made him do a certain amount and say to him, 'Look you have got to have a go,' because he just thinks, 'I am Dean Watts and I don't do any homework. Everybody else has to but I don't have to.' That's his label and he has kept that the label. 'I'm the one who does not do homework. Everybody else does and I don't.' ... The trouble is for me I couldn't monitor his homework and tell him what to do because that is not my role. He does not see me as a teacher. I feel I can't really tell him off about his homework. I mean, I do say to him, 'Well why did you not do your homework Dean?' If it was made clear to him in front of me then possibly it would be different, but I feel that he needs that discipline from the other teachers. The teachers need to reprimand him more. I know it is difficult but he has not got any boundaries in that way. That is the trouble.

The greatest problem for me in this work is that I feel I'm a nobody. I walk out of the classroom feeling I am more like one of the kids. The kids are my friends. The teachers don't consult me very often. It's up to me to go to the teacher all the time. It is very much down to me to find out what is going on and what have you. I need to go up to the Special Needs area at break time and lunch time just to know what is happening. Quite honestly, to increase the respect and status of the position, the way I feel about it really when you are going up there at lunch time and talking to staff and talking to kids and helping kids, I really ought to be paid for it. I mean, we found out that they are paying 6th formers to stand at the top of the stairs and just stand there, and we aren't paid for helping kids and finding out what we are supposed to be doing at lunchtime. Why could not they offer us that job? I mean, it bloody annoys me that we are another stage up with the ancillary staff.

Another reason why I feel I am a nobody is that they have OFSTED meetings going on with ancillary staff and we were not included, the support staff. When we went to ask we were told. 'Yes, go along,' but the next minute there were other meetings going on with sort of representatives from different areas like the office and what have you but we were not asked. So I felt, well, you know, nobody had ever taken us into account. People seemed to be aware of us wanting to know, but we just were not included in things. I don't know how it works though.

The most important things I feel I do with Dean are to encourage him and to start him off and get him thinking about things. Some days I'll suggest things and he will come up with things of his own that are similar and that is great. Other times he just won't want to do it. I do get a bit annoyed with some of the teachers because they seem to think my job is to stand over Dean all the time and make him work, but that really is not my job. It is as if if he does not do things it is my fault, and I have got three others in that class. One of them, Paul, is quite childish in his thinking and actually, you know, I got on very well with him at first, but he has become quite abusive to me lately. He will say, 'I don't need help I am fine' when I know very well he can't understand and he can't do it. He would rather copy off other children than accept help from me, and been seen to take help from me. I feel quite honestly that I just can't do enough for the four of them in that lesson. I feel Paul deserves better than I can give him at the moment. He needs more support. He needs someone to discuss things with on his own level.

I think it would definitely help if kids were allowed to talk to each other more about things and help each other more, and were not just expected sit there and get on silently and independently on their own. I think it is partly to do with the organization of the lesson. ... There is so much variation amongst the statemented children. I mean John is very intelligent and able to work things out for himself. His basic Maths and English aren't very good but his understanding is good and his understanding of what he has got to know is quite good as well. He often puts up his hand and answers questions and things in class. He just needs help with the reading of things and writing it down. What makes me angry is that most of them are really very practically orientated but nobody is playing to that strength. It would be easier for me to have them all on on one table to give then the help they need, rather than have to walk halfway round the room from one to the other. The trouble is if it was any other kid in the room and they went up to a mate and said, 'Can you help me out?' I would think it was all right. There does seem to be a problem with the labelling of statemented kids. I do make an effort to help the rest of the class and sometimes the rest of the class help do ask me to help them.

When there are four of them in the class I just don't have time to stand over them and check their spelling but I don't really think that that is my job. I just don't have the time to go through every single piece of their work and say this is wrong, and this is wrong and I don't think that is my job. If their writing is totally illegible I will say change this or change that. I think they need a time to get themselves in balance a time to get themselves sorted. I think it helps if they know that I will help any one in the class and not just them. I help them with understanding what they have got to do, that is the kind of thing they ask me about.

There are some situations in class where I absolutely can't operate at all, depending where you sit in the classroom. For example, it can be awkward if you think you are interrupting the teacher and what they are doing. The kids will ask you a question, they are in the middle of asking you a question and the teacher will say, 'Right, I want everybody silent,' and I mean how do you get the question out of them? I quite often feel as if I am one of the kids because the teacher will say, 'Now shut up all that talking,' and it's me. It's me explaining to the kids things about what they have got to do, because you know they ask you a question and you are a teacher and you have got to answer it.

I think probably a lot more of my role than should happen goes into the discipline side. When I first started I was told that I was a support assistant and it was not my job to discipline kids but you know in the end you have to discipline them. In some lessons I find myself doing the teacher's job, quite honestly. I mean, the teacher is sitting down marking and I am walking around helping all the kids in the class and I do get annoyed at that sometimes because I don't feel that's my place and it happens with the same teachers over and over again. There is one particular department where every single member of the department is always ten or fifteen minutes late at the beginning of the lesson. You get three classes arriving together and I am the only adult there, and there am I running from one to the other controlling three classes all together and quite honestly that is not my job and then you know I am so angry because I have shouted at the class two or three times. ... So the net result is I just hang around for at least five minutes after the bell before going into the classroom.

Generally, I think the idea of support teaching is very effective, actually. Just having someone there for them is very good for them, but I just feel we could do so much more. The difficulty in History and Geography is the reading side of things. I am always going around the room and they may have two pages there that they have got to read and they don't understand what is on the page anyway. I'll ask them if they want help reading and they say. 'No,' because they don't want to be seen as having help with their English by their friends. A number of pupils in that class really do value having it read out to them as well. In History in particular I spend so much of my time in class going over what they should be doing. The thing is, I go up to a kid and say, 'Do you want help with the reading?' and it is quite hard and none of them say they want help. But if they can't do the question then I will help them and then they will let me help them. There are a number of pupils who really are very intelligent, but then there are a large majority of pupils who really can't or don't. The trouble is even if the work was differentiated so that different groups in the class were given different work to do it would create problems because they would each be comparing with the others what they were doing.

I had a job description when I first went there but I have never actually looked at it since. Definitely to begin with that booklet was of value to me right at the beginning to understand more about the school, the position of the support teacher and what have you, because what you are expected to do in different lessons does vary.

The lesson I enjoy being with kids most is in Maths, I think. It is a very small class and you can really get down to sorting them out and helping them and you can see them understanding it and getting on with it at their level. There are only about ten or twelve pupils in that group. Even so, I spend quite a lot of time with Dean but not as much as I do in other lessons because there are other pupils there, like John, and they also need help in Maths, and there are other pupils not on statement who also need help.

Being a smaller group, I also get on very well with the teacher who does that class. We just get on and work together and she lets me mark their work. I get a lot of responsibility in that class. I walk round, she does not leave me just with Dean. She helps him as much as I do, which I think is very good for them, and very good for me, and for my relationships with them and her relationships with them. I wish that a lot more teachers would take more notice of those pupils that I am supporting and don't just leave it up to the support teacher. You know, it is as if some teachers think, well, there is a support teacher with them I don't need to look at them. I don't need to be with them. Yet it would help them a lot if the main teacher paid them a lot more attention, but teachers just don't bother.

I feel very happy in that lesson. I feel things are a lot better balanced. I feel a lot more valued as a person. I feel like it's a lot more positive, it's like in the other lessons I can't do things that I feel I ought to do. She always discusses beforehand what she is going to do if there is time anyway, and she reflects on the kids' progress with me as well. She does that at the beginning and the end of the lesson and she finds time in the lessons when the kids are working as well and she talks to me about all the kids in the class and what is going on. In a bigger class some teachers try but it is time for them that makes it difficult. Others just don't. That is a different situation because it is a small class anyway, and both of us know them and we both know that we are both there very much to help the class, make things possible for them.

One of the important issues here is how far difficulties are created for Susan because she is paid merely as an assistant who, in a highly academic secondary school, will necessarily be accorded little personal status. It has to be said, however, that in this particular school another support teacher who is a fully qualified teacher and paid as such, reports similar difficulties. One might well wonder how the model might look, and what implications for practice there might be, if the perceptions of support staff, mainstream teachers and students were all taken into account – a 'whole-class', inclusive approach. Very little seems to have been written combining the perceptions and concerns of all three sides simultaneously. Susan's salary was funded from monies coming into the school as a result of provision specified on Statements, implying the 'conventional' model above, which provides one-to-one, input to the student, rather than extra support for all pupils. However, some pupils actively resisted seeking help in front of their peers. She often therefore ended up helping other pupils and not assisting the one for whom this extra resource should have been targeted. Where the child was on Statement but refused her help she was left wondering whom she was there to serve, especially where her aims appeared to be different from the pupil's.

The SENCO in one upper school in the East Midlands, when first introducing support assistants to classrooms in the school, offered the following advice to staff:

- **discuss with the classroom assistant the work you will be expecting in your classrooms**

- **set aside specific time to discuss/plan together without interruption where possible**

- **a notebook can be useful for jottings or reminders etc. when it is not possible to talk**

- **classroom assistants should not be expected to work beyond their paid hours**

- **remember, you prefer time to prepare before a lesson, so will the classroom assistant**

- **plan work for/with the classroom assistant and give clear guidelines**

- **make sure the classroom assistant knows exactly what is wanted from the students. The classroom assistant may not have been in the classroom when you were talking with them**

- **discuss in advance where, within the class, the classroom assistant is going to work.**

  (Wearmouth, in press)

Advice from OFSTED: Key features of effective in-class support

Richmond (2000) notes that a survey (OFSTED 1996a) evaluating the effects of recent legislation which coincided with the implementation by schools of the Code of Practice (DfEE 1994) identified the features of lessons in which high quality provision was made using in-class support for pupils with SEN:

- good team working between support staff and class teacher (joint planning)

- support staff supplied with information about the work to be attempted

- support staff introducing additional materials and strategies (often of use to a wider group of pupils) to enable pupils with SEN to take part

- support staff working with a more able group to enable class teacher to focus on those who need more help

- ensuring that pupils of all abilities are adequately challenged to solve problems, reflect, formulate strategies and act independently: it is not helpful to a pupil if the support staff do the work for the child

- ensuring the integration of pupils into the whole class.

Managing support for pupils in the Literacy Hour

One area of particular current concern to SENCOs is that of how to manage support for pupils who experience difficulties in literacy development during the Literacy Hour. Before turning to issues of appropriate support for pupils during the Hour, it is necessary first to examine what this initiative is attempting to achieve.

Overall aims of the National Literacy Strategy

The overall aims of the National Literacy Strategy as outlined in the guidance manual are twofold:

- Improvement of the quality of literacy teaching in the classroom.

- Improvement of the management of literacy at whole-school level.

In the National Literacy Strategy, literacy is defined as:

Literacy unites the important skills of reading and writing.

It ... involves speaking and listening which ... are an essential part of it.

Good oral work enhances pupils' understanding of

- **language in oral and written forms**

- **the way language can be used to communicate.**

Good oral work is an important part of the process through which pupils read and compose texts.

(Adapted from National Literacy Strategy, DfEE, 1998)

Clearly this definition unites the skills of reading and writing and involves speaking and listening. It also makes reference to the importance of literacy in communication. However, there is no clear statement of what is the bedrock of the perspective underlying the Strategy. We are not offered any particular orientation here.

It is important to reflect on one's personal understanding of what constitutes 'literacy' and one's own interpretation, and views on, the government perspective because these will be directing principles and practice in teaching, planning and liaising with other staff and with parents.

A small group of teachers involved in a training session on special educational needs and the Literacy Hour came up with the following definitions of literacy:

Literacy is …

- functional: it relates to

  - the economic situation, both nationally and personally. The more literate the population, the better equipped it is to contribute to the nation's economy; the more literate the individual, the more employable.

  - one's personal learning. A high standard of literacy is necessary to be well educated.

- cultural: it is important for

  - personal identity and a sense of self

  - the formal recording of culture

- related to power/status: it is associated with

  - inclusion within a society, or separation from it

  - both control through particular uses of text, and liberation through offering personal choice

- pleasurable: it offers opportunities for

  - personal fulfilment

  - enjoyment of leisure time

- essential for the organisation of society: it is important for mass communication.

The National Literacy Strategy is intended to achieve improvement of the quality of literacy teaching in the classroom through:

i) direct teaching

ii) clear, planned objectives.

OFSTED findings from its evaluation of the first cohort of pupils in the pilot projects around the country (Nov. 1998) concluded that, in Cohort 1, there were:

- improved reading scores among all groups of pupils 'only modest improvement' in a 'stubborn minority of schools'

- some pupil negativity owing to slow pace and ineffective classroom management

- word level work sometimes superficial and unsystematic

- noise disrupted some guided reading

- teacher-questioning sometimes shallow

- less progress among

  - boys compared with girls

  - pupils on free school meals

  - pupils at Stages 3-5 and Statemented, especially where LSA was unavailable

  - English as first-language children compared with *very fluent* English-as-first-language pupils

  - English as foreign language pupils just developing English

- high teacher turnover and recruitment difficulties in some disadvantaged areas.

The implications of the OFSTED research appear to be that there is a need for:

- urgent action to improve unsatisfactory classroom teaching, especially at word level

- recognition of aspects of the Hour creating barriers to individual pupils

- collaboration between English-as-first-language staff, SENCOs, LSAs and classteachers

- clear recognition of importance of language fluency in literacy development

- action to address weaknesses in low-attaining year groups from earliest stages

- concentrated, co-ordinated support to improve leadership where improvement in standards is insufficient. Head teachers must: negotiate staff support for the National Literacy Project, agree implementation strategies, monitor classroom work and offer constructive feedback

- action to address teacher-recruitment and retention in some areas.

Research into the effective teaching of literacy

To fulfil a role as SENCO, and to be able to make informal decisions, it is useful to be aware of the results of other research into the effective teaching of literacy. A SENCO may well find her or himself in a position of influence in deciding what kind of training might be the most appropriate for teachers in supporting children's literacy development needs.

Research findings from the project *Effective Teachers of Literacy,* (Exeter Univiversity, sponsored by TTA, 1998) into what effective primary school teachers of literacy know, understand and do come to the following conclusions.

Findings

Effective teachers have:

- a coherent personal philosophy about how literacy should be taught which guides pedagogy: the purpose of teaching literacy and of activities at word, sentence and text level should be made explicit. Decoding and spelling should be systematic, highly structured and presented to pupils in a way that clarifies their significance

- considerable knowledge about literacy which enables them to see and help pupils make connections between word, sentence and text level

- experience of personal professional development in the area.

Effective Practice in Literacy Teaching

Knowledge and understanding of literacy development consistently and coherently informs practice in:

- teaching of literacy embedded into the wider context

- modelling extensively used; reading and writing regularly demonstrated, with simultaneous verbal explanations

- less focus on written paper exercises

- connections between word, sentence and text level made explicit

- literacy in environment emphasised and brought to children's attention

- phonics taught within context of a text

- 'short, regular teaching sessions'

- 'brisk pace' with 'clear time frames'

- children regularly brought back to task

- varied support between pupil groups

- 'systematic record-keeping' using 'focused observation'.

The Audit Commission (Audit Commission/HMI 1992) provides a telling example of the reading attainments of pupils over a period of 4 years in similar primary schools. Some features which lifted performance in the more successful school were:

- the provision of extra support at Key Stage 1

- a system of recording progress which included records of the teaching approaches

- the use of reading tests to monitor school performance

- a significant level of parental involvement

- opportunity to practise reading silently every day.

In contrast some characteristics depressing school performance in another school were:

- the inadequacy of passing information about pupils with reading difficulties from teacher to teacher

- low expectations of what pupils could achieve

- no teacher with a school oversight of reading policy

- the use of library and books was unsupervised

- school to home reading initiatives were not pursued

- pupils with serious learning difficulties were not identified

- insufficient money for support assistance for weak readers.

The effective deployment of classroom assistants during the Literacy Hour

The issue of assessing and meeting individual pupils' literacy needs was discussed above. Cable (1998) offers advice to classroom assistants on the kind of role they might have in supporting pupils who experience difficulty in literacy development. It is noticeable that issues related to the need to make time for prior planning are similar to those already discussed. Cable makes the point that it is very important for classroom assistants to be present for the whole hour and not to be distracted by tasks such as clearing away the debris from other activities because:

- **(CAs) need to know and understand what the teaching objectives are for the class as a whole and for the week and (they) can learn this best by being in the classroom and observing the teacher.**

- **(CAs) need to know and understand the approaches and strategies that the teacher uses and wants the children to learn so that (they) can use similar ones when (they) are working with the children.**

- **It is important for children's learning, motivation and behaviour that they receive consistent teaching and do not get different messages from (the CA) and the teacher.**

- (CAs) need to know and understand the new terminology that the teacher is using and teaching so that you can feed back meaningful comments to the teacher about the progress and achievement of children you have been working with.

For those with a special concern in reviewing and evaluating support for pupils during the Literacy Hour, particular activities have been included in the final section of this chapter below.

Summary

Funding in-class support for pupils is an expensive option for schools. All too often in the past insufficient rationale for using support teachers or assistants has underpinned their use in particular schools. There is research to show that this kind of provision can facilitate the learning of pupils who experience difficulties, but clear justification must be given and a clear role for the support teacher or assistant must be negotiated and agreed with all concerned.

Suggested Activities: Reflection and Discussion

1. Evaluating the use of in-class support

Below is a list of questions relevant to a review of the usefulness of support staff:

- What are the distinctive contributions that can be made to pupils' learning by support staff?
- Is compatibility of educational ideals an essential ingredient to harmonious relations between mainstream and support staff?
- Have issues of status, sharing of workload, who has expertise in what, and mutual respect been addressed adequately? If so, how?
- How is the issue of discipline and control in the classroom viewed by all the participants?
- How do teachers and support staff view the refusal of some pupils to accept help in class? What is it about the nature of the support offered that 'makes' some pupils refuse help, while others accept it?
- What are the qualities in the individual support teacher, or the factors in what is being offered, that students really value?

2. Evaluating good practice in support work

(Cont...)

For those with a responsibility for monitoring support work with pupils, it might be useful to reflect on practice in the school against the features of lessons in which high quality in-class support was made, as identified by OFSTED (OFSTED 1996a). What improvements might be made to the support provision with which you are familiar:

- in the short-term

- in the medium-term

- in the long-term?

3. Evaluating whole-school needs in relation to the development of literacy

For any teacher with whole-school responsibilities in relation to the Literacy Hour and pupils' special learning needs, the following checklist (Melidis and Wearmouth, 1999) adapted from the Literacy Framework document might be a useful starting point to determine the areas of particular concern in literacy development across a year group:

The National Literacy Project

	Literate primary pupils should	Concerns: fraction of pupils in year group
1.	Read and write with confidence, fluency and understanding	/
2.	Be able to combine a full range of reading cues (phonic, graphic, syntactic, contextual) to monitor and self-correct their own reading	/
3.	Understand the sound and spelling system and use this to read and spell accurately	/
4.	Have fluent and legible handwriting	/
5.	Have an interest in words and meanings, and a growing vocabulary	/
6.	Know, understand and be able to write in a range of genres in fiction and poetry, and understand and be familiar with some of the ways in which narratives are structured through basic literary ideas of setting, character and plot	/
7.	Know, understand and be able to write a range of non-fiction texts	/
8.	Plan, draft, revise and edit their own writing	/
9.	Have a suitable technical vocabulary through which to understand and discuss their reading and writing	/
10.	Be interested in books, read with enjoyment and evaluate and justify their preferences	/
11.	Through reading and writing, develop their powers of imagination, inventiveness and critical awareness.	/

(Cont ...)

Completing a check list across groups of children will give some indication of where one might wish to place a particular emphasis on improving standards of literacy development for all the children in your school.

4. Difficulties associated with SEN and the Literacy Hour

Classifying what is believed to be at the root of a difficulty experienced by children can be helpful in deciding how to conceptualise strategies appropriate to the level at which the problem is thought to be located. Staff teaching pupils in the Literacy Hour might be asked to complete the following form:

Difficulties in learning experienced by pupils during the Literacy Hour		
Within-child	Teacher/classroom level	School level

5. Implications of the OFSTED research into the effectiveness of the Literacy Hour

Read through the list of findings of the OFSTED research into the effectiveness of the Literacy Hour as outlined above.

Note down what you feel may be some of the implications of these findings for your own school.

11 Liaising and working with outside agencies

There are many reasons why pupils experience difficulties in learning. In addition, the difficulties experienced by particular pupils vary and it may be impossible for families or schools to sort out the complex interaction of factors which produce, or result, in a learning difficulty without the involvement of others. The probability that a pupil, and his or her family, will be involved with other agencies in addition to the school, depends of the complexity and severity of the difficulty. More complex and severe difficulties (as well as some medical conditions associated with learning problems) are generally identified before school age. For teachers co-ordinating the provision offered in school, knowing when and how to interact with the vast array of outside professionals who may become involved with a particular child and family can be confusing and time consuming. Nevertheless it is very important to the pupil's welfare and progress.

Models of inter–agency work

There is a long history of problems in the exchange of information between agencies and of disputes over responsibility for offering particular services; sometimes with duplication of interventions by different agencies working on the same case. Different agencies operate to different legislative frameworks with different priorities and definitions of what constitutes a need. Recent research by Dyson, Lin and Millward (DfEE, 1998) re-states the need for closer co-operation between agencies which exist to support children in difficulties and their families or carers.

Three overlapping but distinct models (multi-disciplinary, inter-disciplinary and trans-disciplinary) for interagency work are in common use though the terminology used in the professional literature may differ (Florian and Rouse 2000). In practice each model is often used inter-changeably by practitioners, creating some confusion about the role expectations professionals have of each other.

Under the *multi-disciplinary approach*, specialists from different disciplines evaluate a particular child and make recommendations often without knowledge of, or consultation with, other specialist providers. For example, a speech and language therapist and a physio-therapist may each evaluate a child and make recommendations for intervention without involving each other or the school in the evaluation, recommendations or interventions.

Under the *inter-disciplinary approach*, specialists conduct their assessments independently but share their results with each other at team meetings. By sharing their results, they aim to develop co-ordinated and individualised interventions for particular children.

The *trans-disciplinary approach* involves professionals from different disciplines working together with families to gather information about a child and develop intervention strategies. The responsibility for the interventions is also shared. Under this model, the speech and language therapist and the physio-therapist would have consulted with each other, the family and the other professional team members as part of the assessment process. They would also develop a strategy of sharing responsibility for intervention so, for example, the classroom teacher may implement a recommendation aimed to remediate an articulation difficulty.

The type of model encountered or developed within a particular school will depend on such factors as the size of the school and the proximity of other agencies. Each model has advantages and disadvantages which give rise to a variety of problems and solutions. For example, while a multi-disciplinary approach may limit the amount and quality of information exchanged by professionals when compared to other approaches, the team meetings required by the inter-disciplinary and trans-disciplinary approaches may be too time consuming and/or difficult for teachers to attend. On the other hand, developing interventions which can be implemented by non-specialists at home and in school may produce better results than those obtained by direct therapy when the pupil is removed from the classroom and misses other learning opportunities.

Taking a slightly different approach to their analysis of ways of working, Dyson, Lin and Millward identified four underlying models of co-operative practices in their study of practice in ten local education authorities:

- The 'mutual co-operation model' where agencies act independently, respect each others' statutory responsibilities, but have effective systems for co-operation when their statutory responsibilities require joint action, for example in the assessment procedures under Part IV of the 1996 Education Act. The disadvantage of this model is the contraint on co-opartion, but the advantage is the freedom for proactive individuals to initiate activity locally.

- The 'shared responsibility' model where agencies devolve autonomy to locally-based, multi-professional teams, for example Family Support Centres. Whilst this model facilitates a preventative approach based in the community, rational planning across a whole area may not be possible because local demand drives provision.

- The 'natural lead' model where each agency takes a leading responsibility in co-ordinating provision at different stages of a young person's life, for example

Health in infancy, Education in the years of compulsory schooling and Social Services in early adulthood. The advantage of this model is its clarity and the degree of co-ordination established because individual agencies have a lead at particular times. The disadvantage is possible breakdown at points of transition and unwillingness of agencies to commit resources when they do not have the lead responsibility.

- The 'community services' model, where centralised management structures are progressively dismantled and inter-agency services are devolved to 'identifiable areas', for examples clusters of schools. The main advantage is the comparatively high level of participation by local users of the system. The disadvantages are the difficulty in monitoring overall quality of service provision, differences in levels of resourcing across communities and the potential for services to be fragmented.

Guidance in the Code on inter-agency work

Commenting on the manner in which inter-agency work is framed within the Code of Practice, Roaf (2000) quotes the Code in pointing out that effective implementation of policy will only be possible:

> **... if schools create positive working relationships with parents, pupils, the health services and the local authority services departments (SSD), as well as with LEAs and any other provider of support services...**

(DfEE, 1994, 2.27)

However, as Roaf notes, the exhortation to co-operate is tempered by a proviso:

> **... while section 2.38 sets out the duties placed by the 1989 Children Act and the 1993 Education Act on schools, LEAs, the health services and the social services to co-operate, it does so with the let out clauses reminiscent of the 1981 Education Act: 'so long as the request is compatible with their duties and does not unduly prejudice the discharge of any of their functions' (1989 Children Act, Section 27), or 'subject to the reasonableness of the request in the light of available resources'.**

(Education Act 1993, Section 166)

Roaf goes on to comment on the fact that guidance is given about the kind of reciprocal relationship that should exist between education authorities, health and social services, with regard to pupils with special educational needs relating to physical, mental health or social difficulties. However, the processes by which this relationship should be established are not specified. She notes that the 1998 Action Programme to meet special educational needs, does nothing to strengthen this exhortation beyond committing the Government to 'promote 'joined up thinking' between central Government Departments in the development of policy [and] … improvements locally, both in relation to strategic planning and effective delivery of services' (DfEE, 1998, Section 5). It does not advocate a legal requirement that joined up thinking should be turned into joined up practice nor specify how to do this.

Identifying problematic factors

Among agencies themselves, problems in working collaboratively are often attributed to difficulties with individuals or one particular agency. A whole agency may be made the scapegoat for the failure of an inter-agency project, partly as a result of the fact that each agency might have problems defining what they offer in terms that the others understand:.

> Agencies can spend too much time working on their own with a client and too little time working together.

> They find it difficult to agree joint procedures for action. Each agency has its own culture, language, aims and priorities. This makes its difficult for practitioners working together to see the young person as a whole and to offer a 'seamless service'.

> There was also limited understanding of what inter-agency work means in terms of skills and practice and of its potential to alleviate the problems of the agencies as distinct from those of the young people

> *(Roaf and Lloyd, 1995)*

Roaf (2000) suggests that the literature in the field, and also practical experience, suggest that factors contributing to success and the problems encountered can be classified into four areas which, in the school context, concern: 'policy, organisational structures, professional practice and financial arrangements'. With regard to policy, the three primary care agencies, Education, Health and Social Services have different priorities:

> … with Education being in a somewhat anomalous position. Social Services and Health are primarily concerned with risks to life, where Education is concerned with life chances. This contrast governs some of the disparity between these three agencies in terms of their priorities, and explains the frustration experienced by, for example, the teacher who cannot understand why Social Services has closed the case of a child regarded as educationally at risk for lack of adequate care at home. However, Education's objectives, intensified in schools, have traditionally tended to be based on concepts of excellence and norms which

depend on abstractions, ideas of what can be achieved by some, and of what behaviours are to count as 'normal' and 'manageable'.

(Ibid)

Where core values are so different it is not obvious how practitioners from the agencies concerned can be expected to co-operate without friction between them.

A further difficulty exists within agencies themselves to prioritise 'universal, preventative work and individual case (and crisis) management' (ibid). The tension generated, especially when resources are under pressure, can be considerable. The loser is the client and his or her parents or carers. Roaf (op cit.) quotes the frustration of one young person's parents:

> He was offending while truanting from school. A mixture of the two. In the end we felt like tennis balls because Education said it was a social problem and Social Services said it was an education problem, and we were just going backwards and forwards from one to another.

(Roaf and Lloyd, 1995)

If there is no adequate inter-agency organisational structures disputes over responsibilities are highly likely, especially where precious resources are involved.

Models of professional practice also vary across agencies. Roaf (op cit.) quoting Wilson and Charlton (1997) acknowledges that interpersonal skills are of crucial importance in the development of partnerships across agencies in different sectors and disciplnes, public, private, voluntary and community.

> One cannot ignore the importance of interpersonal skills in any management process. These are skills which can be taught and can be acquired. … But skills cannot be bolted on where there is no willingness to be open about one's own position or to the different views of others.

(Wilson and Charlton 1997, p. 50)

The finances needed to establish inter-agency co-operative practices have not been forthcoming. Independent funding-providers have financed short term pilot projects but have not been willing to support work which, in their view, should be the responsibility of central government.

Identifying 'good practice'

The 'single most important factor' underpinning the inter-agency work identified as successful in the above study was the existence of a clear inter-agency structure where a policy and planning group with members drawn from all the agencies supported a multi-agency, multi-disciplinary team. An effective net-working system provided feedback about gaps in provision, identified needs and resources and facilitated the free flow of information among a wide range of practitioners. In general, effective structures of this kind:

- are solution focused

- provide opportunities for creative thinking

- challenge professionals to overcome inter-agency boundaries/professional jealousies/vested interests

- invite professionals to consider, and support them towards, more collaborative ways of working

- maintain progress in the face of political change or vacuum.

The study found that examples of good inter-agency practice had a number of characteristics in common. These were:

- **formal commitment and support from senior management and from political to practitioner level**

- **formal and regular inter-agency meetings to discuss ethical issues, changes in legislation and practice, gaps in provision and information-sharing at all levels to develop short- and long-term strategies**

- **common work practices in relation to legislation, referral/assessment, joint vocabulary, agreed definitions, procedures and outcomes**

- **common agreement of client group and collective ownership of the problems, leading to early intervention**

- **mechanisms for exchange of confidential information**

- **framework for collecting data and statistical information across all agencies that can inform all practice including ethnic monitoring**

- **monitoring and evaluation of services in relation to inter-agency work**

- **joint training in order to understand each other's professional role.**

> *(Roaf and Lloyd, 1995)*

Parallels with special needs departments

Roaf (op cit.) compares the guidelines for successful inter-agency working with the organisation of a secondary school special needs department and highlights a number of parallels:

A strong expression, in the SEN policy, of commitment to equal opportunities and a school ethos valuing diversity.

Commitment from governors, headteacher and senior management to uphold and monitor the policy. A group representative of the school community appointed to oversee policy making in relation to SEN and equal opportunities, to review priorities and ensure these are entered in the school development plan will enhance this further.

A multi-disciplinary team of practitioners (i.e. with a range of teaching skills and experience of diversity) including, for example, Learning Support Assistants, counsellor, youth workers and volunteers, to whom teachers, parents and children themselves may refer for advice, support and active intervention in the form of specialist teaching, counselling or referral to outside agencies. The work of this team becomes more effective if it is jointly funded by a partnership of schools (Cade and Caffyn, 1994).

A meetings structure enabling external agencies to meet regularly with heads of year, SENCO and other relevant staff. Current practice in this respect varies. In some LEAs, Special Educational Needs Support Services (SENSS) arrange termly meetings for each of their schools, or families of schools, at which policy is reviewed, trends noted, training needs identified and referrals recommended for individual cases requiring attention from services such as Educational Psychology, E2L, EBD and other SEN outreach services. These regular round table consultation meetings ensure a co-operative approach to a school and a more holistic response to young people's needs. Educational Social Workers tend to require more frequent, weekly meetings in school but benefit similarly if they can meet heads of year in the company of the SENCO and where, they exist, the school counsellor. Traditionally, the ESW came into school to meet with each head of year separately. Schools bringing heads of year together for this purpose with the SENCO have found that the combined experience and different viewpoints in the group has many benefits. Heads of year, ESW and SENCO can agree support packages, can take prompt action which can be followed up in the next weekly meeting. Challenges to school ethos, policy and accepted practice can be tackled in a safe environment and mutual support offered to colleagues, including those from outside agencies, undertaking difficult casework. Although the cost, in staff time, may seem high, it is repaid in effective case management, the maintenance of staff morale, school ethos and efficient working relationships with outside agencies. These meetings encourage the development of creative solutions and ensure a range of opinion is heard. The decisions then made are more likely to ensure a fair outcome since the SENCO, as advocate for the young person and holder of additional resources is present and can relieve a head of year who may well be under pressure from classroom teachers to exclude a child from a particular class for a while, or from the school.

SENCOs provide the LEA, governing body and head teacher with a detailed analysis of student and school needs on which to base the allocation of delegated funds to promote the objectives of the SEN policy. The management of resources and funding is transparent and SENCOs and governors responsible for SEN play a full part in their allocation.

Summary

There is a long history of problems in inter-agency work which relate to: the exchange of information, 'boundary' disputes over responsibility for offering particular services, and different agencies operating to different legislative frameworks with different priorities. The net result has been that, at times, the system has failed the client. Pilot studies have shown that these difficulties are not insurmountable. However, to date, consistent central funding to support development in effective collaborative working practices has been unforthcoming.

Suggested Activities: Reflection and Discussion

Developing collaborative inter-agency working practices

A number of factors appear to be important in establishing and maintaining effective collaborative practices between the agencies:

- efficient information management within and between agencies

- specific locations and opportunities within which co-operation can develop

- a clearly defined focus which is of significance to each participating professional

- some means of countering the tendency of agencies to pursue separate objectives within separate organisational frameworks - such as common geographical boundaries, agreed definitions of client groups and shared aims

- the intervention, in some cases, of one or more proactive individuals who can provide an initial stinmulus.

(Dyson, Lin & Millward, 1998)

(Cont...)

An additional factor identified by some researchers is that of a clear organisational structure to support collaboration.

Reflect on the extent to which, in your own experience, inter-agency practices compare favourably with the above factors. What action might be taken in relation to working practices with which you are familiar:

- in the short term
- in the medium term
- in the long term?

Needs Analysis

Evaluating the use of support services

Read the guidance offered in the Code of Practice, section 2:58, which relates to the use of external support services.

With colleagues at your school discuss and complete the questionnaire *Whole-school needs assessment 8: Support services* that you will find in the Appendix.

List, in order of priority, areas that you will target for improvement.

12 Resource Management

Co-ordinating provision for pupils to meet special educational needs requires a flexibility of approach in incorporating and embedding additional and/or unfamiliar resources into the curriculum in ways that address identified needs. It also requires a thorough understanding of what resources are available, human, physical and financial, how they are allocated and how they might be re-allocated to improve educational outcomes for pupils.

There are generic principles which might be applied to a consideration of any form of alternative or additional resources provided for supporting pupils' learning. For the current purpose, the resources under consideration are those related to information and communications technology. Many of the issues discussed below in relation to the effective use of ICT relate to the effective use of other resources also.

Issues of equal opportunities

Whenever there is a question of resourcing or allocating additional, alternative or 'special' resources to particular pupils, inevitably the issue of equality of opportunity arises. There is a view, already discussed in Chapter 7, that those who gain most from additional resources are the children of the more literate, persistent and articulate parents (Gross, 1996). The Audit Commission (1992) also noted the admission by some local education authorities that factors bearing little relation to the severity of a pupil's 'need' were highly influential in decisions to maintain a Statement with its consequent resource implications. Examples given of the factors were the 'determination' of the parents and representation by a lawyer. In a climate of increasing accountability and recourse to litigation, parent power has to be taken very seriously.

From a slightly different perspective, Salmon (1995) comments on the way in which the kind of special provision which a pupil is deemed to 'need' or deserve implies a value that is being attributed to that pupil. This issue is clearly important in relation to the cost or availability of particular equipment.

For these reasons, therefore, it is vital that those responsible for requesting, or overseeing the allocation of, additional or special resources are very clear in their procedures and practice which must be open to scrutiny.

Justifying additional resources

'Access to the curriculum' is often used as a justification for providing additional or alternative resources for pupils in schools. What the practical implications are of putting this principle into practice will vary across schools, depending on the context, the aspect of the curriculum under consideration and the severity of an individual pupil's need. For example, there are schools where many of the pupils experience very great difficulty in communication with others, in mobility and in being able to control anything at all in their environment. Hence 'access' may imply ways of being able to express a need, want or choice to someone else. It also may imply means by which to move oneself about or to control aspects of the environment, to turn on a light or stimulate a sound, for example. For some pupils with the most profound difficulties in communication it is possible to devise sequences of communication systems from single pre-set greetings activated by a switch through to e-mail messages associated with voice simulation programmes and/or symbols representing individual words or whole concepts.

Developing a strategy

Phillips, Goodwin and Heron (1999 pp. 123–5) suggest that the SENCO develop a strategy for resource allocation. As these researchers caution, the strategy must be justifiable in terms of the Code of Practice and it may need to be negotiated with the headteacher, other colleagues and school governors. Consulting with and involving these people in the development of the strategy will help to ensure its success (Florian, in press). The five steps below have been adapted from Phillips et al's recommendations (op cit) and should support those with responsibilities for resource allocation to plan a stragegy for meeting pupils' needs within a school:

1. Consider the needs of all the pupils known to experience difficulties in learning in the school. Take note of the nature, severity and range of difficulties experienced by these pupils. Note also the distribution of these pupils across teaching groups

2. Identify the principles and criteria that will support a clearly specified rationale for resource allocation.

3. Carry out an audit of available human and material resources. Make a distinction between staff support from within the school and external to it. Note the financial implications of both. Consider the implications for space, time and for additional human support of the use of physical resources. For example wheelchair use by pupils might necessitate a particular the arrangement of furniture, access to printing facilities at specific times during the school day might be needed for efficient use of IT, support from classroom assistants might be necessary for certain types of adaptive devices, for example a brailler.

4. Consider how much time is available from external/internal support teachers, assistants, other professionals.

5. Take into account the way in which pupils are grouped for learning in the school: use made of small groups, individual work, the support available to different kinds of group.

The use of information and communications technology

The rationale for using ICT to meet particular needs exemplifies a focused way of thinking about how, in general terms, resources might be harnessed to facilitate access to the curriculum. Many writers have noted the potential of Computer-Assisted Learning as a tool for overcoming barriers to learning in three domains: physical, cognitive and affective (Singleton, 1994, Moseley, 1992). Although these domains have been considered separately below, it is clear that their effect is mutually interactive.

Enabling physical access

The kinds of physical access that are available through ICT can, at the extreme, 'liberate' pupils from physical barriers to their learning:

> **A pupil who cannot use his (sic) hands can control the computer by pressing a switch with hbis head. Through the computer, he can learn to make choices and to select words and images for his own purpose. A youngster who has problems with fine motor control can use a tracker-ball to move a pointer across the screen. He can select the options in a drawing package to draw a series of geometric shapes, with a confidence that the quality of the results will do justice to his intentions.**

> *(NCET, 1995, p. 4)*

Affective Considerations

Motivation

Some schools have developed a highly sophisticated approach to the use of ICT. However, even the most highly developed support system will be useless to a pupil unless she or he wishes to learn to use it. Any individually-devised programme for a pupil must take into account that pupil's motivation to use the particular support systems. It is important to think about whether to find out the pupil's views before designing a programme, or, alternatively, to attempt to motivate the pupil after the programme is set up.

There is evidence that some secondary age pupils prefer working with a computer rather than having intensive tuition from a teacher, which they feel is too similar to their primary school experience (Hartas and Moseley, 1993). There is no stigma attached to its use; indeed it may be seen as a high-status piece of equipment (Brown and Howlett, 1994). ICT can motivate learners to acquire specific skills for reading, spelling and writing, as well as giving more general support in the curriculum (Singleton, 1992). The use of a word-processor can encourage students whose writing or spelling skills do not adequately reflect their higher general level of performance and can produce results which may look as good as that of peers (Singleton, 1991).

Overcoming fear of failure: building self confidence

Fear of failure is often thought to prevent some learners from making the effort which is needed for them to succeed (Lawrence, 1996). Part of the attraction of computers is their emotional neutrality. The word-processor, for example, may avoid the aversion that is often produced by pen and paper: the computer provides a safe environment for students who can take their time without holding the rest of the class back and make mistakes in private, without fear of humiliation. The learner with a history of failure is enabled to avoid situations of public failure and consequent damage to self esteem. The computer enables learners to pace themselves and puts the learner in control of the learning situation, unlike the usual teaching situation where the teacher has the power and control (Brown and Howlett, 1994).

Computer-based activities can allow learners with poor self-esteem to experience the success needed to boost their confidence, allowing written work to be presented to a high standard (Singleton, 1991, Thomas, 1992b). Using a word-processor improves the content and presentation of work; students are therefore more likely to experiment with their writing and to express themselves confidently. The student who has failed to learn adequate literacy skills over an extended period can explore ideas in a supportive environment. Anecdotal evidence from secondary classrooms suggests that ICT may be particularly effective in encouraging older pupils to complete written coursework:

> L.C.: Please can you run me off another copy (a piece of extended coursework in English Literature)?

> Shirley: Why, L.?

> L.C.: Because I want to take it home to show my Mum. (Never been known before!)

> One of the lads, S.: Look at how much I've done. I've never written ten pages before.

> *(Wearmouth, 1996)*

ICT can support cognitive access by enabling concepts, skills and knowledge to be presented in a variety of ways:

> **The pupils use a computer to drive a robot round an obstacle course on the floor, directing its movements from the keyboard, by telling the robot how far and in which direction to travel. In this way, they are encouraged to develop an understanding of estimation and direction in a practical setting. On another occasion, exploring a picture of dangers in the home on the overlay keyboard can reinforce messages of health and safety. The pupils can review their ideas and discuss differing viewpoints by collaborating on the task. By experiencing learning in an active way, they are helped to identify similar situations in the world around them.**

(NCET, op cit.)

Having said this, however, the use of ICT is no substitute for real life. One might think of a number of instances of where using this medium is inappropriate. As an IT co-ordinator in a residential school for pupils with complex physical disabilities commented recently, for example, it is patronising to suppose that a computer simulation of a bus ride will substitute in every respect the real experience of it for pupils who find independent movement difficult.

The use of content-free software such as word processing packages which provide an environment aimed at facilitating the writing process is increasing in education, particularly as the hardware has become more powerful, enabling the creation of ever more complex software engineering, such as word prediction and speech feedback.

Connecting the process with the skill

Research on ways in which ICT can support the learning of pupils experiencing difficulties in acquiring and using literacy skills is sometimes dichotomised between that intended for the remediation of basic skills, for example phonic awareness and spelling, and that intended to offer support and access to the curriculum. Individual programmes to support the development of specific skills have been evaluated in their own terms. The special value of didactic software for dyslexics, for example, has been identified as offering practice in basic skills in a convenient, enjoyable, and cost-effective manner (Singleton, 1991a, 1992).

For most people the 'lower' skills of writing are automatic, and their focus is therefore on the higher level skills involving, for example, the manipulation of ideas. However, for many learners, the lower level skills take over the task and block the ability to produce interesting written work. The possibility of drafting and re-drafting enables writing to become more closely connected to thought because the writer is able to focus on the content of the text before considering issues of presentation, spelling and punctuation (NCET, 1992). Pupils can then begin to expand on some of the higher level skills such as considering audience or organising thoughts coherently. They can perhaps even begin to see themselves as successful writers. In addition, the screen can also provide a distancing effect which increases self criticism and helps to develop a sense of audience (NCET, 1993).

Spelling

Some writers have noted how software support such as spelling checkers and word prediction facilitate the growth of the learner's communicative skills (Newell and Booth, 1991; Nellar and Nisbet, 1993). The main difficulty for a spell checker is the writer with faulty auditory perception/articulation who uses bizarre spellings or has inconsistent errors. Many spell checkers expect the first letter to be typed correctly at least, yet many learners with literacy difficulties do not. Other strategies will be needed by the writer. Even more useful is a spell checker that will speak the words as well, so that a writer does not have to rely solely on the visual medium to pick out the correct spelling. It is unclear, however, how far a facility of this type can be used by older pupils. Another useful tool for those with writing difficulties is the spelling predictor which predicts the word based on the first letter(s) typed. An 'intelligent' predictor will also learn the words commonly used, and put them near the top of each list.

Support for reading

The use of symbols on some computer programmes acts as scaffolding for reading. Symbols can be used with one pupils and gradually withdrawn until those pupils can read without them. This therefore provides an alternative method of teaching reading.

The left-right directionality of reading can be reinforced through the *Clicker* programme. A *Clicker grid* can be adapted for each individual pupil according to their own interests. When both *Clicker* and *Symbols* are loaded and used together, pupils can then write and have their work read back immediately. There is a difficulty in the use of voice recognition software to support the writing of text where pupils' speech is unclear and their words are not sufficiently differentiated, clear or consistent to be encoded into text.

Sound to support reading and writing can be used in many different ways. Word-processors with speech synthesis can be very powerful. Learners can hear what they have written, either as they are writing, or hear the whole text after they have finished.

Sound can be introduced to text by dropping it into a standard text to speech utility or talking word processor. The text may also be dropped into a programme such as *Writing with Symbols* (Widgit Computing) which gives a symbolic version that can be printed out and spoken aloud. Talking word-processors may be particularly useful tools in the future to enable pupils to decode text downloaded from the Internet.

Specific uses of ICT: use of the Internet

One aim of the (1998) NCET-sponsored research project into the use of Internet curriculum service providers in schools (EISPP) was to investigate the extent to which use of the Internet can help to overcome the special barriers to learning faced by some pupils. If use of the Internet were to be considered as a form of pedagogy for pupils who experience difficulties in learning, factors that might need to be taken into account are:

- how far pupils' access to the Internet is constrained by the nature and severity of the barriers to their learning which might be cognitive and/or physical

- how far use of the Internet has the potential to enhance all pupils' learning

- the kind of pedagogy that would enable pupils to engage most effectively with their learning.

Findings from the 1998 NCET project indicated that important issues associated with the use of the Internet in relation to meeting pupils' special learning needs are that:

- 'Real' time access to raw information from the Worldwide Web is unrealistic for many pupils. This means that teachers will need to find time to save to disk for future use any material that they or pupils have found interesting or useful.

- The manner in which pupils are given choice of e-mail and video-conferencing partners is very important. This is the kind of consideration that tends to generate very strongly-held feelings about who, among the pupils, is allowed to be put into contact with whom.

- Where pupils are isolated from peers for whatever reason, for example the location of their home, or difficulties with mobility, it may be especially important for pupils to make contact through e-mail or video-conferencing with peers elsewhere.

- Use of e-mail provides purpose for reading and writing skills and is highly motivating to pupils. An e-mail system which integrates the use of a concept keyboard, symbols, a talking word-processor and text, and which automatically deletes headers when messages are received would be useful.

- The creation of the schools' own website functions to advertise the school, publish students' work and, perhaps most importantly, reduce the isolation of a special school context by promoting e-mail links.

- There appears to be the potential for groups of teachers involved in modifying curriculum materials to share those materials in order to reduce time demands.

- There is a serious concern over the issue of equal opportunities where use of the Internet has a clear contribution to make to the learning of pupils with a wide range of needs but many schools do not have the necessary prerequisites for its development: a member of staff who is knowledgeable and highly skilled in ICT to act as the catalyst, a computer network, adequate resources, support from senior management, time and resources for staff training

Embedding the use of unfamiliar resources into the curriculum

Developing ways of working with any unfamiliar resource is not easy. One head teacher has described crucial factors in the development of ICT provision to meet special learning needs as sheer 'bloody-mindedness', keeping the development of technology under control, stimulating interest among the staff by focusing on authentic, relevant uses of ICT, giving staff 'something that will work the first time' and offering staff training from well informed sources are emphasised as important factors in promoting the use of ICT in a school (Wearmouth, 1999, in press).

Incorporating the use of new resources requires a great deal of careful planning. NCET (1995) has set out a very useful checklist to assist the process of matching IT resources to the educational objectives set out on a pupil's Individual Education Plan, and on identifying appropriate strategies for support:

Context

- **What evidence is there to support the need for IT?**

- **Why isn't the present provision adequate?**

Purpose

- **What does the learner need to achieve?**

- **What else, apart from IT, is needed to meet the learner's needs?**

- **Is the IT provision linked into the learner's Individual Education Plan?**

Resourcing

- **Is the IT already available in the school/classroom being fully utilised?**

- **Is the provision appropriate for the learner's age and stage of development?**

- **Is any proposed equipment compatible with the IT already available in the school?**

Support

- Is the learner familiar with any proposed resources?
- Can all adults working with the learner use the equipment appropriately?
- Do staff know where to find help?

Expectations

- Have the learner's views been taken into account?
- Have the parents been involved in the discussion over provision?
- What are the class teacher's expectations?

Management

- Are all staff committed to supporting a learner with IT provision in the classroom?
- Who will take responsibility for ensuring that the equipment is functioning correctly?

Monitoring

- What criteria will be used to monitor the effectiveness of the provision?
- What criteria will be used to monitor the learning targets?

Transition

- What planning is in place for considering the changing needs of the learner?
- What planning is in place to consider changing needs, both in school and beyond school?
- What planning is in place to consider developments in technology?

(NCET, op cit., p. 8–9)

The principles outlined in this checklist have a generic value in that they can be applied to any other form of resource which might be considered appropriate to meet particular learning needs. There is obviously the question of how far the particular resource can facilitate the individual pupil's access to the curriculum. There is also the issue of the time required for staff development and, crucially, that of budgetary implications.

The school budget for special educational needs

The issue of the school budget in the realm of special educational needs can be particularly contentious. As in other areas, the school governing body has the ultimate responsibility for oversight of these funds. The Education (SEN) (Information) Regulations 1994, quoted in the Code (DfEE, 2:10) state that school special policies must provide:

Information about the school's policies for:

- **the allocation of resources to and amongst pupils with SEN.**

The Education (SEN) (Information) Regulations, regulations 5 and Schedule 4 prescribe that the governing body's annual report must include information on:

- **how resources have been allocated to and amongst children with special educational needs over the year.**

However, as OFSTED (1996) has shown, governors themselves are not always clear about their exact duties.

In their research into school policies on special needs, Tarr and Thomas (1998) found 'little or no information on budgets for SEN'. This finding is of particular concern. If there is no clear statement on budget allocation for special needs in policy documents, there is less chance of transparent accountability for the use of monies assigned to the school for this purpose. The corollary of this is that local education authorities are much less likely to assign additional funds to schools because, without this transparency, it is difficult to justify extra.

Tarr and Thomas (op cit.), commenting on Vincent et al's (1995) finding that school budgets are 'impenetrable and intricate', feel that most SENCOs will not suspect that senior management will 'cheat' on the special needs budget. However, they also mention the 'fears' of some researchers and writers that funds intended for special educational needs will be siphoned off into other areas. As a result of competition between schools, there has been added pressure on school resources and an increased demand for statements for pupils who achieve standards which are lower than those of peers. In this climate this fear may become particularly acute.

Clearly it is in the interest of special needs co-ordinators to be aware of the amount of money that may arrive at the school from a number of different sources to support pupils' learning needs. Advice offered by Tarr and Thomas (op cit.) is to set up 'transparent procedures that describe how funding comes to the school and how it is thereafter spent'. This may not be easy in a school, given the findings above and given the type of management structure that might exist. It may have to be a longer-term goal and a matter for negotiation and discussion within an understanding of the individual school's priorities and the requirements of the law.

Summary

Managing resources for pupils requires a clear understanding of a number of issues. Among these are accountability to pupils, parents, the school and the local authority, the principle of equal opportunities, the nature, availability and function of resources, human, physical and financial, ways of embedding the use of unfamiliar technology into the curriculum, and strategies for resource allocation. How a balance is achieved between finite resources, people, space, time and money, and the individual needs of pupils who are experiencing difficulties in learning will vary from school to school. It is very likely, however, that the SENCO will play a key management role.

Suggested Activities: Reflection and Discussion

1. Developing a strategy for resource allocation

If you have a responsibility for resource management in a school you might choose to:

- re-read the five steps in resource allocation outlined by Phillips et al. above

- compare this strategy with yours and identify any areas for improvement in either of them.

2. Using information and communications technology

Reflect on:

- ways in which ICT is currently being used to meet particular learning neds in a school with which you are familiar

- uses that might be made of ICT to enhance special learning needs in the school

- the factors that would have to be taken into account to extend the use of ICT.

3. Using a checklist to assist the planning process

For those with a responsibility for co-ordination of special provision:

(Cont...)

- re-read NCET's checklist for matching IT resources to the educational objectives set out on a pupil's Individual Education Plan, and on identifying appropriate strategies for support. Try applying it to the use of another form of reource that you are considering for a pupil.

- reflect on the usefulness, or otherwise, of a checklist such as this.

4. The school special needs budget

Those with a co-ordination responsibility in a school might like to reflect on:

- the variety of sources from which money comes to the school for the purpose of supporting pupils' special learning needs

- the amount of money available for additional resourcing in the special needs area

- the way in which priorities are set out for the use of this funding.

If any of this information is unforthcoming, consider what action might be taken about it in a diplomatic manner.

Needs Analysis

Evaluating the use of additional resources in schools

Those with a responsibility for overseeing the use of additional resources in a school might decide to evaluate its effectiveness by discussing with colleagues and completing *Whole-School Needs Assessment 9: Resources to support learning needs,* in the Appendix.

Conclusion

The co-ordination of special educational provision in schools is a complex task. It involves an understanding of policy development and management issues, as well as considerations of curriculum, pedagogy, assessment and planning for learning.

The 1997 Green Paper *Excellence for All Children,* the *National Standards for Special Educational Needs Co-ordinators* (TTA, 1998a) and *Meeting Special Educational Need: A programme for action* (DfEE, 1998) indicate the extent to which the co-ordination of special education provision has been prioritised for scrutiny. Further expectations and increased responsibilities have followed the government's focus on 'inclusion', particularly 'in the unwritten understanding that the SENCO would be a figurehead for developing inclusive practices' (Garner, 2000).

At the root of the education system is a fundamental principle of universal access to education. The current system attempts to reconcile principles of individuality, distinctiveness and diversity with inclusion and equal opportunities, and is therefore bound to be characterised by tensions and contradictions (Norwich, 1996). Ultimately, as discussed in Chapter 1, the dilemmas created in schools by what often appear to be somewhat fragmented and contradictory government policies may be insoluble. These dilemmas are particularly problematic for those involved with co-ordinating special provision. The encouragement of competition between schools, league tables and an ever-increasing focus on academic league tables is at odds with the principle of inclusion of pupils experiencing difficulties in learning.

The law currently in operation, and the Code of Practice associated with it are based on the rights of the individual child. The individualised approach to overcoming barriers to learning through identification of 'special educational needs' brings with it both advantages and disadvantages. It may, paradoxically, lead to a greater degree of labelling than formerly where more pupils attended special schools. Although the Code has advisory status only it is used as a shared text during school inspections and therefore its advice needs to be taken very seriously indeed in schools, as outlined in Chapter 2. A number of recommendations for revisions and amendments to the Code have been made following a number of studies into its working as well as the consultation document *Excellence for All Children* (DfEE, 1997).

The duties of the special needs co-ordinator as outlined in both the Code of Practice and also the *Standards for Special Educational Needs Co-ordinators* (TTA, 1998) are multi-faceted and imply a dual approach to overcoming barriers to pupils' learning: meeting individual learning needs and supporting work across the curriculum in liaison with other teachers, sometimes acting as a change-agent. As discussed in Chapter 3, some of the issues underlying the role as defined are problematic, for example the question of status and resistances to change in the school. Additionally, there is an implication in the Standards document that the co-ordinator alone is responsible for the progress of pupils identified as having special learning needs. Clearly this cannot be the case in the institution of school.

Policy in relation to special educational needs at school level should be compatible with the overall School Development Plan as well as other related policies such as those on assessment and equal opportunities. It should also take into account both local authority policy in the area and national requirements. Chapter 4 discusses the challenges facing schools in achieving this compatibility and developing a process by which policy can be evaluated and improved on a regular basis.

Whatever views any individual may hold, the current individualised approach to supporting children's learning is underpinned by law and reinforced by inspection procedures, and therefore must be respected by professionals. The current OFSTED inspection framework is problematic in some respects, for example, the rigid assumption that the quality of pedagogy influences the attitudes, behaviour, development, attendance and progress of pupils in a simplistic cause-and-effect manner: the higher the pupils' attainment, the better the pedagogy, the unfairness of comparative attainment data as a measure of the effectiveness of a given school because like is obviously not compared with like, and the narrow view of achievement. Despite the critiques, those responsible for co-ordinating special educational provision in schools would do well to prepare very carefully for OFSTED inspections, as outlined in Chapter 5. They should ensure, for example, that they have clear evidence of pupil progress in the form of records of monitoring procedures and outcomes, and the proceedings of review meetings.

Translating the current ideology of inclusion into practice in schools is not easy and will vary from one school to another. Chapter 6 outlines a number of factors which make schools more or less hospitable for some pupils, for example approaches to target-setting, certain aspects of classroom pedagogy and types of pupil grouping arrangements.

Meeting the Code's expectation of engagement with the perspectives of both parents and pupils is one of the major challenges facing those co-ordinating special provision. Conventionally, however, teachers see themselves as professionals whose function and responsibility it is to make informed decisions on the basis of their knowledge and experience. Justification for greater pupil and parent participation on ethical, moral, and legal grounds in addition to considerations of models of children's learning have been offered in Chapter 7. Issues related to specific parental concerns have also been addressed.

Questions of assessment and planning for pupils' learning are of particular consequence for those with responsibilities for pupils identified as having special learning needs, particularly as OFSTED had emphasised that assessment must be embedded within whole-school pratices and clearly linked to purpose. Topics raised in Chapters 8 and 9 included statutory requirements in the assessment process as well as particular issues related specifically to the assessment of special educational needs. Integrating a range of considerations into the planning process is not easy, and a practical framework for this was suggested.

In the current climate of accountability in schools there is a clear need to offer a rationale for the use of additional and alternative resources, human and material, to support learning. Developing a clear strategy for resource-allocation is essential and might follow the five steps suggested by Phillips et al. (1999). The development of collaborative arrangements between schools and outside agencies has, historically, been problematic. Chapters 10, 11 and 12 have exemplified concerns that need to be addressed if support staff and special resources are to be used to maximum advantage. Factors highlighted by research as important in establishing effective collaborative practices with outside agencies need to be taken into account by schools, for example the development of an effieient information management system.

Education is crucially important to overall life chances for the majority of pupils. The responses to issues related to special educational needs by all teachers in a school have important implications for school effectiveness and individual pupil-progression. Relationships with teachers influence pupils' attitudes to learning, fostering disaffection or engagement. Whole-school approaches to providing for the learning needs of those who experience difficulties do not succeed in an ethos that these approaches are the SENCO's sole responsibility. The far-reaching nature of legislation, and particularly the guidance enshrined within the Code of Practice means that responsibility for its effective operation cannot simply be the duty of the special needs co-ordinator.

As the movement towards educational inclusion gathers pace in the new century it is apparent that success will be measured just as much in terms of the actions of 'non-specialist' teachers, and those operating outside the mainstream, as it will on the work of Sencos.

(Garner, 2000)

In the face of all these demands, to survive, maintain self esteem and respect *and* carry out a function that is of benefit to pupils, parents/carers and colleagues in a school, any current, or aspiring, special needs co-ordinator might do well to follow two particular pieces of advice given by the three co-ordinators mentioned in the introduction to this book:

- network with colleagues who value what you do

- remember that the pupil is the most important person. The co-ordinator must not distance him or herself.

Appendix

Whole-school needs assessment 1: Responsibilities and roles in special educational provision in schools

1. How well acquainted are the following members of staff with their responsibilities towards pupils with special learning needs:

   - classroom teachers

   - classroom assistants

   - learning support staff

   - curriculum leaders

   - pastoral staff

   - special needs coordinator

   - head teacher

   - governors

Areas of strength:

Areas of weakness:

2. What arrangements exist for supporting staff to fulfil their responsibilities?

Areas of strength:

Areas of weakness:

3. How do pastoral, curricular and learning support staff co-ordinate their efforts to support the learning of all pupils?

Areas of strength:

Areas of weakness:

Whole-school needs assessment 2: School special needs policy documents

Check your policy documents on special educational needs very carefully against the requirements laid down in Circular 9/94.

Areas of strength:

Areas for improvement:

Whole-school needs assessment 3: Staff development

1. How are staff development needs identified in respect of making appropriate provision for pupils with special learning needs?

How does the school meet these staff development needs?

Areas of strength:

Areas for improvement:

2. How are these staff development needs related to the school's overall staff development plan?

How are these needs related to areas prioritised within the school development plan?

Areas of strength:

Areas for improvement:

3. How does the induction of new teachers support them in fulfilling their responsibilities towards pupils with special learning needs?

What opportunities exist for new and experienced staff to learn collaboratively?

Areas of strength:

Areas for improvement:

4. On which agencies does the school draw on to support staff development in respect of pupils who have special learning needs?

How does the school share training opportunities with other schools?

Areas of strength:

Areas for improvement:

5. How does the school's approach to staff development take account of national and local priorities?

Areas of strength:

Areas for improvement:

Whole-school needs assessment 4: Pupil involvement

1. How does the school involve pupils in the process of decision-making at the level of:

 - the individual learner
 - the class
 - the year group
 - the whole school?

Areas of strength:

Areas for improvement:

2. In what ways are pupils encouraged to express any concerns they may have about their own work and progress?

Areas of strength:

Areas for improvement:

3. How are pupils encouraged to engage with the process of identifying and assessing any special learning needs they may have?

Areas of strength:

Areas for improvement:

4. How are pupils enabled to contribute their own views during the process of decision-making about any additional or special provision that is to be made for them?

Areas of strength:

Areas for improvement:

5. In which ways are all pupils involved in monitoring their own progress?

In which ways are pupils for whom additional or special provision has been made involved in monitoring their own progress?

Areas of strength:

Areas for improvement:

Whole-school Needs Assessment 5: Parental involvement

1. How does the school involve parents or carers in the progress and development of their children?

How are parents or carers involved when the school is concerned about a child's progress?

Areas of strength:

Areas for improvement:

2. What opportunities are there for parents or carers to express a concern about a child's progress?

How does the school respond?

Areas of strength:

Areas for improvement:

3. How does the school attempt to involve parents or carers in planning provision to meet the special learning needs of a child?

How does the school work with parents or carers to plan short-term targets and to review progress?

Areas of strength:

Areas for improvement:

4. What information is made available to parents or carers about special educational provision at the school, and in the local authority?

How are parents or carers informed of appropriate sources of support that may be available to them?

Areas of strength:

Areas for improvement:

5. What is the procedure for parental or carers' complaints about the effectiveness of the special provision made to meet pupils' special learning needs?

How is this complaints procedure evaluated?

Areas of strength:

Areas for improvement:

Whole-school Needs Assessment 6: Assessment and planning

1. What forms of assessment of pupils' attainments are in use in the school?

Do they allow for the progress and achievement of all children to be recognised?

Areas of strength:

Areas for improvement:

2. What information do teachers record about the progress and achievement of all children?

How far is there a common system of record-keeping across the school?

Areas of strength:

Areas for improvement:

3. How is recorded information used in planning future learning:

    • for groups and classes?

    • for individual pupils within each group?

Areas of strength:

Areas for improvement:

4. What sources of information does the school use to decide whether a pupil is experiencing difficulties in learning?

How far is the information drawn together in a coherent manner?

Areas of strength:

Areas for improvement:

5. When individual pupils' behaviour is perceived as unacceptable, to what extent is an audit of the learning environment the first response from the class teacher?

How far is there a co-ordinated response from pastoral and learning support staff when there is continued concern about the behaviour of particular pupils?

Areas of strength:

Areas for improvement:

6. How far arc all pupils involved in decision-making with regard to activities relating to their own tutor group, year group and the whole school?

To what extent are all pupils involved in monitoring their own progress?

Areas of strength:

Areas for improvement:

7. To what extent are individual pupils who experience difficulties in learning encouraged to engage in the decision-making processes with regard to special provision to meet their own learning needs?

To what extent are individual pupils who experience difficulties in learning involved in the monitoring and evaluation of their own progress?

Areas of strength:

Areas for improvement:

8. To what extent are all staff aware of the agreed procedures for identifying and assessing the aspecial learning needs of pupil?

How successful are the arrangements for reviewing the progress of children identified as having special learning needs, including annual reviews for pupils with statements?

Areas of strength:

Areas for improvement:

9. How far does the school's current approach to identifying and assessing children's special learning needs reflect the:

    - guidance in the Code of Practice?
    - guidance from the local authority?

Areas of strength:

Areas for improvement:

10. How far do teaching approaches and learning activities enable all pupils to demonstrate what they know, understand and can do?

Are there any pupils for whom access to the broad balanced curriculum is limited in some way? If so, what barriers to their learning do they experience?

Areas of strength:

Areas for improvement:

11. To what extent is the development of individual planning for pupils who experience difficulties in learning an integral part of curriculum planning for all pupils?

How does the school's practice on support/withdrawal affect access to the full breadth of the curriculum for any pupils?

Areas of strength:

Areas for improvement:

12. To what extent do existing curriculum policies meet the diversity of learning needs in the school?

How do curriculum leaders encourage the development of teaching strategies, learning activities and support materials for pupils who experience difficulties in learning?

Areas of strength:

Areas for improvement:

13. To what extent is the special educational needs coordinator able to support staff in the development of teaching strategies, learning activities and support materials across the curriculum for pupils who experience difficulties in learning?

Areas of strength:

Areas for improvement:

Whole-school needs assessment 7: Individual Education Plans

1. To what extent are IEPs designed to meet the specific needs of individual pupils?

How far does the process actively seek to engage with the views of the pupils themselves?

Areas of strength:

Areas for improvement:

2. What arrangements does the school have in place to ensure engagement with parents' or carers' perspectives?

How far does this reflect arrangements for parents of all pupils in the school?

Areas of strength:

Areas for improvement:

3. To what extent do IEPs address both short-term and long-term goals for the learner's future progress?

How clear are the targets?

Areas of strength:

Areas for improvement:

4. How far do the IEPs take into account individual pupil learning needs and also issues related to access to the whole school curriculum?

To what extent are resources for pupils used effectively and efficiently?

Areas of strength:

Areas for improvement:

5. How are issues related to the IEP process integrated into the assessment policy at whole-school and department level?

How far do they feature in the school's overall plans for raising the achievement of all pupils?

Areas of strength:

Areas for improvement:

6. How far is there clear definition of roles and responsibilities of all staff in the IEP process?

What opportunities exist for staff to share ideas and understanding relating to IEPs?

Areas of strength:

Areas for improvement:

1. What information does the school have about the range of services available locally from the different support agencies: learning support, educational psychologist, educational welfare, health services, social services, voluntary organisations?

What is the nature of existing links the school has with these support services?

Areas of strength:

Areas for improvement:

2. How does the school assess its need for these services?

Is external support targeted at individual pupils, groups of pupils, staff development, curriculum development, organisational development?

Areas of strength:

Areas for improvement:

3. How does the school monitor and evaluate the services it receives?

How are staff included in discussions about the ways in which support services can work in the school?

Areas of strength:

Areas for improvement:

4. Does the school consult with other schools, including special schools, to maximise efficient use of resources and expertise in meeting pupils' special learning needs?

Areas of strength:

Areas for improvement:

5. How may the school need to develop its arrangements for linking with other agencies in the light of

- the Code of Practice?
- views about the effectiveness of current arrangements?

How will any such development be managed?

Areas of strength:

Areas for improvement:

Whole-School Needs Assessment 9: Resources to support learning needs

1. How are decisions made about the allocation of resources to support pupils' learning needs?

Which of the following criteria exist for allocating resources:

- identified pupil learning need
- the level of need in teaching groups
- the needs of curriculum areas
- values and principles expressed in the school's SEN policy
- other?

Areas of strength:

Areas for improvement:

2. On what basis is support divided between:

- individual pupils

- in-class support
- pupil withdrawal
- curriculum support?

Areas of strength:

Areas for improvement:

3. What arrangements exist to ensure that funds delegated by the local authority to support the learning needs of pupils with statements are used for the designated purpose?

Areas of strength:

Areas for improvement:

4. What arrangements exist to review the management and allocation of additional resources in the school?

Areas of strength:

Areas for improvement:

5. By what means is the effectiveness of the use of additional resources evaluated?

Areas of strength:

Areas for improvement:

References

Ainscow, M. and Tweddle, D. (1979) *Preventing Classroom Failure*, Wiley: Chichester

—— (1988) *Encouraging Classroom Success*, London: Fulton

Ainscow, M. (ed.) (1991) *Effective Schools for All*, London: David Fulton

Allan, J. (1995) 'How are we doing? Teachers' views on the effectiveness of co-operative teaching, *Support for Learning* 10 (3), pp. 127–132

Armstrong, D. (1995) *Power and Partnership in Education*, London: Routledge

Audit Commission. (1992) *Getting in on the Act: Provision for pupils with special educational needs*, London: HMSO

Bailey, J. (1998) 'Medical and psychological models in special needs education', in Clarke, C., Dyson, A. and Millward, A. *Theorising Special Education*, London: Routledge

Barton, L. and Tomlinson, S. (eds.) (1984). *Special Education and Social Interests*, London: Croom Helm

Beard, R. (1999) *National Literacy Strategy: Review of research*, Sudbury: DfEE

—— (1990) *Developing Reading 3–13*, Hodder: London

Bearn, A. and Smith, C. (1998) 'How learning support is perceived by mainstream colleagues', *Support for Learning*, 13(1), pp. 14–20.

Beckman, P.J. (ed.) (1997) *Strategies for Working with Families of Young Children with Disabilities*, Baltimore: Paul Brookes.

Beresford, P. and Campbell J. (1994) 'Disabled People, Service Users, User Involvement and Representation', in *Disability and Society*, 9(3)

Best, R. (1991) 'Support Teaching in a Comprehensive School', *Support for Learning*, 6(1)

Bibby, G. (1990). 'An evaluation of in-class support in a secondary school', *Support for Learning*, 5(1)

Bines, H. (1986) *Redefining Remedial Education*, London: Croom Helm

Birmingham Local Education Authority (1996) *Strategy 2000*, Birmingham: Birmingham City Council

Booth, J., Simmons, K. and Wearmouth, J. (2000) *The Legal Framework and the Code of Practice*, Milton Keynes: Open University

Booth, T. (1991) 'Integration, disability and commitment, a response to M. Sacter,' *European Journal of Special Needs Education*, 6(1)

Booth, T. (1981) 'Demystifying integration,' in W. Swann (ed.) *The Practice of Special Education*, Oxford: Basil Blackwell

Booth, T., Simmons, K. and Wearmouth, J. (1996) *How Should We React to Government Policies? Responding to the Code of Practice*, Milton Keynes: Open University

Boothroyd, C., Fitz-Gibbon, C., McNicholas, J., Stern, E., Thompson, M. and Wragg, T. (1996) *A Better System of Inspection?* London: Office for Standards in Education.

Bowers, T. (1989) *Managing Special Needs*, Milton Keynes: Open University Press

Bradley, C. and Roaf, C. (1995) 'Meeting special educational needs in the secondary school: A team approach', *Support for Learning*, 10 (2), pp. 93–99

Broadfoot, P. (1996) *Education, Assessment and Society*, Buckingham: Open University Press

Bronfenbrenner, U. (1979) *The Ecology of Human Development*, Cambridge, Mass: Harvard.

Brown, J. and Howlett, F. (1994) *IT Works*, Coventry: NCET

Bruner, J. (1985) 'Vygotsky: A Historical and Cultural Perspective' in J. Wersch (ed.) *Culture, Communication and Cognition: Vygotskian Perspectives*, Cambridge: Cambridge University Press

Cable, C. (1998) 'Working in the Literacy Hour' in Specialist Teacher Assistant Course Guide, Milton Keynes: Open University

Clark, C. Dyson, A. and Millward, A (1998) *Theorising Special Education*, London: Routledge

—— (1997) *New Directions in Special Needs*, London: Cassell

Clay, M. (1993) *Reading Recovery: A guidebook for teachers in training*, Heinemann: Auckland

Cline, T. (ed.) (1992) *The Assessment of Special Educational Needs*, London: Routledge

Cocker, C. (1995) 'Special needs in the infant school', *Support for Learning*, 10(2)

Collins, J. (1993) *Beyond the Word-processor*. Computer ed., February 1993

Cooper, P. (1993) *Effective Schools for Disaffected Students*, London: Routledge

—— 'Learning from the Pupils' Perspectives. *British Journal of Special Education*, Volume 20 Number 4, December 1993

Corbett, J. (1996) *Bad-Mouthing: The language of special needs* London: Falmer Press.

—— (1999) 'Special Needs, Inclusion and Social Exclusion', in A. Hayton (ed.) *Tackling Disaffection and Social Exclusion*, London: Kogan Page

Cornwall, J. and Tod, J. (1998) *Emotional and Behavioural Difficulties*, London: Fulton

Cowne, E. (1998) *SENCO Handbook*, London: Fulton

—— (2000) 'Inclusive Curriculum: Access for All – Rhetoric or Reality?' in E831 Professional Development for Special Educational Needs Co-ordinators, Milton Keynes: Open University

Crowther, W. H. (1959) 'A Report of the Central Advisory Council for Education'. Department of Education and Science. London: HMSO

Dale, N. (1996) *Working with Families of Children with Special Needs: Partnership and practice*, London: Routledge

Daniels, H., Hey, V., Leonard, D. and Smith, M. (1995) 'Gendered Practice in Special Educational Needs', in L. Dawtrey, J. Holland, M. Hammer and S. Sheldon *Equity and Inequity in Educational Policy*, Clevedon: Oxford University Press

Davies, J., Garner, P. and Lee, J. (eds) (1998) *Managing Special Educational Needs: The Role of SENCO*, London: David Fulton.

Day, A. (1989) 'Reaching out: The background to outreach', in Baker, D. and Bovair, K. (eds.) *Making the Special School Ordinary*, Lewes: Falmer Press

Department for Education and Employment (1994) *The Organisation of Special Educational Provision*, Circular 6/94, DfEE: London

—— (1994a) *Code of Practice on the Identification and Assessment of Special Educational Needs*, London: HMSO

—— (1994b) *Pupils with Problems*, Circulars 8/94–13/94, London: DfEE

—— (1997) *Excellence for All Children: Meeting Special Educational Needs*, Sudbury: DfEE.

—— (1998) *Meeting Special Educational Needs: A programme for action*, Sudbury: DfEE

—— (1998) *National Literacy Strategy*, London: DfEE

—— (1999) *Consultation Document on the Proposed Revision of the Code of Practice*, London: DfEE.

Department of Education and Science (1989) *Discipline in Schools: (The Elton Report,)* London: HMSO

Derrington, C., Evans, C. and Lee, B. (1996) *The Code in Practice: The Impact on Schools and LEAs*, Slough: NFER

Digby, B., Lewis, G., Taylor, A. and Yates, G. (1999) 'Classroom Teachers' Knowledge and Application of the Code of Practice', Internal Report, Brunel University School of Education.

Dockrell, J. and McShane, J. (1993) *Children's Learning Difficulties: A cognitive approach*, Oxford: Blackwell

Douglas, J.W.B. (1964) *The Home and the School*, St Albans: Panther

Duffield, J., Riddell, S. and Brown, S. (1995) 'The post-Warnock Learning Support Teacher' in *Support for Learning*, 10(1)

Dyer, C. (1995) 'The Code of Practice through LEA eyes', *British Journal of Special Education*, 22(2).

Dyson, A. and Gains, C. (1993) *Rethinking Special Needs in Mainstream Schools*, London: Fulton

—— 'The role of the special needs co-ordinator: poisoned chalice or crock of gold?', *Support for Learning*, 10(2)

Dyson, A. (1997) 'Social and educational disadvantage: Reconnecting special needs education', *British Journal of Special Education*, 24(4)

Dyson, A. and Millward, A. (1997) 'The reform of special education or the transformation of mainstream schools' in Pijl, S., Meijer, C. and Hegarty, S. (eds) *Inclusive Education: A Global Agenda*, London, Routledge.

Dyson, A. Lin, M. and Millward, A. (1998) *Effective Communication between Schools, LEAs and Health and Social Services in the Field of Special Educational Needs*, Research Report No 60, London: DfEE

Education Committee (1996) *Special Educational Needs: The working of the Code of Practice and the Tribunal. Session 1995-96. Report together with the Proceedings of the Committee, Minutes of Evidence and Appendices*, London: HMSO

Edwards, J. (1993) 'The emotional effects of dyslexia'. In S.F. Wright and R. Grooner (Eds.), *Facets of Dyslexia* Basle: Elsevier

Evans, R., Docking, J., Bentley, D. and Evans, K. (1995) *Review of Policy and Practice in Five Authorities*, London: Roehampton Institute Research Centre.

Exeter University (1998) *Effective Teachers of Literacy*, Exeter: Exeter University/TTA

Fish, J. (1985) *The Way Ahead*, Milton Keynes: Open University Press

Florian, L. and Rouse, M. (2000) *Investigating Effective Classroom Practice in Inclusive Education*, final Report. Cambridge: University of Cambridge School of Education

Florian, L. (in press) Contribution to Wearmouth, J. (in press) 'Course Guide, E831 Professional Development for Special Educational Needs Co-ordinators', Milton Keynes: Open University

Ford, J, Mongon, D. and Whelan, M. (1982) *Special Education and Social Control*, London: Routledge

Foucault, M. (1980) *Power-knowledge: Selected interviews and other writings*, 1972–1977 Brighton: Harvester Press

Fraser, B. (1986) *Classroom Environment*, London: Croom Helm

Fraser B.J. and Walberg, H.J. (1984) 'Co-operative learning environments: Review of Slavin's "Co-operative Learning" and Johnson et al's "Circles of Learning: Co-operation", *Contemporary Education Review*, 3, 253–260

Friend, M. and Cook, L. (1996) *Interactions: collaboration skills for school professionals* (2nd edition), White Plains NY: Longman

Fulcher, G. (1989) *Disabling Policies: A Comparative Approach to Educational Policy and Disabilities*, London: Falmer

Fullan, M. and Hargreaves, D. (1996) *What's Worth Fighting for in Your School?* New York: Columbia Press

Fullan, M. G. (1992) *The New Meaning of Educational Change*, London: Cassell

Furlong. V.J. (1985) *The Deviant Pupil: Sociological Perspectives*, Milton Keynes: OU Press

Gains, C. (ed.) (1994) *Collaborating to Meet Special Educational Needs*. Special issue of Support for Learning, 9(2).

Galloway, D.M. and Goodwin, C. (1987) *The Education of Disturbing Children: Pupils with learning and adjustment difficulties*, London: Longman

Galloway, D.M., Armstrong, D, and Tomlinson, S. (1994) *The Assessment of Special Educational Needs: Whose Problem?* Harlow: Longman

Gardner, J. et al (1992). *Pupils' Learning and Access to Information Technology: An Evaluation*. School of Education: University of Belfast

Garner, and Sandow, S. (1995) *Advocacy, Self Advocacy and Special Needs*, London: Fulton

Garner, P. (2000) 'The teacher as the key or the teacher as the padlock? Attitudes of mainstream teachers towards inclusion of children with learning difficulties'. Paper to be presented at ISEC 2000, the International Special Education Congress, the University of Manchester.

—— (2000) 'What's the Weight of a Badger?' in *E831 Professional Development for Special Educational Needs Co-ordinators*, Milton Keynes: Open University

Gattegno, C. (1969). *Reading with Words in Colour: A scientific study of the problem of reading*, Reading: Educational Explorers

Gersch, I.S. (1987) *Involving Pupils in their own Assessment*. Chapter 10 in *Special Educational Needs and Human Resource Management*. Edited by Bowers, T. London: Croom Helm. 149–170

—— (2000) 'Listening to children: an initiative to increase the active involvement of children in their education by an educational psychology service' in *E831 Professional Development for Special Educational Needs Co-ordinators*, Milton Keynes: Open University Press

Gillborn, D. (1998) 'Racism, selection, poverty and parents: New Labour, old problems?' in *Journal of Educational Policy* Vol 13, No. 6 pp 717–735, London: Taylor and Francis Ltd

Gipps, C. and Gross, H. (1987) 'Children with special needs in the primary school', in *Support for Learning*, 2(3)

Glynn and McNaughton (1981) *Parents as Remedial Reading Tutors: Issues for home and school*, Wellington, NZ: NZ Council for Educational Research

Gosling, P., Murray, A. and Stephen, F. (1996) 'Planning for Change', in D. Clarke, and A. Murray (1996) *Developing and Implementing a Whole-school Behaviour Policy*, London: David Fulton

Green Paper, (1997) *Excellence for All Children*, DfEE

Greenhalgh, P. (1996) 'Behaviour: roles, responsibilities and referrals in the shadow of the Code of Practice', *Support for Learning*, 11(1)

Gross, J. (1996) 'The Weight of the Evidence', *Support for Learning*, 11(1)

Hallam, S. (1996) *Grouping Pupils by Ability: Selection, streaming, banding and setting*, London: Institute of Education

Halpin, D. and Lewis, A. (1994) 'The impact of the national curriculum on twelve special schools in England, *European Journal of Special Needs education*, 11(1)

Hargreaves, D.H. (1967) *Social Relations in a Secondary School*, London: Routledge

Harlen, W. and James, M. (1997) 'Assessment and learning: differences and relationships between formative and summative assessment', *Assessment in Education*, 4(3)

Hart, S. (1992) 'Differentiation – Way forward or retreat?' *British Journal of Special Education*, 19(1) pp. 10–12

—— (1995) 'Differentiation by task or differentiation by outcome?' in National Children's Bureau (1995) *Schools' Special Educational Needs Policies Pack*, London: National Children's Bureau

Hartas, C. and Moseley, D. (1993) 'Say-that-again, please: A reading program using a speaking computer' in *Support for Learning*, 8(1)

Heitler, S.M. (1990) *From Conflict to Resolution: Skills and strategies for individual, couple and family therapy*, New York: W.W. Norton Co

Hewton, E and Jolly, M. (1991) 'Making time for staff development'. A report for the DES. Sussex: Institute of Continuing Development, University of Sussex

Hopkins, D. (1991) 'School improvement and the problem of educational change' in C. McLaughlin and M. Rouse (eds) *Supporting Schools* London: David Fulton.

Hopkins, D. and Harris, A. (1997) 'Improving the quality of education for all, Support for Learning' 12 (4) pp 162–165

Hopkins, D., West, M. and Ainscow, M. (1996) *Improving the Quality of Education for All: Progress and challenge*, London: David Fulton

Hornby, G., Atkinson, M. and Howard, J. (1997) *Controversial Issues in Special Education*, London: David Fulton Publishers.

Independent Panel for Special Education Advice (1997) *'Rights at Risk? A response to the Green Paper 'Excellence for all children'*, Independent Panel for Special Education Advice

Ingram, E. (1994) 'Trends in educational software'. In C. Singleton (Ed.), *Computers and Dyslexia.* Hull: University of Hull

Johnson, D., Johnson, R., Johnson J. and Anderson, D. (1976) 'Effects of co-operative versus individualised instruction on student prosocial behaviour, attitudes towards learning, and achievement', *Journal of Educational Physchology*, 68

Johnson, D., Marvyama, S., Johnson, R., Welson, D. and Skon, L. (1981) 'The effects of co-operative, competitive and individualistic goal structures on achievement: a meta-analysis', *Physchological Bulletin*, 89

Kelly, B. (1999) 'Circle Time, a systems approach to emotional and behavioural difficulties', *Educational Psychology in Practice*, 15(1)

Lang, P. and Moslcy, J. (1993) 'Promoting pupil self esteem and positive school policies through the use of circle time', *Primary Teaching Studies*, 7(2)

Lawrence, D. (1996) *Enhancing Self Esteem in the Classroom*, London: Paul Chapman

Lewis, A. (1991) *Primary Special Needs and the National Curriculum.* London: Routledge

—— (1995) *Special Needs Provision in Mainstream Primary Schools*, Stoke: Trentham

Lewis, A., Neill, S. and Campbell, R. (1996) *The Implementation of the Code of Practice in Primary and Secondary Schools: A National Survey of Perceptions of Special Needs Co-ordinators*, Coventry: University of Warwick, Institute of Education.

Lovey, J. (1995) *Support Special Educational Needs in Secondary School Classrooms*, London: Fulton

Loxley, A. and Bines, H. (1995) 'Implementing the Code of Practice: professional responses', *Support for Learning*, 10(4).

Lunt, I. (1993) 'The Practice of Assessment' in Daniels, D. *Charting the Agenda: Educational activity after Vygotsky*, London: Routledge

Lunt, I., Evans, J., Norwich, B. and Wedell, K. (1994) *Working Together: interschool collaboration for special needs*, London: David Fulton.

Male, D. (1996) 'Special needs co-ordinators' career continuation plans', *Support for Learning*, 11(2).

McIntyre, D. and Cooper, P. (1996) 'The classroom expertise of Year 7 teachers and pupils', *Education*, 24(1) 3–13

Mehan, H. 'Beneath the Skin and Between the Ears' in Chaiklin, S. and Lave, J. (1996) *Understanding Practice: Perspectives on activity and context*, Cambridge: Cambridge University Press

Meijer, C., Pijl, S., and Hegarty, S. (1997) 'Inclusion: implementation and approaches' in Pijl, S., Meijer, C., and Hegarty, S., (eds.) *Inclusive Education: A Global Agenda*, London: Routledge

Mercer, N. (1995) *The Guided Construction of Knowledge*, Clevedon: Multilingual Matters

Merrett, F. (1998) 'Helping readers who have fallen behind', *Support for Learning*, 13(2)

Mittler, P. (1993) 'Special needs at the crossroads', *Support for Learning*, 7(3), pp. 145–51

—— (1999) 'Equal Opportunities – for whom?' *British Journal of Special Education*, 26(1)

Mortimore, P. Sammons, P., Stoll, L., Lewis, D. and Ecob, R. (1988) *School Matters: The Junior Years*, Wells: Open Books

Moseley, D.V. (1992) 'Visual and linguistic determinants of reading fluency in dyslexics: A classroom study with speaking computers', in R. Groner (ed.), *Reading and Reading Disorders: International perspectives*, Oxford: Elsevier

Moss, H. and Reason, R. (1998) 'Interactive group work with young children needing additional help in learning to read, *Support for Learning*, 13(1)

National Curriculum Council (1989) *An Introduction to the National Curriculum.* N.C.C.

—— (1992) *The National Curriculum and Pupils with Severe Learning Difficulties.* Inset Resources

National Union of Teachers (NUT) (1998) The submission of the NUT to the House of Commons Education and Employment Sub-committee inquiry into the work of OFSTED, London: NUT

NCET (1993) Portable Computers in the Curriculum: the PLAIT Research Project, Coventy: NCET

Nellar S.V., and Nisbet, P.D. (1993) *Accelerated writing for people with disabilities*, CALL Centre: University of Edinburgh

Newell, A.F., and Booth, L. (1991) 'The use of lexical and spelling aids with dyslexics', in C.H. Singleton (ed.) *Computers and Literacy Skills*, Dyslexia Computer Resource Centre: University of Hull

Norwich, B. and Daniels, H. (1997) 'Teacher support teams for special educational needs in primary schools', *Educational Studies*, 23(1)

Norwich, B. (1994) 'Differentiation: from the perspective of resolving tensions between basic social values and assumptions about individual differences', *Curriculum Studies*, 2(3) pp. 289–308

—— (1996) *Special Needs Education, Inclusive Education or Just Education For All?* London: Institute of Education: London University

O'Brien, T. (1998) 'The millennium curriculum: Confronting the issues and proposing the solutions, *Support for Learning*, 13(4) pp 147–152

Office for Standards in Education (OFSTED) (1993) Framework for the Inspection of Schools, London: HMSO.

—— (1995a) Framework for the Inspection of Schools, London: HMSO

—— (1995b) The Annual Report of HMCI of Schools, London: HMSO

—— (1995c) *The OFSTED Handbook, Guidance on the inspection of Nursery and Primary Schools*, London: HMSO

—— (1995d) *The OFSTED Handbook, Guidance on the inspection of Middle and Secondary Schools*, London: HMSO

—— (1995e) *The OFSTED Handbook, Guidance on the inspection of Special Schools*, London: HMSO

—— (1998a) *Inspection '98, Supplement to the inspection handbooks continuing new requirements and guidance*, London: OFSTED

—— (1998b) *Judging Attainment. An occasional paper on the relationship between inspectors' judgements and school results*, London: OFSTED

—— (1996) *Implementation of the Code of Practice*, London, HMSO

—— (1996a) Promoting High Achievement For pupils with special educational needs in mainstream schools. A report of the Office of Her Majesty's Chief Inspector of Schools, London: HMSO

—— (1996b) Update. Nineteenth Issue. Summer 1996 London: OFSTED

—— (1996c) Update. Twentieth issue. Winter 1996 London: OFSTED

Ogilvie, V. (1957) *The English Public School*, London: Batsford.

Phillips, S., Goodwin, J. and Heron, R. (1999) *Management Skills for SEN Co-ordinators in the Primary School*, London: Falmer Press

Pickles, P.A.C. (2000) 'Including Special Therapeutic Provision for Pupils with Severe Motor Difficulties in the Mainstream Curriculum' in *E831 Professional Development for Special Educational Needs Co-ordinators*, Milton Keynes: Open University Press

Powell, J.L. (1985a) *The teacher's craft*, Edinburgh: Scottish Council for Research in Education

—— (1985b) *Ways of teaching*, Edinburgh: Scottish Council for Research in Education

Pyke, N (1994) 'Needs tribunals set for flood of appeals', *Times Educational Supplement*, February 25, p.8

Ravenette, A.T. (1984) 'The recycling of maladjustment', *A.E.P. Journal*, 6(3), 18–27

Reindal, S.M. (1995) 'Discussing disability – an investigation into theories of disability', *European Journal of Special Needs Education*, 10(1)

Reynolds, D. (1976). 'Schools do make a difference', *New Society*, 37, 223–5

Richmond, R. (2000) 'Inclusive schools, the quality of education and OFSTED school inspection' in *E831 Professional Development for Special Educational Needs Co-ordinators*, Milton Keynes: Open University

Roaf, C. (2000) 'Working with outside agencies: the SENCO role' in *E831 Professional Development for Special Educational Needs Co-ordinators*, Milton Keynes: Open University

Roaf, C. and Lloyd, C. (1995) 'Multi-agency work with young people in difficulty' *Social Care Research Findings* No. 68, June 1995, York, Joseph Rowntree Foundation

Rogers, R. (1980) *Crowther to Warnock. How Fourteen Reports Tried to Change Children's Lives*, London: Heinemann Educational Books

Rosenthal R. and Jacobson, L. (1968) '*Pygmalion in the Classroom*', New York: Holt, Rinehart and Winston

Rutter, M., Maughan, B., Mortimore, P., Ouston, and Smith, A. (1979). *Fifteen Thousand Hours: Secondary Schools and Their Effects on Children, Wells*, Somerset: Open Books

Rutter, M., Tizard, J. and Whitmore, K., (1970) *Education, Health and Behaviour*, London: Longman

Salmon, P. (1998) *Life at School*, London: Constable

—— (1995) *Psychology in the Classroom*, London: Cassell

Sammons, P. Hillman, J. and Mortimore, P. (1995) *Key Characteristics of Effective Schools*, London: Institute of Education

Sassoon, R. (1995) *The Acquisition of a Second Writing System*, Oxford: Intellect Books

Scottish Office Education Department (1993) I*nspection of Provision for Pupils with Special Educational Needs*, Edinburgh: SOED

Sebba, J. and Sachdev, D. (1997) *What Works in Inclusive Education?* Ilford, Essex: Barnardos

SEN Tribunal (1995) 'Annual Report', London: SEN Tribunal

SEN (1999) *Code of Practice and Associated Legislation: proposed changes and areas for revision*, London: DfEE

Shaw, K.E. (1982) Rediguide 24. *Researching an Organisation* Oxford: TRC Rediguides Ltd

Simmons, K. (1996) 'In Defence of Entitlement', *Support for Learning*, 11(3)

Simmons, K. and Thomas, G. (1988) 'Assessment, Special Needs and the Education Reform Bill', *Support for Learning*, 3(3)

Singleton, C.H. (1991) *Computers and Literacy Skills*, Hull: BDA

—— (1991a) 'A rationale for computer-assisted literacy learning' in C.H. Singleton (Ed.) *Computers and Literacy Skills*, Dyslexia Computer Resource Centre: University of Hull

—— (1991b) *Computer applications in the diagnosis and assessment of cognitive deficits in dyslexia* in C.H. Singleton (ed.) Computers and Literacy Skills Dyslexia Computer Resource Centre: University of Hull

Slavin, R.E. (1987) 'Grouping for Instruction: Equity and Effectiveness', *Equity and Excellence*, 23(2)

—— (1983) *Co-operative Learning*, New York: Longman

Soder, M. (1991) 'Theory' Ideology and Research: a response to Tony Booth', in *European Journal of Special Needs Education*, 6(1)

Stansfield, J. (1991) 'Use of speech with computers for pupils with specific learning disabilities' in C.H. Singleton (ed.), *Computers and Literacy Skills*, Dyslexia Computer Resource Centre: University of Hull

Tarr, J. and Thomas, G. 'Compiling School Policies for Special Educational Needs', in J.D. Davies, P. Garner, and J. Lee, (1998) *Managing Special Needs in Mainstream Schools*, London: Fulton

Teacher Training Agency (1998a) *National Standards for Special Educational Needs Co-ordinators*, London TTA.

—— (1998b) *National Standards for Special Educational Needs (SEN) Specialist Teachers* (Consultation), London: TTA

Thomas, G. (1992a) 'Evaluating Support', *Support for Learning*, Vol 5(1)

—— (1992b) *Effective Classroom Teamwork – support or intrusion?* London: Falmer

Thomas, G., Walker, D., and Webb, J. (1998) *The Making of the Inclusive School*, London: Routledge.

Tilstone, C., Florian, L. and Rose, R (eds) (1998) *Promoting Inclusive Practice*, London: Routledge

Tod, J. Castle, F. and Blamires, M., *Implementing Effective Practice*, London: Fulton

Tomlinson, S. (1981) *Educational subnormality: A study in decision-making*, London: Routledge and Kegan Paul

—— (1982) *A Sociology of Special Education*, London: Routledge

—— (1985) 'The expansion of special education', in *Oxford Review of Education*, 11 (2), pp. 157–165

Torrington, D. Weightman, J. and Johns, K. (1989) *Effective Management*, New York: Prentice Hall

Turnbull, A. and Turnbull, H.R. (1990) *Families, Professionals, and Exceptionality: A special partnership* (2nd ed.), New York: Merrill

Understanding the Development of Inclusive Schools (UDIS) (December, 1998) *Investigating Effective Classroom Practice in Inclusive Education*, Cambridge: University of Cambridge School of Education.

Underwood, J.E.A. (1955) *Report of the Committee on Maladjusted Children*, London: HMSO

Warnock Report, The (1978) *Special Educational Needs, Report of the Committee of Enquiry into the Education of Handicapped Children and Young People*, Cmnd. 7212 Department of Education and Science, London: HMSO

Watson, D. (1993) *The Impact report: An evaluation of the impact of information technology on children's achievement in primary and secondary schools*, London: Kings College.

Wearmouth, J. (1999) 'Another One Flew Over: maladjusted Jack's perception of his label', *British Journal of Special Education*, 26(1)

—— (1997) 'Pygmalion Lives On', *Support for Learning*, 12(3)

—— (1996) 'Registering: for what purpose?', *Support for Learning*, 11(3)

—— (in press) 'E831 Professional Development for Special Education Needs Co-ordinators', Milton Keynes: Open University Press

Wedell, K. (2000) Contribution to Wearmouth, J. 'Course Guide' in *E831 Professional Development for Special Educational Needs Co-ordinators*, Milton Keynes: Open University

Weiner, G., Arnot, M., and David, M. (1997) 'Is the Future Female? Female Success, Male Disadvantage, and Changing Gender Patterns in Education', in Halsey, A.H., Lauder, H., Brown, P., and Wells, *A.S Education: Culture, Economy, Society*, Oxford: Oxford University Press

Wexler, P. (1992) *Becoming Somebody: Toward a social psychology of school*, London: Falmer

Wheal, R. (1995) 'Unleashing individual potential: a team approach', in *Support for Learning*, 10(2)

Whittaker, J., Kenworthy, J. and Crabtree, C. (1998) *What Children Say About School*, Bolton: Bolton Institute

Wilson, A. and Charlton, J. (1997) *Making Partnerships Work*, York: York Publishing Services

Wiltshire, A. (1998) 'A wider role for special schools?' in Tilstone, C., Florian, L. and Rose, R. (eds.) *Promoting Inclusive Practice*, London: Routledge

Wolfensberger, W. (1989) 'Human Service Policies: the rhetoric versus the reality', in Barton,L. (ed.) *Disability and Dependency*, London: Falmer

Woodbridge, Wade, B. and Moore, M. (1993) *Experiencing Special Education: What young people with special needs can tell us*, Buckingham: Open University Press

Index